Kwame Adapa

Awakening to your Nature as a Spirit Being Incarnated on Earth

Copyright © 2022 Kwame Adapa

The moral right of the author has been asserted.

All rights reserved. No part of this publication may be reproduced, stored in or introduced into a retrieval system, or transmitted, in any form or by any means (graphic, electronic, mechanical, photocopying, recording or otherwise), without the prior written permission of the copyright owner.

ISBN-13: 978-1-952228-07-0

Preface

At some point in our lives, we may have stopped to ask ourselves or to contemplate some those "big questions": I am alive now. Where was I before I got here? What happens once my present consciousness passes away? Is there something afterwards? Is this all there is? Some of these questions may bring about fear of the unknown, because answers may not be readily available. This fear of the unknown can lead a conscious mind asking these questions to give up, or to return to what is more familiar, and less disturbing.

The probing questions about existence often take a back seat in favour of more pressing everyday concerns. For some, this back seat may be short lived. For others, it could take a long time for consciousness to return to asking these important questions. Other questions of importance may take precedence, and often those questions have to do with the "real world" that can be perceived by the 5 senses.

Rather than bring about an expression of fear when these big questions are posed, other minds may instead want to probe and explore more. These other minds may want to unravel more of the mystery surrounding life and death. The mystery surrounding our condition of existence.

I call it a mystery because it is the kind of enquiry that has intrigued or some may even say plagued the human mind for as long as we can remember. The mystery surrounding the condition of our existence as conscious beings that we know ourselves as, as humans, has spawned various philosophies, religions, and spiritual viewpoints among the different peoples who have lived on Earth. So, this topic of the conditions surrounding our existence is an old one indeed.

This book is about various thresholds of viewpoints I have surmised as a result of my own life experiences and my research, which I believe speaks to understandings of ways in which we can view the world and our place in it. Given that we are all born or at least come into incarnation one way or another, to what degree do we become aware of what is happening to us, and around us, as we go about living our lives? How much do we realize what the experience of living is about, what the influences are, and to what degree do we feel comfortable penetrating the mystery of life and of existence? For some of us, we choose to or prefer to delve into this mystery as deeply as we can. For others, we are satisfied to live our lives according to standard or relatively standard understandings of things, without probing too deeply. There is no correct or incorrect approach. In my experience, it all depends on the needs of the spirit entity incarnating within a certain context of time, place, gender, cultural, economic, political, and social circumstances in surface Earth life.

I am writing this book for spirit beings on the human journey who fall somewhere either on the standard or on the nonstandard side of the spectrum of stable viewpoints about the world and our place in it. The standard viewpoints tend to relate to very much to five-sense perceptual reality, and what the "common sense" opinions are about things. The standard viewpoint is less well versed in explaining non-physical (energetic and spiritual) aspects of reality. As you may have guessed, nonstandard viewpoints tend to include esoteric or occult explanations of reality. The earlier chapters start off with an examination of the more standard aspects, and then the book progressively advances into nonstandard aspects, getting into the deeply esoteric in the later chapters. This way, I imagine that most readers would relate to some of the earlier chapters in the book, because those earlier chapters are about experiences most if not all of us go through, once we enter into incarnation on Earth during these modern times. Other readers may resonate with most or even all of the content, from the earlier to the later chapters.

Therefore, in this book, I present some of what I have tried to work out as a conscious human being who has been intrigued by some of those "big questions" that many of us ask ourselves as we go about living our normal, daily lives. Over the past few decades, I have come up with working hypotheses as responses to some of these questions. It is my aim to present several of these working hypotheses I came up with which I have been able to explain coherently to myself and which I can hopefully explain to others as well. The idea is to stimulate the thinking and discovery of other conscious minds who are more intrigued than afraid to explore some of the big questions.

The very nature of this work is limited by the lens of my own mind, my experiences and my thoughts. I write as one who has been on a journey of discovery and is at the present time attempting to communicate some of this process. I do not claim to be writing an "objective" work about the nature of reality. Instead, the method I am adopting in this shared work is to draw on logic and on common human experiences. These experiences comprise mine and other individuals I have encountered or researched. Through these affordances, I pieced together some of what I have discovered or thought about, which I imagine conscious or awakening humans can also relate to. In particular, this work is meant for Earth humans who live or have lived their human experiences on the surface of planet Earth.

From the broad approach of discussing experiences and ideas pertaining to the standard approach that most of us can relate to, I shall progressively get into particular details concerning nonstandard ideas and experiences of an esoteric nature that fewer readers would relate to, form their own thoughts and experiences. I adopt the approach of presenting the discussions in this book from being about standard ideas and experiences to delving progressively into the nonstandard ones because it parallels my own experiences of awakening. In other words, when I first began to seriously ask questions about the nature of existence, I started with examining the ordinary world of sense perception. I then continued delving deeper into the world of the occult, of spirit, of energy, and of nonstandard epistemologies. I read a great deal about ancient history, about nonstandard science, and about the different spiritual traditions of the world. It was only after doing the broad sweep that I found specific aspects of interest and narrowed in on those. Once I arrived in the nonstandard space, I increasingly exchanged experiences and notes with other awakening individuals on their own journeys. That process continues to this day. Fortunately, a fair number of these awakening individuals have a firm footing in both the world of standard ideas and experiences and the world of the nonstandard. It is from interacting with these individuals that I nurtured the notion that there must be many more individuals out in the world who are at different stages of their own awakening, and who can appreciate in part or in full, a work such as I intend to present in this book.

The reader will also find that I draw on philosophical ideas and spiritual traditions developed in the intellectual and spiritual traditions of Africa, America, Asia, Europe and among

Indigenous peoples of various parts of the world. The ideas and traditions cited in this work were at various stages were crucial in assisting me formulate and understand the stable viewpoints I have surmised and now share with a wider audience.

Dedication

I would like to dedicate this book to all spiritually oriented people on Earth, who are on a path to greater spiritual awakening and enlightenment.

Table of Contents

1. **INTRODUCTION** 3

2. **SUMMARY OF THE RINGS** 22

3. **THE RING OF CHILDHOOD** 26
   - 3.1 The spirit realm
   - 3.2 Coming into incarnation
   - 3.3 "Growing up"
   - 3.4 Adult-child

4. **THE RING OF POLITY** 47
   - 4.1 Diverse circles
   - 4.2 Living a "normal life"
   - 4.3 Disenchantment
   - 4.4 Sovereign lifestyle

5. **THE RING OF THE FIVE SENSES** ... 68
   - 5.1 "Common sense" perception
   - 5.2 Concrete knowledge and the real world
   - 5.3 Altered states of consciousness
   - 5.4 Being of two worlds
   - 5.5 Energy work

6. **THE RING OF LIFE AND DEATH** 89
   - 6.1 God and science save us
   - 6.2 "New age" paradigms
   - 6.3 Transcending religion
   - 6.4 Metaphysics and spiritual science

7. **THE RING OF THE HIGHER SELF** 108
   - 7.1 The totally trustworthy parent-spirit
   - 7.2 The hierarchy of Higher Selves
   - 7.3 Alignment
   - 7.4 Integration

8. THE RING OF THE SEPARATE SELF
.... 116
    8.1 Physical and spiritual identities
    8.2 Approaching oneness
    8.3 The universal self
    8.4 Healing polarities

9. THE RING PASS-NOT 129
    9.0 Prelude
    9.1 All manifestation is illusion
    9.2 Exiting creation
    9.3 The unspeakable
    9.4 Becoming God

AFTERWORD 242

SOURCES 243

ABOUT THE AUTHOR 247

1

INTRODUCTION

As I progressed along to discover clues and answers to some of the "big questions" that intrigued my mind from a young age, I came to realize that there is a manifest reality that I was experiencing. Now, one would say that this is kind of obvious, right? Of course, there is a manifest reality. It is called the "real world" Yes, I agree that there is a commonly shared experience of a reality that at the time of writing this book, has been called the "real world". What is this real world? I suppose I can say that it is the world that is experienced through our five senses. It is the world of tangible objects and things. Tangible means something that can be touched. Something that is of material existence. But touch is not the only quality of objects in the real world. Some things in the real world can also be seen, or smelled, or tasted. There are things that can be touched but cannot be seen, for instance air, although some gases can be seen. There are some things that can be heard but cannot be seen or tasted, under normal circumstances. One such thing is the sound of thunder.

I include "under normal circumstances" because there are indeed abnormal circumstances under which normal phenomena may behave differently. One example is the condition known as synesthesia. Synesthesia is an experience that is brought about when the senses behave differently from their normal function. For example, synesthesia can bring about the experience of seeing sounds or of hearing lights. There are several variations of the experience of synesthesia. One quality all the variations seem to have in common is that sense perception from "reality" or the "real world" cannot always be placed neatly into categories such as touch, taste, smell, sight or hearing. There are some possible implications here, one of which is that the manner in which most of us learn to process sensory data into neat categories in order to experience the "real world", is learned behaviour. That behaviour can be disrupted under certain conditions. One such condition is when a child is first learning to assemble reality. Another is when an adult is under the influence of certain mind-altering substances such as cannabis. If the behaviour itself is learned, leading to other experiences outside the commonly learned behaviour, then the reality being processed does not necessarily conform to the neat sense-perception categories of the learned behaviour. Put another way, the reality out there does not necessarily exist as "sight", "sound", "taste", "smell", and "touch". It is something else, that we learn to put into these five categories, and in a minority of circumstances, we blur or mix up some of the categories. So, one assumption underlying this work, is that there is a "real world", and our experience of it is learned.

Another assumption is that if we limit our experience and understanding of the real world to mean that world which we can experience with our five senses, then there are realities or worlds besides this real world. Again, one may claim that this is obvious. Anyone can imagine whatever world they want to, and these have been called imaginary worlds. Add to the imaginary worlds we can access in our daydreams those that that are also accessible during night time dreams, and that gives a great variety of worlds besides the real world that we can access as part of the common experience of surface Earth humans. Include those spiritual and transcendental experiences that one can have consciously or that one may experience accidentally and we have a great range of potential realities outside real world perceptions that can be experienced by a conscious being having a human experience.

I chose the words of the last sentence carefully because they constitute another assumption of this work. That assumption is that through my own experiences, through those that have personally been shared with me by others, and through findings from the research of others, I have come learn and to understand that I am much more than my physical body. I have come to learn that in addition to having a physical body, I am also a spirit being, that in fact I am an increasingly conscious spirit being having a human experience. What it means to be a spirit being will be discussed more extensively later in this work. Not only am I a spirit being. I have also interacted with several other humans who are consciously aware of, or at least aware to a certain degree, that they too are spirit beings having a human experience. As a spirit being having a human experience, I have learned that the societies within this "school of learning" that we call modern day surface Earth life, at least at the time of writing this book, actively and formally teach an incarnated human being how to survive and function in the real world, but not so much how to survive and function in those other worlds outside the real world that include the worlds of spirit.

There are of course exceptions to this rule. This seems to be the case in some parts of our modern world that still have strong influences from or representation by indigenous societies. In these indigenous societies, which often comprise not very large groups, there are forms of education involving initiation of younger members of the community into indigenous knowledge that often has spiritual components. The nature of the education differs from community to community. Two examples that I have learned about on my own path are the experiences that Malidoma Somé shared in his book *Of Water and the Spirit* about his initiation experiences within the Dagara indigenous group of West Africa, and the experiences that James Neal shares in the book *Jungle Magic*, of the initiation of girls of the Krobo ethnic group of Ghana during the Dipo ceremony. There are other indigenous groups around the planet that carry out similar forms of education for young community members through forms of initiation. Much of surface Earth today however gets "modern" education.

A fourth assumption in this work, and this is a major one that draws on earlier assumptions, is that within the real world, much of what we experience as cultural, economic and social realities are artificial constructs created and maintained by consensus. The consensus is manifested in the dominant modes of acceptable beliefs and opinions of the human minds of souls currently incarnated at a given period of time within a given society. Put simply, you, me, all our friends, family, and everyone out there who believes in democracy, or communism, or that wearing a suit and tie is more fashionable and good-looking than wearing a jumpsuit, or who prefers a Bentley or a BMW car to a Fiat Punto, or who gets upset when stocks tumble, collectively contributes to maintaining the consensus. All these prevailing attitudes of beliefs, opinions, and things that matter, this is what is taken to be the definition of "life" at a given time in surface culture on planet Earth. These prevailing beliefs and attitudes obviously change over a period of time, and that change is often seen as "progress". For example, a few hundred years ago, it was perfectly acceptable for disputes among men in the US to be settled through a gun duel. For earlier periods of human history, it has also been perfectly acceptable among many communities for one group of people to have the status in society as slaves to another group of people. Now, over time, these beliefs and opinions change, so that at this time of writing it is no longer acceptable in modern society to hold others as slaves because of current prevailing beliefs in regard to human rights.

Meanwhile, human life is currently "owned" by the state. Once a person is born, that individual, in order to move around and to function in the state, gets some country or state identification which comes with certain implications. One of those implications is that the individual can no longer attempt to take their own life, or others' lives for that matter, without dire consequences. If they try, and fail, they can be severely punished by the state. The offending individual's physical body can for instance be taken into custody and incarcerated, or put to death. It appears to me that in these modern times, not only is an individual's physical body the property of a state once the individual is born and signed up to a particular birth certificate, what is more is that the individual also theoretically and practically exists to serve the state. Theoretically because the individual can theoretically be called upon to enlist in an army and compelled to fight for the state in times of war. Practically because once the individual is of age to no longer be under the legal guidance of their parents but now under the legal guidance of the state, they are often required to pay taxes in support of the state. And so on. Perhaps a thousand years from now, the prevailing view at that future time would look upon this current condition perhaps as barbaric, as very liberal or as something completely different depending on what the prevailing beliefs and opinions at that future time are.

The point of the fourth assumption, however, is that the prevailing mass attitudes, beliefs and opinions of a particular age can be thought of as models for experiencing interactions between peoples in societies of that age. We incarnate into a given age (e.g., stone age, Greek and Roman age, medieval age, modern age). When we arrive, we find that there is a particular orientation of thought and action in the society our spirits incarnate into. We then learn these orientations of thought and action in order to participate in and contribute to the culture of the society we end up in. In that regard, the attitudes, beliefs and opinions of a given society within a given age can be thought of as being "artificial" in the sense that they are models of living that are created, maintained and evolved by the people and the communities of the respective age. As such, because these are modes of living rather than aspects of function, people can change their minds about them. Aspects of function are for instance the manner in which our body's blood circulation system works, or the manner in which gravity influences objects in space. I use this term "artificial" in respect to attitudes, beliefs and opinions of a given society loosely, I must admit. Artificial because they are very much manmade, versus an object or an aspect of function that is independent of human thought. For example, people can change from being in support of capital punishment to being against it. People can change from being against abortion to supporting it. Possible reasons why people change their minds could be a result of their own experiences, logical deductions or insights, those of others that were found convincing, or a host of other reasons. Thus artificial, due to the changeable nature of thoughts and actions. Opinions are not necessarily set in stone. They can change. This is as opposed to natural laws that govern objects and phenomena existing in nature. Rocks, oceans, and solar orbits can be studied by coming up with natural laws that govern their existence. These natural laws can be distinguished from artificial phenomena because they are about objects in nature. The planet was around long before any of us showed up, and will probably still be here long after we are gone.

These prevailing mass attitudes, beliefs and opinions that serve as models that govern the dominant modes of personal and community life of a given age or time are taken seriously by the people who hold them dear and who propagate them. A spirit being that incarnates into a surface Earth human body of that age is enculturated into these viewpoints, and the societal laws that enforce community consensus. Deviating from these viewpoints within a given society, especially in ways that may be deemed threatening, brings potential consequences to the physical existence of the transgressor, consequences that are upheld by consensus. It can thus become dangerous to have alternative viewpoints. The danger is at least two-fold. On one hand, the individual having divergent views can be seen as a threat to the order of things in a society. On the other hand, the introduced viewpoint can itself be a danger to established or prevailing viewpoints, depending on how different or opposed the new viewpoints are to the prevailing ones. This is where societal laws come in, and also the idea of the social contract, which has existed in the European mind on ideas about government at least since the time of ancient Greek philosopher Plato in his work titled *Crito*, and has been a subject of discussion among philosophers of the European tradition over the past few centuries. Given that the dominant models of government of today's modern societies across most parts of the world appear to be strongly influenced by models promoted by European thought, I have thought it fit to study these models (but not only them) as part of my process of awakening. This is by no means a book that only studies European ideas.

In all of this, is there anything then that is "true", independent of the age or time, or of the current understandings of philosophy, of science or of spirituality? That is a question I have sometimes asked myself. There has been talk of the timeless or ageless wisdom, propagated by arcane schools. Wisdom that at least attempts to describe or to elucidate a viewpoint about the nature of reality. Since we surface Earth humans for the most part arrive into incarnation without active memory of prior existences, we must resort to examining and integrating viewpoints we acquire or develop on our journey as humans. We learn to figure out what to make of all the experiences we perceive. We do this right from childhood, and we may continue this process of unravelling reality, which can be an iterative process of formulating stable viewpoints of the way the world works and what our place in it is. Arriving at convictions of how the world works may occur as a tacit understanding for some individuals or as an active process of thinking, philosophizing and conjecturing for others. Realistically, it is likely a mix of both for most individuals. There may be different times in our lives when our stable viewpoints about the world are disrupted and stimulated to change. The process may never occur, may occur once or on a few or on several occasions until we reach a stage where we become comfortable with a new view. The depths to which we strive to penetrate the mysteries of manifest experience will as such differ from one individual to another. I would imagine that for most people, the process occurs at least once in a given lifetime. Once we arrive at a stable viewpoint, we tend to work with it as our model for understanding the world and our place in it, unless or until life brings about circumstances that disrupt the previously stable viewpoint, leading to a period of uncertainty until a new stable viewpoint can be established, or the individual remains in the uncertain space.

At this juncture, I would like to introduce an allegory that has had an impact on my quest to penetrate questions involving the mysteries of reality. This allegory is known as "the Allegory of the Cave". It has been made famous by the ancient Greek philosopher Plato, who wrote about it in his book *The Republic*, over two thousand years ago, detailing a conversation between Glaucon, Plato's brother and Socrates, who was mentor to both Glaucon and Plato. I bring up this allegory because I find it to be central to the fourth assumption I stated above. Paraphrased, the allegory of the cave portrays a situation whereby individuals find themselves in a dark cave. When individuals are born, they are free, however after living in the cave for a while, they become chained and imprisoned. This imprisonment begins from childhood. The nature of their imprisonment is such that the individual is chained at their legs and at their necks, while forced to view a wall ahead of them, rather than being able to view around the cave, at one another, or even at themselves. Behind the imprisoned individuals there is a fire, an artificial light created by humans, and between the fire and those in chains is a raised walkway and a low wall. There are people walking behind the low wall who place objects and puppets on the wall, so that the shadows of these objects and puppets are projected onto the wall that the chained individuals are affixed to gaze at. The low wall also keeps the shadows of those putting the objects and puppets on the low wall hidden from being projected onto the view wall. As such, the imprisoned individuals do not see the manipulators' shadows. Those controlling the objects and puppets make sounds that the chained individuals believe are coming from the shadows they see on the wall.

Interestingly, the chained individuals believe that the shadows are real, rather than being shadows of real objects. This is because they have never seen real objects, having had their vision and attention fixated on the wall and on nothing else. One can gather that this first part of the allegory details the reality of the nation where citizens get fed the official line through the media. Behind the media are those manipulators who decide what the "objects" and the "puppets" are to be, that get projected onto the viewing wall. Brings to mind L. Frank Baum's book *The Wonderful Wizard of Oz*, where an "all powerful" but unseen wizard (who turns out to be just an ordinary human) and who, through appearances, manipulates things in the city of Oz from the background. It amazes me that this allegory that was told to Plato and Glaucon over two thousand years ago parallels circumstances in modern times. The comparison goes right down to television in modern times versus a wall on which shadows are projected, in the time of Ancient Greece.

In recounting the allegory of the cave, Plato also holds that few humans manage to leave the cave. Most will remain chained, continuing to view the wall as the only reality they know. There would of course be the few "artists" who have taken it upon themselves to maintain the illusions on the wall. In comparison with the chained people, these are much fewer. In the allegory, Plato does not appear to say whether the artists are chained or not. One would imagine that the artists have a greater degree of freedom than those that are chained. However, being part of the "control structure", they would likely have their own freedoms curtailed to a certain degree as well. Those few humans, previously chained, that manage to truly leave or to escape the cave, according to Plato, are those few philosophers who have had decades of preparation. It is not an easy task, and these are few and far between.

Then it gets interesting. Plato next supposes that one of the previously chained people gets released. What happens then? Having spent a lifetime viewing shadows on the wall as the only reality, this individual will have their eyes hurt as they attempt to turn around to view the artificial light as well as the objects and the puppets on the low wall. If told that this light and these objects are more real than the shadows on the view wall, after a lifetime of wall viewing, the freed individual may not believe it to be so. The freed individual may even want to return to the circumstance of viewing in the wall, being more accustomed to that prior to being freed. Even more drastic would be the reaction of the freed individual, if they were to be forcibly dragged out of the cave, past the artificial light of the manipulators and progressively toward the exit of the cave, into the light of the sun. Plato explains that the freed individual would be indeed be angry along the way, would struggle in pain and would resist being brought into the natural light. What is more, their eyes would hurt even more than they did when first released to view the artificial light in the cave.

Eventually, once the freed individual becomes accustomed to the reality outside the cave, they would see a bright and beautiful world. This could bring the freed individual into a state of wonder. A vast world they had never experienced. The now freed individual would want to return to the cave to free others who, once like herself or himself, were subject to the limited views of the shadows on the cave walls. Plato then explains that upon re-entering the cave, the dim light that once felt comfortable to the individual would now be blinding, having spent time in the light of the sun. Those in the cave who notice the returning individual blinded by the darkness of the cave would infer that the journey outside of the cave was harmful to the individual and would thus want to avoid such a journey themselves. Plato ends by indicating that the still imprisoned individuals, if they could, would move to kill anyone who attempts to free them, in order to drag them into the light of the outer world.

This allegory is still apt for us in this modern time that I shall draw upon it as one of the ways I frame the discussion in this book. One of the major themes in the allegory is that of awakening to the nature of reality, which is the theme of this book. There is also the idea of being born free, but then becoming chained after that. It brings to mind the words of French philosopher Jean-Jacques Rousseau, who stated that "man is born free, but everywhere he is in chains." Perhaps Rousseau had read Plato's Republic, if he did not otherwise come up with this idea himself.

So, a major point in regard to the allegory, and another assumption in this book, the fifth, is that the incarnational game appears to be rigged. Rigged, in the sense that spirit beings that come into the world to have a human experience in recent times often find themselves entering a prison world. There are important reasons why this appears to be the case. The short reason is that in certain societies on surface Earth, members do or did not always get support needed to aid a spiritual being in following its development to reach its potential. Where there should have been support to follow one's path in order to blossom, there was rather the need to conform and to work toward maintaining an artificial system. Such conditions are frequently found in the complex city-states and metropolitan areas where the inhabitants have to work in order to support the system. One runs the risk of becoming a cog in the machine. At the other end, within indigenous settings, some cultures made provision for meeting the educational and spiritual needs of community members, rather than training them to become a cog in the machine. Of course, there can be exceptions on either side, however this is really about knowledge of the nature of reality and of one's purpose in a given lifetime versus ignorance of these things and just living to survive.

So, as a summary, the allegory of the cave given by Plato tells us that the world is not what it seems to be. That, although humans are born free, they soon emerge as imprisoned individuals before their lives end. That there is an "evil" hand at play, that purposely keeps people chained and in ignorance. Plato perhaps meant this to be a description of the condition among Western societies, or at the very least, ancient Greek society. Today, much of the world, especially in urban areas, is heavily influenced by the culture, religion, social and political thought of the West, which is itself heavily influenced by the culture and the traditions of Ancient Greece. The culture of the West, that developed in Europe over past centuries and that culminates in Western pre-eminence on the world stage today is dubbed the 'modern' era. For example, much of the world has adopted ideals of democratic governance and ideals that have been strongly promoted by Western thinkers. In most places, formal attire in business, political and other professional settings follow Western styles. Systems of schooling, scientific and industrial approaches, and much else globally builds on the Western way. It can be said that in the current age which we call the modern age, the life model that holds the greatest sway on the global stage is the model that developed for centuries in Europe prior to the modern time. Western thinking has itself been strongly influenced by the culture and thinking that prevailed in ancient Greece (not only Greece but Asia as well to a certain extent, especially the Muslim world). As such, this problem of imprisonment in chains after birth that Plato described in his book over two thousand years ago has now become a problem that is found no longer only in Western societies, but also in many other societies around the world.

In addition to the allegory of the cave, another conception I shall draw on in this book in order to frame experiences and ideas is that of the Hero's Journey. Also known as the monomyth, the hero's journey is a framework for understanding a common theme that runs through the journey of discovery that includes initiation into non-ordinary knowledge. The term has been made popular through the work of the late Joseph Campbell, a professor of literature who specialized in comparative religions. Campbell, who also drew on the works of earlier authors as well as drawing inspiration from Jung's work, noticed that the heroes of religions the world over experience journeys that have follow a similar pattern. He cites Gautama Buddha, Huang Ti, Jesus, Mohammed, Moses Osirus, and Tezcatlipoca among others to support his pattern. The pattern includes three broad stages: departure, initiation, and return. Each stage consists of substages that detail the occurrences within the stage. Altogether, Campbell came up with seventeen substages detailing his version of the hero's journey.

Since Campbell, other authors who were inspired by him have come up with fewer substages for the Hero's Journey that still have the three main stages. One of those authors is Christopher Vogler, a Hollywood screenwriter, who came up with twelve substages. In this book, I shall draw on some of Vogler's substages in connecting them with the allegory of the cave. Specifically, the departure stage of the Hero's Journey can be likened to unchaining an individual in the cave and proceeding to exit the cave. In Plato's allegory, the ordinary life situation of the chained individual involved being shackled while gazing at the wall. This was the stable and unruffled situation of the imprisoned individual. Once newly freed, however, the individual becomes reluctant to leave while struggling to acclimatize to the new circumstance of being freed. This part of Plato's allegory corresponds to three substages of the Hero's Journey: ordinary world, call to adventure, and refusal of the call. Experience of the ordinary world is when the prisoner simply viewed the shadows of the wall, thinking that was all there was. The unchaining event is the call to adventure, and the struggle of the newly freed individual is the refusal to leave. So, these three, ordinary world, call to adventure, and refusal of the call, are substages within the departure stage of the Hero's Journey framework.

The next stage in the Hero's Journey is the initiation stage. During the initiation stage, the Hero goes through some trials which, if handled successfully, lead to some reward. Three of the substages within the initiation stage are: tests, allies and enemies, the ordeal, and reward. Returning to Plato's allegory, after the prisoner is freed, he or she is progressively moved toward the light, in a journey to exit the cave. During this phase, the newly freed individual resists, gets angry and struggles to return to the familiar condition of being imprisoned. This part of the allegory corresponds to the tests, allies and enemies substage. Now begins the arduous journey to exit the cave. During this period, learning is an uphill battle. The individual struggles, fumbles and may experience disorientation on the journey to reach the exit point. This is the part of the allegory corresponding to the ordeal. Finally, the freed individual, after expending effort and with much perseverance, reaches entrance and exits the cave. Once outside the cave, the freed individual would at first struggle to see in the light, however after adjusting to the brilliant light of day, this individual would set eyes on the beauty and the wonder of their surroundings. They would be overjoyed, to experience the freedom and the beauty of the natural world. Herein likes the freed individual's reward.

This leads us to the sixth assumption. The sixth assumption in this work is that the experience of being human on surface Earth necessitates successive and iterative awakenings through which the spirit being incarnated as a human gains increasingly greater awareness of self and of the world. Each awakening is like going through an unchaining process, and being taken up to a new level. In Vogler's rendition of the Hero's Journey, the departure stage comprises the five substages: ordinary world, call to adventure, refusal of the call, meeting with the mentor, and crossing the first threshold. The initiation stage has three substages, the first being tests, allies, and enemies, the second being the ordeal and the third being reward. Finally, the return stage has three substages, which are the road back, the resurrection, and return with the elixir. For example, imagine for a moment that you are an individual who is very much normal and worldly. You enjoy a great time with family and friends, and you are intensely motivated to build your business. You do much of what normal people do. In your younger years, you went clubbing a lot, and still do on occasion. You love to cook, to be in a relationship, to tease your friends, and to get into occasional arguments with family members. Ordinarily, you have almost no pressing interest to explore existential questions outside of normal, regular life. You would much rather spend that time doing some marketing for your business or as quality time with your friends, or even your partner. And then you have a life experience that forces you to re-examine your beliefs and your entire orientation with life. On one ordinary day, you unfortunately become a victim of a motor vehicle accident. The accident is severe enough that the car gets mangled. Luckily, you do not lose your life. In fact, you are so incredibly lucky that you escape with escape with only minor injuries. What you had not previously imagined is that you could one day get into a coma. The impact of the accident leaves you in a coma for two weeks. Your physical recovery after the coma is remarkable, however there has been one very important change during the experience. This is that you had what is known as a "near death experience", often abbreviated as "NDE". The NDE is a well-known and often documented experience wherein an individual who experiences a brush with death also experiences a separation of the physical body from what has been called soul, or spirit. These two terms tend to be used interchangeably in normal (non-esoteric) speak, but in a number of spiritual traditions that I have studied, they are not exactly the same thing. In any case, during an NDE, experiencers have been documented to perceive phenomena happening in the real world of five senses even when in a coma and their five senses are shut down. For example, they may see the emergency response individuals who handled them at the accident site or carried them to the hospital even while unconscious. Often, it has been documented that NDE experiencers can identify individuals or speak to a whole series of events that they claim they witnessed even though their physical bodies were unconscious. That begs the question of who, or rather what, is doing the perceiving. The who, or the what, is this phenomenon some have called soul, or spirit.

In many places and times in this book, we will discuss this phenomenon of soul or spirit, which we can simply term 'consciousness' and which seems to be able to perceive independent of a physical body. The consciousness experiencing an NDE may also interact with other nonphysical consciousnesses, and upon waking up, can recount the experience in great detail. Imagine further that you had this NDE and upon being revived from the coma, you found yourself to be a different person. Before this time, you had little to no interest in spiritual things, however something happened to you. Something that you cannot ignore. During the NDE, you were able to perceive things that you later on confirmed happened while you were "under". Ordinarily, such perceptions are not supposed to be possible. Now, your reality is all mixed up. For the next month and a half, you find yourself to be not quite the self you were mentally, before you had the vehicle accident. You are quiet and withdrawn, but also very calm and serene. You had a powerful spiritual experience in the spirit world. You cannot shake it off, and in addition to that, you have a strong interest in seeking answers to bridge your knowledge gap. After a month and a half of being in this calm and serene, semi-altered state of mind, you are more or less back to your old self. You are back to having fun with your friends, drinking, cooking and talking about business. But one thing has changed fundamentally in you. You now have a seemingly insatiable desire to learn more about the NDE condition, about out of body experiences, and about life after death. Not only that, you are also highly intrinsically motivated to learn how to reproduce the experience of being in the spiritual states you experienced during the two weeks in a coma. You are actively learning techniques for bringing about an out of body experience, or OBE as it is commonly known. This is when one learns to project consciousness out of their physical bodies.

At this juncture, although I asked you to imagine this situation, I would like to alert the reader to the fact that this is actually a true story. This experience happened to a friend of mine, and not just any friend. This was actually a friend I was living with at the time. So, I was a close part of this story. As close as one can get without experiencing the collision, coma, NDE and recovery firsthand. I cite this story to demonstrate one instance of how an individual can awaken to a new view of the world. In a manner of speaking, my friend experienced the hero's journey. The departure phase was brought about by life's experiences, a call to adventure of sorts, that one would otherwise want to refuse. While his consciousness was behind the veil, he had some peak spiritual experiences that were deeply impactful to him. Once he regained consciousness, he was a changed individual. He had experienced something that would stay with him for the rest of his life. He however had to find his way back to normalcy. That road back did not happen immediately. It happened in stages, from the stage of his calm, serene self, to the stage where he was once his gregarious self, talking about all the normal, mundane things he used to talk about, and back to his interest in business. But he brought something back with him in this experience. He brought back a newfound interest in spirituality, with a wider view of reality and what is possible. For him, spirituality was no longer a fringe interest or some far off theory. A physically and spiritually relevant experience happened to him, and he survived it. Where once, his views and orientation were almost completely within five-sense perceptual reality, now he was a mundane man, and more. In his case, he succeeded in attaining a new stable viewpoint after a period of uncertainty (i.e., those six weeks during his calm, serene self, when he engaged in discussions in order to understand what had happened to him and in order to widen his views about reality). My friend is a hero, and I was fortunate to be at the right place, at the right time to also experience this unique event. To this day, my friend's interest in the aspect of spirituality known as OBEs remains very strong. His views on the nature of existence have permanently changed. This is a powerful example of what I mean by an awakening that can be brought about by life experiences. As I will discuss in coming chapters, many awakenings bring about a greater spiritual awareness but the first few awakenings to be shortly discussed pertain more to the physical world and to understanding it, and navigating it, than they do transcending the physical world to the spiritual. I will discuss seven different thresholds of awakenings. The first three are more or less rooted in the real world. Among the experiences of the fourth kind are those similar to what my friend experienced. I chose to share his experience because the fourth kind of awakening sits right between the physical world on one hand, and the spiritual world on the other. It hence highlights aspects of both.

The seventh and final assumption in this work is that the successive awakenings of spirit having a human experience can occur over different lifetimes and multiple incarnations or within a single lifetime. This assumption also implies the reality of reincarnation, or of multiple incarnations. If we think of the entire journey a spirit entity undertakes to become human as one big hero's journey, within which are several smaller hero's journey iterations, then in order for the spirit entity to return with its final gift, which is the reward of having earned lessons in the "school of life" called surface Earth existence, it could take many, many iterations to learn those valuable lessons. Lessons such as compassion, perseverance, love, cunning, courage may need several lives to master. Add to that this idea that within this one big hero's journey that you and I and others as spirit beings having human experiences take, we tend to forget ourselves during the journey. Regaining the knowledge of who we are while in the midst of the experience may take many iterations. Indeed, the multiple nature of incarnational lives for a given spirit being is confirmed by research data from hypnotic regressions, research which I shall also delve into as I progress through the chapters in this book. One of the intriguing things is that for some individuals, successive awakenings happen within the same lifetime. This seems to be the case when that individual has had many other lifetimes, and has thus learned some of the lessons in previous lifetimes so that the reaching the threshold for attaining a certain type of awakening may be faster, therefore many of which can happen in the same lifetime. This seems to be the path I have been on, in this incarnation. This reality may be similar, or different, for others.

2

SUMMARY OF THE RINGS

Have you ever had one of those night time dreams where, while still in one dream you fall asleep and then awaken into another dream? That is, one dream nested within another? It is one of the most fascinating experiences one can have. Fascinating because upon waking up from the second dream, one wakes into the first dream, and depending on one's degree of consciousness, it may be apparent to one that one is dreaming. Or not. I have had a number of these "dream within a dream" experiences and I have also interacted with other individuals who have had such nested dreams. A nested dream is where there are one or more layers of dreams within dreams.

Better yet, have you ever heard about or watched Christopher Nolan's movie *Inception*? It came out in 2010. In that movie, there are individuals who do the nested dream realities several levels deep. As a Hollywood movie, it has a plot with an action theme, however the idea of nested dreams is an experience that individuals in the real world have. Movies are a great way that some truths are shared with the public. To date, apart from Inception, I can think of at least three movies that show the use of technology to access other realities while within a dream state. The first of those movies is *Total Recall*. In this movie, a person can have a technologically assisted mental experience of an otherworldly place like the planet Mars while dreaming. *The Matrix* is a famous movie that was released in 1999, where humans can live their entire existence in a state of sleep, all the while thinking that they are awake and living a regular life. In the third movie, Avatar, technology assists an individual in a state of sleep to access an avatar's body and to have physical experiences through that body.

Is Hollywood onto something? One could say that they often are. Regardless, this notion of dream experiences spawning other dream experiences that appear very real to consciousness having those experiences is one that has been pondered for a long time. Typically, the consciousness in the innermost dream reality is unaware of the dreamer in the immediate outer layer dream within the nested dream reality. For example, the ancient Chinese sage, Chuang-Tsu, is known to have written in his book *Zhuangzi* about a dream wherein he was a butterfly. While he was the butterfly, he had no notion of himself as Chuang-Tsu. Upon waking up, Chuang-Tsu pondered whether he was dreaming the butterfly, or whether it was indeed the butterfly that was dreaming his life. Similarly, we are typically not aware of the dreamer who is dreaming our real lives.

I bring up the notion of dreams and their possible nested nature because I would like to draw a parallel between the nature of consciousness experiencing manifest reality and this notion of nested dreams. Specifically, I would like to propose an idea, which is that the life we are living now, which we are so fully engrossed in, with some of us thinking that it is so real and all that there is, could in fact be the dream of another version of ourselves. That self, could also be the dream of yet another version of ourselves. At a certain point, the self that wakes from the dream is Source itself.

This idea of dreaming other aspects of ourselves, or even of entire realities, is not an arbitrary one. Apart from the nested dreams I and others I have interacted with have had, and noticing that Hollywood has made a few movies connecting dreaming on one hand with living conscious existences within the dream on the other, there are two sources I draw from, in making this analogy between nested dreams and the possible situation of our lives as being the dreams of other versions of ourselves. One source comes from conversations I have had with friends who are members of esoteric orders and who share that opinion as part of their esoteric knowledge, and the other source is at least one experience I had during a consciousness exploration exercise where I projected my consciousness far beyond the confines of this galaxy and into the higher spiritual worlds.

That being said, as a working hypothesis, I would like to propose a scenario where you and I, and the people we know in our lives, are conscious to one degree or another in our current incarnation. Yet, by becoming aware we are conscious in our current lives, and while still alive, it is possible to progressively backtrack with our consciousness to other aspects of ourselves that through their dreaming are contributing to our current life. We will find that these other aspects are in a state of sleep, or meditation. Their dreams ultimately contribute to our lives. If they were to wake up, our lives would come to an end. This is a similar idea to seeing yourself asleep while you are projected out of body, for those who have either had the experience or are aware of the phenomenon. The secret then, if we are to progressively gain greater awareness of ourselves, is to learn to merge with these aspects of ourselves that are dreaming our existence.

Herein comes the rings. What are these rings? They can be thought of as filters of the reality we experience, similar to the idea of dreams within dreams. In terms of the hero's journey, each ring represents going through the entire cycle of departure, initiation, and return. When we come full circle within the ring, we acquire the gift that the ring has to offer. Ring one is the ring of childhood. This is the ring that we engage as a child, which defines our childhood world. Ring two, the ring of polity, is the ring we engage as adults in society. Ring three is the ring of the five senses. It is the ring we engage as the human mammal living in the real world. Ring four is the ring of life and death. It is the ring where we go beyond the physical world into the worlds of spirit where we reside before life and after death. Ring five is the ring of the higher self. It is the ring wherein we engage a broader spiritual identity beyond the soul that incarnates multiple times on Earth. Ring six is the ring of the separate self. It is the ring in which we realize that there are other selves with their higher selves, and that ultimately these other selves with their higher selves are also ourselves. Ring seven is the ring pass-not. It is the ring we engage as the creator within its own manifested illusion. Each of these rings will be discussed at length in chapters that follow.

3

THE RING OF CHILDHOOD

A human being is born into the world as we know it without any prior knowledge of what came before entrance into the world. The human being from the period of being a baby into adulthood undergoes continuous programming from the environment in order to acquaint the human its new surroundings. The programming is arguably an essential tool for the new human to quickly reach a point where communication with other human beings can take place. After the preliminary stages of language are taught the child learns symbolic manipulation of verbal, quantitative, spatial and other modes to enable the child not only communicate with other human beings but to also take in information encoded by other human beings that constitutes recorded human knowledge. The child also learns how to be emotionally intelligent when communicating with other human beings and sometimes with other living creatures such as animals. In our current modern age, the child starts school at a young age since the increasingly complex society means that to guarantee the best success and survival rates, the logical thing for the child to do is to get the best encoding of information through education and enculturation. In addition to school, the child attends church, mosque, synagogue or temple and also participates in out of school activities among family and friends. Education culminates with the opportunity to secure a means to maintain the child's livelihood, once the transition occurs from childhood to adulthood. During childhood, at the current time, the family unit, typically led by biological parents, is responsible for housing and supporting the child as it grows and matures. Upon reaching maturity, the child, now an adult typically leaves home in order to set up its own home. Typically, the human who is now an adult also has children of their own, and the cycle continues. Most adults will still be welcome at the home they grew up in, and most will still remain the children of their own parents.

This is one description of the standard lifestyle in modern times that most of us experience and can relate to. Within this cycle, we rarely think about what challenges there must have been for our child selves, or indeed for our spirits that incarnate and start their journeys as children. Imagine appearing in a new physical body once again, and having to figure it all out once again. It must be quite an experience. Our child selves give us the first experience and opportunity to be heroes. In this chapter, I shall explore details of the hero's journey as it pertains to the ring of childhood. The hero undertaking the journey is the spirit coming into incarnation on surface Earth, either for the first time, or for a repeat experience.

3.1 The spiritual realm

As we saw earlier on, the third assumption I made in the introduction to this book is that I am a spirit being having a human experience, therefore I am much more than just my physical body. For me, this assumption is based on my actual spiritual experiences. I have experienced being in my spirit body and out of my physical body, on several occasions. I have also interacted with other individuals who have had and have shared their spiritual experiences.

For the reader, however, the idea of being a spirit being having a human experience may still be just an idea, not one backed by actual spiritual experiences. I would therefore ask both readers who have had experiences confirming their existences as spirit beings, and those who have not had such experiences, to entertain the possibility of there being such a situation as having your conscious awareness exist and be able to perceive reality independent of your physical body.

If you can perceive reality without your physical body, then there is a nonphysical version of you that an exist in its own reality. Let us call that reality the spiritual realm. Now, what do we know about the spiritual realm? Well, my experience of education and schooling, and my study of modern school systems leads me to believe that in the modern education system, there is almost no place for spiritual education. This is because the modern education system has inherited ways of learning and teaching from Europe, and the European system of knowledge is built around an epistemology that has no place for spirit. The science and the philosophy that is taught publicly dwell on logic and rationality, not on the esoteric and on the mystical.

This is no accident. The ways of learning and education that developed in Europe at a certain stage focused almost entirely on reality that can be perceived and studied by the five senses. The view of the world, from those influential philosophers in Europe, became one that is materialistic. Those European philosophers like Descartes and scientists like Newton, focused on materialism of the observable real world. The dominant ontology of the modern European knowledge system, and its associated epistemology, became one based on materialism. Ontology is how reality is viewed, and epistemology is how knowledge is derived from that view of reality.

To be fair, some European thinkers at different times over the past millennium have advocated a focus on both physical and nonphysical realities as realms for gaining and building knowledge about the world. It just turns out that the bias towards materialistic existence won over the alternative. Materialistic science has since been quite successful in advancing categories of knowledge but even with this success, there have been anomalies and phenomena that could be explained by incorporating an acknowledgement of spirit as an assumption.

We find that other peoples around the world, some of them with knowledge systems as ancient as those of the Europeans or in some cases arguably more ancient, these people had different ontologies. Different starting assumptions. Starting assumptions are important, because they determine the scope of what is possible within a given system of knowledge. This is the reason why I stated some underlying assumptions at the start of this work. The late African high shaman of the Zulu people, the Sanusi Vuzamazulu Credo Mutwa wrote clearly in part 4 of his book *Indaba My Children* that the ways of a people are influenced by their starting assumptions. I agree with this position.

There are well developed ontologies of other cultures outside of Europe that include not only the material world but the nonmaterial world as well, which we can call the spiritual world. Among the peoples of Africa, spirit plays a crucial role in understandings about existence and reality. Every African group I have learned about engages in spiritual practices as part of traditional life within the community. Credo's writings show a deep and well-developed ontology and epistemology that incorporates worlds of matter and spirit. My own people, the Akan of West Africa, have a clearly well-developed ontology wherein the material world is only a small fraction of a much wider reality, much of which is spiritual, beginning with an infinite creator, and various hierarchies of spirit beings and existences, and ending with the physical world in one nonseparated existence. In Asia as another example, there are various peoples and cultures with well-developed ontologies and epistemologies that give the spiritual existence a much larger and broader representation within their knowledge systems. One example is the Advaita Vedanta system of India, advanced by sages such as Gaudapada and Shankara.

We shall return to more in-depth treatments of ontologies later in this book. The reader would find that in this book, we start with discussing spirit, and we end with discussing spirit. For now, I merely aim to encourage the reader to entertain the possibility of there being spirit worlds where spirits reside in prior to being born into incarnation. Along with this exhortation of the reader, I would also like to bring attention to the works of some Western scientists who have applied their skills for creating new knowledge not only within materialistic science but also to the realm of spirit. One such individual is the social scientist Helen Wambach, a modern-day clinical psychologist and one of my favourites when it comes to using research methods to learn about consciousness. Wambach built her research around using hypnosis methods to help individuals explore early memories, past lives, and even previous existences just before birth. The first published book by Wambach that I read was titled *Reliving Past Lives*, which was fascinating in its own account. In *Reliving Past Lives*, much data is presented to support the existence of spirit, the survival of the death experience, and the reality of multiple incarnations that a spirit has experienced. Sometimes Wambach managed to corroborate her collected accounts with independent evidence from the real world.

However, for this present book on awakening, it is Wambach's book titled *Life before Life* that I would like to highlight, because she presents what I think are truly fascinating accounts of what happens not only before birth but also as the baby is being born, and soon after. If you do get to read this book, you may not think about babies the same way again. The book asserts the existence of spirits in the spirit world that frequently receive counseling from other spirits on the life they are about to live during incarnation. Of course, a child does not typically remember what it agreed to as a spirit, because of the birthing process. Think about it, the spirit enters a baby that had spent most of its time sleeping in the womb, and even more time sleeping after birth. Most of us rarely remember what we did a day or two ago, not to mention a week ago, how much more after many weeks and months of sleeping during the first year after birth. During the post-birth period, the child has other challenges to overcome. It has just been taken out of an environment that it was very comfortable in, and now it is expected to learn how to exist and to survive in a new and largely unfamiliar world. Tough chance to remember your life purpose and goals discussed with your spirit committee prior to uniting with the baby's physical body. Yet, another fascinating facet of this situation is that although we may not consciously remember these happenings, under the conditions of hypnosis, it is possible to recollect that information. Nothing is lost to our subconscious mind, which records everything.

So, in *Life after Life*, we learn that there are spirit worlds, that they are populated by denizens who understand that they will be incarnating into physical bodies, and that these denizens can and do receive advice from other spirit beings on the incarnation process. The purpose of speaking about spirit worlds, or the possibility of them, to begin with, is to set the stage to understand the first hero's journey that I believe we all undergo. That hero's journey, is the journey of being born and coming to life in the physical world. Remember that I assume we are spirit beings having a human experience. Not everyone believes this, or even entertains such thoughts. This section of chapter three is an attempt to provide an alternative view, which I argue is in fact an old view, or perhaps *the* old view, that prevailed long before materialistic thinking encouraged by materialistic philosophy and science mostly developed in Europe took over and has now become the norm in modern contexts around the world. The old view, simply stated, is that human beings have souls. The soul is a kind of spirit. For now, the purpose of this section is simply to encourage the reader to entertain the possibility of spirit.

The hero's journey framework begins with an ordinary world. If we think of ourselves first as spirits and second as humans, then our ordinary world is the world of spirit. Coming into incarnation can be seen as a call to adventure. If you do read *Life before Life*, you will learn that not all souls that are currently incarnated wanted to be born. In some cases, the hypnosis accounts report of resistance by the soul to be born, or to be born again. This is similar to refusing the call at the onset of the hero's journey. Before moving on to the next section on the process of coming into incarnation, I would like to draw attention to two works that provide more data on the existence of spirit worlds, and of the process that precedes birth. The first is a book by the late Robert Monroe, titled *Far Journeys*. Now, this book *Far Journeys* is about a lot more than just what happens before we are born. It is really about very interesting accounts of a man who learned how to project his consciousness out of his body, and became quite famous for his ability to do so and to help others also gain experiences beyond the five physical senses. Bob Monroe set up the Monroe Institute in Virginia in the USA. To this day, the institute continues to conduct research aimed at exploring and expanding consciousness states. Back to Bob's book, however. In it, there is a detailed account, from the perspective of spirit, of spirit beings entering into incarnation on Earth, and being assisted by groups of beings that oversee and assist the process. The gist of the process is that spirits come this "school of learning" known as surface Earth life. These spirits experience numerous incarnations. Eventually, just like it occurs in schools in real life, the spirits reach graduation. They graduate, and then leave to continue their journeys elsewhere, beyond the surface Earth life school.

The second book I would like to draw attention to is entitled *The Magic Bag*. It is a book that was dictated to a man named Mark Probert, via clairaudience, over a five-year period, starting in 1947, by nine beings known as the "Inner Circle". More will be said about the contents of The Magic Bag when discussing ring seven, in chapter nine. What I would like to bring attention to, is that in this book there is mention of yet more information on how spirits enter into incarnation. Specifically, the opinion of the spirit sharing the information is that once a spirit in the spirit world decides it is ready to come into incarnation once again, it falls into a sleep-like state, after which it gets into incarnation. I found this to be interesting because of some of the earlier material I presented regarding the use of technology to get humans into a sleep state, after which they experience dream worlds such as were shown in the movies Total Recall, The Matrix and Avatar. It was quite fascinating to me then, that a spirit coming into incarnation goes into something like a sleep state and perhaps dreams its way into incarnation. That brings back thoughts of the Chinese sage Chuang-Tzu who asked whether he was dreaming the butterfly, or whether the butterfly was dreaming him. With that being said, let us proceed to the next section on what coming into incarnation entails.

3.2 Coming into incarnation

There is a longstanding curiosity, which is the question around when a spirit enters the body. This is of course assuming that we are spirit beings. If so, when do we come into incarnation? Do we come in during pregnancy, at the time of birth, or shortly thereafter? In the studies that Wambach carried out for her book *Life before life*, we learn of an interesting result, which is that prior to being born, as spirit beings we are aware of ourselves, even if we do not remember that we are, after we come into incarnation. We can learn the following from Wambach's research:

"The response of my subjects to the question: "When does your soul enter the fetus?" provides an interesting answer to this question. My subjects were perhaps more pro-abortion, as a group, than a cross-section of the American public would be. Yet among the 750 subjects were some practicing Catholics, many Christians, and others who believed that abortion was a form of murder. Yet the 750 subjects were nearly unanimous on one key point. They felt that the fetus was not truly a part of their consciousness. They existed, fully conscious, as an entity apart from the fetus. Indeed they frequently reported that the fetal body was confining and restrictive, and that they preferred the freedom of out-of-body existence. It was with much reluctance that many of them joined their consciousness with the cellular consciousness of the newborn infant.

When all the 750 cases were analyzed, 89 percent of all the subjects responding said that they did not become a part of the fetus or involved with the fetus until after six months of gestation. Even then, many subjects reported being "in and out" of the fetal body. They viewed themselves as an adult consciousness relating to the fetal body as a less-developed form of life." (Wambach, 1979)

There are two comment that I would like to make on from this quote above. The first is that the responses from individuals under hypnosis appear to suggest that they had conscious awareness of themselves and of the foetus at the time the questions were presented during hypnosis. It is also stated that the consciousness preferred the freedom of being out of body to being joined with the foetus. To me, this evidence obtained from subjects under hypnosis speaks to the presence of aware consciousnesses that one may call soul or spirit. These consciousnesses are aware of themselves and of the foetus, to the extent that they are separate entities from the foetus. They also demonstrate adult consciousness compared with the underdeveloped consciousness of the foetus. That is the first comment.

The second comment is in regard to the incarnating consciousness not joining with the foetus until the end of the second trimester of pregnancy, or after six months of gestation and even then, only in-and-out. Beyond the quote, Wambach goes on to indicate that a third of what I would call souls did not unite with the foetus until during birth or shortly thereafter. I find this to be interesting. I find the in-and-out part to also be interesting. Some cultures in West Africa appear to know how to interrogate the incoming spirit before it comes into incarnation. For example, among the Dagara people, the soul can be queried to learn what its life mission is, prior to birth. That mission is then included in the child's name. One such event was reported in Malidoma Somé's book *Of Water and the Spirit*.

So, it would appear that from the world of spirit, souls come into incarnation by merging their conscious with the cellular consciousness of the foetus sometime between the last three months of pregnancy and after the child is born. Once the merging occurs, the soul's consciousness and the body's consciousness pair up. We can take as a working hypothesis that as spirits we fall into something like a sleep state on the spirit side, in order to come into incarnation. And then we arrive here. When we arrive, we don't remember much, because we are sleeping just as the baby spends much of its time sleeping. We become one with the baby. This also means that we become one with the baby's process of growing and awakening. Because the baby slowly develops its body, its brain and neural systems, its limbs and such, we unite with this situation go along. In the early years, the baby simply wants to grow. So, it eats and it sleeps. In between eating and sleeping, it performs other functions that are largely automatic.

I do not know about you, but as a spirit being, I do not remember any of this process of actually being born. I have not been hypnotized and regressed in this incarnation. What I do remember, and this was much later on, was that I met with a spirit being that referred to me as "my son", and told me that I was to go on a mission. I then became very, very small. Imagine a magnifying glass, focusing rays of light into a tiny point. The version of me that was interacting with the spirit being which referred to me as "my son" can be likened to the wide circumference of the magnifying glass. After that, my consciousness got focused into a little point, just like a magnifying glass does with light. I was born a breech baby, and as a child, my parents told me that I did not cry much, or make much noise. Instead, I tended to be quiet, observing everything around me.

Let us return to the baby's development. Eventually the baby grows enough physically that it starts to rapidly learn about its environment. The baby needs to piece together all of the sensory information coming at it, so that it can make sense of the world around it. Part of the process involves the baby learning to walk, to talk and to communicate. The baby becomes successful when it has succeeded in developing enough physically that it can begin to function intelligently in its new environment. Before that time, the spirit incarnating in this young physical body is often just going along for the ride.

Once the baby develops enough physically, it means the spirit consciousness of the baby is also aligned with the consciousness of the baby's physical body. There is not much differentiation, but again that depends from individual to individual. Without education, the baby progresses through the stages of new-born, infant, toddler, pre-schooler, school-aged child, and then adolescent. After adolescence comes adulthood. We have all gone through this.

As we go through these stages, our focus is very much on mastering the physical world. Without spiritual education, we forget about our spiritual selves until we are old enough to start thinking for ourselves, piecing together information and figuring things out. Some never get to this stage, and instead become frightened by spiritual phenomena. I remember the first conscious out of body experience I had as a child. I was so afraid that I freaked out and passed out from mere fright. It was only after I grew into adulthood and had educated myself into understanding what had happened that I was able to properly process his experience from my earlier years. Other individuals may not receive education directly from the community they incarnate into, but may receive guidance from their individual spirit guides. There have been accounts of this happening.

In some of those non-Western cultures of which two examples were mentioned in the previous section, the existence of spirit may be taken for granted as part of their existence and therefore new entrants to those cultures, in addition to growing up learning how to operate their physical bodies also start to learn how to engage their spiritual selves while incarnated. Often, they are taught how to do this, through initiation. What I still find to be one of the most amazing accounts of initiation is the one shared by Malidoma Somé of his own initiation among the Dagara ethnic group of West Africa. The spiritual activities that his ethnic group engage in seem so "far out" from the standpoint of a mind that is primarily fixed on the five-sense world that it may seem unbelievable. That is, until similar accounts are read in anthropological reports from other groups. One such example in Somé's book is an account of his grandfather being made to walk from the hospital where he died at, back to his village. This was done through spiritual means. The description is incredible, almost unbelievable. And then years later, I read in an anthropological journal an account of an American anthropologist named Bruce Grindal who in 1967 witnessed a dead drummer of the Sisala people of West Africa rise and dance to the beat of the drum. Naturally, the anthropologist experienced a freaking out session in response to this situation that is abnormal from the point of view of materialistic reality. Grindal's article is entitled *Into the Heart of Sisala Experience: Witnessing Death Divination*. It was published in the *Journal of Anthropological Research*, in 1983.

In another example, if the culture you grew up in takes as normal routine practice the need for vision quests, such as some of the Native American people do, then it would be a normal thing for you when individuals leave your settlement for days to be out in the wilderness, only to return from the vision quest with success of having had one or more visions and at times also having been led to acquire objects of power of a spiritual nature. There was a period during my awakening that I spent months reading accounts of Native Americans who shared their life stories with American government anthropologists that were sent out into the frontiers. At the time, one group among several that I was particularly fascinated by were the Crow people, whose matrilineal clan system is so similar to that of my own people the Akan. I was fascinated with them also because my Akan clan totem is the crow. I remember reading books such as *Plenty-Coups: chief of the Crows*, by Frank Linderman, and *Two Leggings: the making of a Crow warrior*, by Peter Nabakov. These books presented a reality that was so different from what I have grown up to know in this modern age that I was gripped by it and could not easily put the books down. In the pre-modern reality that these Native American elders lived, life and death were real and immediate, and spirit was as real and as integral to the ontology of these people as it is not in the modern world dominated by materialistic philosophy and science.

At any rate, the point I intend to make is that as we grow up learning how to operate our physical bodies. Without also being taught about our spiritual selves, we run the risk of thinking that the world of the five-senses is all that there is. If that happens, we can be more easily manipulated by the fear of the unknown and also possibly more easily manipulated by those who take it upon themselves to manage the opinions and perceptions of life within the five-sense world. We can end up becoming imprisoned in the manner that Plato describes in his allegory of the cave.

3.3 "Growing up"

In many ancient cultures across the world, it was recognized that the transition from childhood to adulthood was important enough that it needed to be marked by ceremony involving the entire society. The ceremony was initiation. From one culture to the next, the initiation ceremony differed. In many contexts, initiation was a serious matter. The initiate had to prove themselves in ways that sometimes even threatened the individual's life. In some contexts, initiation was merely an acknowledgement by the community that the individual had come of age. There were ceremonies for females as well as for males.

In the context of current modern communities, traditional initiation has become the exception rather than the norm. Although certain communities are still holding out and carrying out traditional initiations, such as the Dipo initiation ceremony for girls of the Krobo ethnic group in Ghana, much of "coming of age" initiation ceremonies now seem to occur within religions. For example, within Judaism, the bar mitzvah and bah mitzvah ceremonies carried out for boys and girls respectively. For Christians, boys and girls that come of age undergo confirmation, and for Theravada Buddhists, there is a ceremony known as shinbyu which some boys go through.

In all of this, there is a recognition that there is a difference in experience between a child and an adult. These ceremonies mark the change. In the traditional versions, the initiate often goes into nature to have the ordeal directly with nature, and then returns if successful. Reverting to Plato's allegory of the cave, that is like the freed individual that is moving to exit the cave. The process of exit can be likened to childhood. In traditional contexts, when the incarnated spirit undergoes initiation during the transition from childhood to adulthood, the spirit is given a chance to experience the spiritual world while attached to a physical body. If the spirit passes the test and the physical body does not die, the spirit gets to remain incarnated while having the ability to return to visit the spiritual world. The incarnated spirit can then return to the rest of the community as an adult, often bringing back knowledge gained during initiation. In this regard, the reward for the spirit is the gift of remaining incarnated while also being aware of its spiritual nature. In the religious versions, nature as the primordial is replaced by the paradigm of the religion.

Interestingly, in secular modern life, such initiations done formally by the community seem to be missing. There are what may be termed informal initiations that happen for instance among gangs whose members have to carry out a dangerous or even criminal task in order to secure their place in the gang. These kinds of informal initiations seem to be filling a void where teenagers would otherwise have been initiated by the society. For formal initiations, it seems the nearest equivalent to an initiation for pre-adult boys and girls is graduating high school prior to or just about the time of reaching legal age. There are certain actions that can occur around this time, such as becoming independent of parents, being able to marry, to be conscripted in a national army, to register as a voter in national elections, to get certain kinds of jobs, to learn how to drive a car in order to get a driver's license, or in some cultures, to be legally allowed to drink or smoke. These can be seen as markers of transitioning from childhood to adulthood. In many cultures, there are also implications for reaching the age of consent and being considered an adult. These markers are significant because they confer on the newly transitioned individual the right to be regarded as an adult and also the responsibilities that come with that conferral.

One way I also view this transition from childhood to adulthood is the transfer of responsibility for the individual from biological parents to the state. Once we reach legal age, we are no longer under the legal guidance of our parents or guardians. We are now under the legal guidance of the state, and can be held accountable by the state in the manner that other adults are. Before this age, at least in many Western countries around the world, children who commit heinous crimes may be treated as juvenile delinquents and sent for rehabilitation rather than being incarcerated with adults. This is because from the perspective of the state, these juveniles have not yet gone through the transition from childhood to adulthood. They have not yet been "harvested" by the state as a unit of production and hence they must be rehabilitated with minimal damage. Oh, oops, I meant it is because the state does not consider juveniles to be mentally developed to the extent that adults are and therefore juveniles must not be held accountable the way adults are. Smile. Final point on this. For most modern states (that is, those that are communist or democratic, but not those that are monarchies), as adults in such states we consciously or tacitly support the consensus that maintains the legitimacy of the state. This is why states feel threatened when individuals go on mass demonstrations. It is also why such a threat can be made real if the size of the demonstration reaches critical mass beyond which the state can be toppled. When that happens, it can be called a revolution. In recent history, we have seen examples of governments ultimately being deposed as a result of revolution. This occurred in Egypt, Libya, Tunisia and Yemen during the "Arab Spring" event of the last decade.

The point here is that individual adults of a modern state together form the power base of the state. It is also individual adults of a modern state who are ultimately the source of legitimacy of the laws that can be enacted in the state. It is important to be consciously aware of this, because without being consciously aware of this, we give our tacit consent to the state, to use for its ends. Those who end up enacting the ends of the state are individuals in power, and this power can be abused. More on that in the next chapter on the ring of polity. Ideally, the modern state exists to ensure the survival and well-being of the individual. In return, the individual is expected (but arguably not required) to give up a certain degree of sovereignty, through which the individual extends its beingness to encompass that of the state. This is the idea of the social contract that I brought up earlier in the chapter on assumptions. If all goes well, if the state is just, then the exchange is also just for the individual. But it can happen that the exchange is not just for the individual for reasons that the state can be blamed for. When that happens, the individual who is aware of it must attempt to hold the state to account, or otherwise seek to withdraw participation in the consensus that maintains the state.

3.4 Adult-child

So, most adults we know of, very likely including ourselves, have survived the ordeal of being born and having grown from childhood to adulthood. Our spirits incarnated into a physical body in the real world, we progressed through the various stages of the growth of the physical body we incarnated into, and even though we may not have undergone traditional or religious initiation, we passed through childhood to successfully arrive at adulthood.

Adulthood is a great place to be, because as adults, we have the chance to express our volition to the greatest extent possible while incarnated. As adults, we also experience the greatest extent of being held liable for our actions, especially when we are of sound mind and body. At the time of writing this book, many people experience the joys of adulthood starting from when they can legally take care of themselves. In those early years of freedom from parents, newly arrived adults get a job or enjoy time at university. In the secular world, some go out clubbing and partying, exploring interpersonal relationships and working to build a career. These tend to be great years when we are at the height of our energies.

At this point, as adults we are expected to gradually start contributing back to society. We are expected to pay our taxes to support the state. We are also typically expected to start building our own homes. Many in urban areas will become first time tenants who pay rent. We may own different types of properties such as a car, our own pets, and others may also buy homes. We would be expected to be responsible for maintaining these.

As an adult, we also get to decide not only how we use our money, but also how we use our energy and our time. As examples, our personalities and needs would reflect in our choices on whether we join a gym, spend much non-work time in friendship or religious social settings or kick back and watch TV shows in our free time. All of these choices would be our prerogative, and even though our friends, our family members and even our parents may try to put pressure on us in attempts to get us to conform to one way or another that suits their tastes, and even when they may resort to guilt tripping or any other emotional games (or they may not do this but rather be very unconditionally supportive, or not care at all, or anywhere in between), they cannot legally compel us to take any actions that we choose not to.

Therefore, arriving at adulthood can be a very empowering time for us as spirits incarnated in the physical. It can be seen as another stage of freedom we attain, as we navigate through the dream of waking life. An earlier stage of freedom was when we finally learned how to walk, talk, jump about and express ourselves as toddlers. Gosh, all that struggle before, when as babies we were hardly understood, and then breakthrough! We can talk! Once we learn to walk and talk, some of us never stop talking for a moment, or running about, being up to no good. The next big stage of freedom is when we are no longer under the supervision of our parents or guardians. Now we can go to the bar or to the club by ourselves! We don't have to experience the "Ferris Bueller scenario" (for those who have seen the movie *Ferris Bueller's Day Off*) to sneak out as teenagers to go have some fun with our friends without parental consent. I have known this scenario that teenagers experience, not only happening in North America but also in Africa, Asia and in Europe.

On the flipside, our parents may also feel relieved to be rid of us! To them, they have done their duty to society by sacrificing their time, money and energy to take care of us all those years. Our parents may also understand our desire to be free and to enjoy our newly found freedom. They too went through a stage like that a generation ago, even though the time and the circumstances were different. We must not forget that our parents were once children, and were also once young adults. Many who transition from childhood to young adulthood end with us will end up becoming parents as well, at some point. Think of Disney's production *The Lion King*, which had a beautiful song about the circle of life. Having just expressed that, I know that it is also not so easy for some parents to let go of their children once the time comes for the children to break free and to be on their own. It depends from one circumstance to the next, but for most people, a time comes when after transitioning from being a child into being a young adult, it is time to live your own life.

So then, we finally become free of our parents, and that becomes a great time! Party time for many! That time could really be a time to wisely use energies and resources but newly minted adults often tend to be high on energy, time and sometimes money, and low on "wisdom". This is especially the case when they have lived in households or even in cultures that they may have deemed oppressive. The extent to which we enjoy and party as a result of the new found freedom of a young adult can be likened to the freed prisoner in Plato's allegory of the cave who finally makes it into the sunlight outside the cave and is overwhelmed by the beauty of the outside world. This is a time to revel in the light!

Eventually, however, the prisoner decides to make the journey back into the cave. Likewise, the young adult, after years of partying and clubbing, is expected by society to "settle down", to get once again into the cycle, only this time the one who was once a child is now an adult, or expected to be one. Mind you, that adult will always be a child to *their* parents, and their parents to their parents. Hence the notion of the adult-child. It is a continuum. Even as adults, if we choose not to have our own children, we can still be considered the children of the generation before us that reared us during their cycle as parents and guardians. On the other hand, everyone, regardless of age, is a "child" of the nation or state.

Given this new opportunity to experience freedom while incarnated as a young adult, one would imagine that the incarnated spirit would take some time out to finally give good thought to some questions of a spiritual nature. For instance, asking oneself, "what's going on here? Why am I in this world? What am I here for?" It is also plausible that we may ask ourselves these questions even as young children or as adolescents. In the modern society that I currently live in, there is little to no requirement by society to seriously address such questions in a spiritual way. If someone has such questions, they may be encouraged to find answers in one of the available religions, or take up philosophy or psychology. Each of these suggestions could in fact help, and could in fact lead the inquiring soul to discover more about themselves. One cannot necessarily figure out what another soul's triggers would be to catalyze their awakening process.

Otherwise, most of us continue along, striving to cope in the world of sense perception, once we first master our bodies as children and then find our way in life. At this stage, most of the concerns are about how to be in the world and to succeed in it, not what we are doing here. With all the enculturation we get from parents, school, religions and society's values, there is more than enough stimulus to keep our minds and bodies engaged in the reality of the real world. And for most of us, this is enough. After all, one of the main reasons why we come into incarnation as souls is to experience physical life. So, once we arrive here and succeed in doing that, why should we be concerned with anything else? Being a normal, regular citizen is enough for most of us, but for a few, it may not be. The condition of going along in life without being aware or conscious of your existence, of who you are on a soul level, and of what this reality stuff is all about, that is like going to bed every night and dreaming but not being conscious in the dream. Some people do not even pay attention to their dreams after they wake up, unless they experience a nightmare, or an unusual dream. If you have experienced lucid dreaming however, you may agree that those can be very memorable, even more so than experiences in waking life.

So, this is the first ring. What I call the ring of childhood. This ring, once we traverse its scope, gives us the basic awareness to function in incarnation. It is the ring that everyone is expected to acquire throughout their lives. This is the "normal life". Most of the people out there in society do not seriously go beyond this ring. Their thoughts, energies and actions are firmly situated within this ring. This means that much of their attention energies are focused on the activities described in this chapter. Moving attention and energy away from this ring into any of the other six rings to be detailed after this one constitutes a deviation from the basic norm. In the next chapter, we shall detail another ring that is closely related to this one so it is not such a big deviation.

4

THE RING OF POLITY

From time immemorial, human beings have been social creatures. We organize ourselves into groups to socialize with one another but to also meet our survival needs. As a group, through division of labour, we can cooperate and collaborate in joint activities toward producing and maintaining our food, clothing, shelter, health and safety. As a group, we stand a better chance at fending off threats to our survival, and also stand a better chance at reproducing and caring for our young so as to ensure the propagation of the species.

Beyond meeting these basic needs, we come together in social groups also to keep one another company and to entertain one another. Working together and sharing experiences with one another enables us more rapidly learn about ourselves and about the world around us. It also gives us an identity through which to relate within the group as well as with other groups outside of our own.

Historically, as groups became larger and more complex, they developed leaders. Traditional societies had leaders who were priest-kings, or warrior-priests. These were individuals who could lead the group both militarily and spiritually. Over time, the priesthood and the political office of leader separated, so that the priesthood became advisors and the warriors became kings, and sometimes emperors. Not all societies adopted this model. Some smaller, often indigenous societies maintained their priest-kings, even to the current time. Today, the imperial model has also been largely replaced by rule by the majority.

4.1 Diverse circles

As we progress through life, we find ourselves interacting in different circles which begins right at home. When we come into incarnation in a modern home, the first social circle we engage with is often the nuclear family. This is natural, as the child is usually born into a family. It is expected that the family will take care of the child. Now, not all children have this experience, granted, but that tends to be the norm. As we grow, we increase the number of circles we engage in. Extended family members and childhood friends become an important next layer of friendships. Then, for those who are religious, there are also religious circles they may belong to. When we are old enough to join sports groups, or other circles such as music, dance, craft, or scouts, we start having experiences within informal circles. Depending on our life circumstances, we have access to greater and greater varieties of circles as we progress through our formative years and into adult life.

So, our adult life becomes an array of influences from diverse circles that we have either been brought up in, or have acquired due to our own interests. These diverse circles are important because they serve as our formal and informal social networks that enable us have access to people and to resources. If you have strong circles, the people in those circles can make a huge difference in your life, especially after you transition from childhood to adulthood.

4.2 Living a "normal life"

Recall in section 3.4 I detailed a scenario that develops for most of us as we transition from childhood to adulthood. We typically experience a brief period of freedom where we are old enough to be on our own, independent of our parents, but perhaps not old enough (experiences vary) to immediately "settle down" to start a family and a life, and to begin the cycle yet again. A similar cycle such as the one we experienced as a child. This brief period of freedom can be powerful in the lives of young people and it often tends to be a time of celebration. It has been termed "living young" by some, and it is often a time when we live mostly for ourselves, even if for a brief period.

Ironically, it is also a time when we are at our strongest, physically and even mentally, some would argue. What we may lack during this time, is experience of life. It is a time we try to find ourselves and get on with life. During this time, modern society tends to be simultaneously lenient and demanding on the individual. Lenient because pressures to marry and settle down may be delayed on a short-term basis because it is understood that the young adult must have a degree of independence to support self and a new family. Therefore, there tends to be demands or pressure instead on "making it" in life, or at least starting off on a firm footing, so that the young individual can be independent of their parents and childhood family situation first of all, and then also that the individual becomes situated to have dependents and to also contribute to society.

So, this becomes "normal life". As young adults, we strive to succeed in modern life. That strife is for the most part focused on survival in the material world. Beyond what is readily available in religious traditions, the modern education system that I am aware of in many countries gives little to no preparation to the incarnated soul which is now finally able to most fully express its choices and its volition, having survived birth and childhood. No urging to stop and say, "hold on a minute. I am here now. Cool. So, what is this all about? Why am I here? Is there something specific I came here to do? Or is it all just what it is right now?" Not much of a chance to seriously engage in such introspection before advancing on to live life fully as an adult. The most that is available in secular education that probes into some of these questions can be found in the discipline of philosophy. Much of that philosophy which is taught to non-specialists at the late high school or college levels is based on ideas related to materialism. With the exception of philosophers such as Friedrich Nietzsche and some of the school of existentialism, very little, in my experience, is taught about soul and spirit, going into those ontological domains I mentioned earlier in the introduction, that can alternatively be found in Ancient Egyptian, Daoist and Vedic philosophies.

This absence of education and prompting to deeply examine existential questions goes to the advantage of the state and society, and to the disadvantage of the spirit incarnated as a human. It is in the interest of society to preserve the order of things in favour of society and not in favour of provoking greater awareness in the individual. By this, I mean modern society, and not all societies that have existed on this planet. Remember that in Plato's allegory of the cave, not only are people chained and fastened securely so that they can only view the wall in front of them, but there are also people in the background, two general groups of people to be exact, that are neither fastened like the majority, or compelled to view just what is being shown on the wall. The first group are those I shall call "the manipulators", as was indicated in the allegory, and the second are those that I shall call "the artists", also indicated in the allegory.

These two groups of people do not want greater awareness in the masses, as is indicated by the masses being chained *and* also being deceived into thinking that the shadows being projected onto the wall in front of them is all that there is. So, we might ask ourselves, why is that? Well, my opinion of why this is, goes back to what societies are, to begin with. At the beginning of this chapter, I started to paint a picture of how societies evolved from the need of groups of people to come together to ensure the survival of the group. Working together became more efficient in helping achieve the common goals of survival and advancement of the group.

And so, each individual played their part. As societies became more complex, specialization of roles in society also became more complex. These roles also included jobs, such as warriors, healers, artisans, herders, farmers, comedians, kings, you name it. You can imagine for yourself some more roles.

Out of this process, especially in larger societies, emerged the notion of the elite. Those who for whatever reason, historical or other, increasingly assumed upon themselves greater privileges in society, including the ultimate privilege of being in control of the social organism itself. Now, different forms of elites emerged in different societies for different reasons. Herein lies my theory. Whether it became part of the mindset of the elites, or whether it just happens to be the manner in which the social organism functions, the requirement that people came together into groups to ensure their common survival and advancement appears to have been overturned, superseded or upended so that now it is rather the individual that exists to ensure the survival of the state.

I must clarify here, again, on two levels. First, that not all societies in the world today are necessarily like this, and second, that I am not speaking in absolutes. In regard to the first, I speak specifically about modern societies and their governments. Those that in large part have been influenced by political ideas that were developed over the past few centuries in Europe. There are other societies and forms of government on the planet that still thrive. Two main kinds that I know of are versions of kingdoms and monarchies on hand, and versions of rule by a council of elders on the other hand. Most places that still run the monarchical model also run some version of modern governments in parallel. Places that have a council of elders typically either tend to be subsumed within a monarchy or within a nation-state. The government by council of elders also tends to be for smaller societies and also for smaller groupings of indigenous people. Monarchies also tend to have council of elders incorporated into the government structure at some level as advisors to the king or emperor.

Secondly, I am not taking an absolutist standpoint when I hold that it seems to me in these modern times that the governments have become powerful to the extent that their own self-preservation ultimately supersedes that of their subjects. I hold this position because I have noticed that even though governments, be they democratic, republican, socialist or communist still discharge their duties, such as providing protection among the citizenry and against foreign threats, providing health services in peace time and relief in wartime and in times of disaster, supporting education and the advancement of individual goals, governments have also developed an appetite for self-preservation, based on the need to keep the individual pliant and productive. One of the best examples I can think of is the prohibition of taking life, either of one's own, or of another within the group. This was not always the case within Western culture or even within some non-Western cultures. In past times, if there was a deep disagreement between two members of a group, it could be settled through a duel. That idea is ghastly to us in modern times, and we think of it as progress. Maybe it is progress. I however think it is ultimately because the state owns the individual's life, once the individual signs a contract with the state. That contract is becoming a citizen of the state. You can neither take your own life nor another's. The citizen exists to produce for the state. This may seem as an extreme position. I only quote it to illustrate the principle.

Another example is that many people fear their states, however the state tends to also be fearful of its citizens. Sometimes even more so than citizens are fearful of the state. This can be seen in states that invest huge resources into not only spying on and monitoring external threats but also spying on their own citizens, especially in instances where there is no need to. The state does this to ensure its own survival.

Interestingly, I see a parallel between corporations and states. Corporations were originally conceived of as temporary entities that were formed to fulfill a particular function. Over time, lawyers and interest groups manipulated events in order to confer on corporations the rights of an individual. Now, corporations are thought of as entities that have individual rights, even though the corporation itself is not a physical being that exists in the real world. Likewise, I understand states to be entities that were originally conceived of so that group action could enhance individual lives. Now, states have become legal entities even though they do not actually exist as physical entities in the real world.

What exists are people, and in both cases, of corporations and states, it is people that run the show. It is people, in those leadership positions, that make the decisions, which then gets relayed at the level of the entity. Since this discussion is about states, I shall leave the corporation analogy behind at this stage, and focus on states. The point I wanted to make was about people. Those in positions of power. Those in the allegory referred to as "the manipulators", and "the artists". The few that decide for the many. The many, who give up their power to the few, to decide for them. This is what we know of as "normal life", and it is what we are enculturated to accept. From the time of childhood, we are trained to accept authority figures. This starts with our parents, and then our teachers, school principals, and religious mentors. Later, after we graduate from childhood, we are then taught to see our spouses, our work superiors, our chiefs and kings, our church pastors and our politicians, local and national, as those we can look up to. These are the one who take care of us, and so we are beholden to them, to support them, so that they support us.

Do not get me wrong, this system can work, and in many cases, it does work. It works when the people in these positions of authority are responsible and selfless, at least reasonably, and ideally, truly so. When that is the case, then those individuals can dispense their responsibilities equal to the charge. Unfortunately, we live in a world where this is not always the case. In fact, it may often not be the case. There is, what has been called "evil" in the world, and this condition has been known and written about for a long time, both in philosophical and in religious treatises. European philosopher David Hume wrote about the problem of evil, but long before him, this was a problem already identified within the Ma'at, the law, of Ancient Egypt. Religious treatises such as the Jewish Torah, the Christian Bible and the Muslim Qur'an all speak of evil. These are just a few examples. So, evil is a condition that has been well acknowledged for thousands of years. A close look at evil shows that it is influenced by two main factors, one of which is selfishness, which can be taken to the extreme, and the other of which is the exercise of control over others.

Now, as it turns out, there are is a percentage of the population within societies which has these two qualities in considerable amounts, and usually a third quality, which is above average to extreme intelligence. These individuals tend to be attracted to positions of leadership and power. The percentage is about 5-6, and that number emerged from an interesting work, a book titled *Political Ponerology*, by Polish psychiatrist Andrew Lobazewski. This researcher set out to study and to understand how evil is applied for political gain.

4.3 Disenchantment

At some point in our development, humans figured out that congregating and living in larger numbers with greater organization increased our chances of survival. This is the idea of safety in numbers. It is the idea that makes one human potentially more powerful than a bear, an elephant, a lion or a tiger. With greater numbers and greater organization, we can draw on our collective strengths to address challenging situations so that in theory the individual can benefit from the strength of the entire group.

Whether it is at the level of paying your monthly premiums in order to benefit from insurance on a "rainy day" or paying taxes so that this contribution to the greater organization of humans will in turn trickle down some advantages to the individual, we are led to believe in a system that takes care of us. Or it could be putting monthly payments into a savings account at a bank, with the intention that the bank will invest the money responsibly, and then share some of those profits by depositing a portion back into the savings account. And in principle, this is how the system is meant to work. But, even with insurance, there is no guarantee that when an insured individual incurs a certain risk that was the target of insurance, that they would get a payout. Under normal circumstances, they would, or should, and normally, that is what happens.

However, there are those situations that are "not normal". In those circumstances, the entire system unravels and the individual is left at a loss. What is the system? The system is a way of thinking, whereby individuals deposit their resources for others acting on behalf of organs of the system (e.g., banks and insurance companies) to take and use hopefully for the benefit of all, but in many cases for the benefit of the few (i.e., the owners or the shareholders). In the case of a bank, an individual may place their home as surety to gain a loan. If they default on the loan, the home, a real asset, can be kept by the bank. If they deposit their savings into the bank, the bank takes that money and then invests it, keeps most of the profits, and then gives back a small cut to back to the savings account, to keep things legit. If however the economy crashes and there is a bank run, and people want their money, the bank has protections in place to avoid or refuse giving that money. Often because they do not have it (even though they can take people's *real* property when those people do not have the bank's "money"). Similarly, in a real disaster, often a natural one, insurance companies may refuse or simply be unable to cover the cost of damage when everyone, or most people, are afflicted. In fact, insurance companies often have exclusion clauses for covering natural disasters for this very reason. All of these are considered "not normal" circumstances. Extending this line of thinking one step further, if there is a natural disaster that threatens the state, and everybody is afflicted, the "big system", the state, may be unable or simply unwilling to help everyone get the help they need. The situation would be seen as one that is "not normal", and so the response would be a "not normal" response, similar perhaps in ways that banks may act during a bank run, or that insurance companies may respond in the case of real and widespread disasters.

With this in mind, a natural conclusion that emerges is that states, insurance companies, banks and other 'organs' of the system are there to assist the individual but to 'fleece' the individual more than they assist, and in ways that work primarily for the system, and only in normal times. The fleecing involves taking resources from the individual and using or investing those resources in ways that for the most part benefit the system. Not always. There are exceptions. For example, credit unions tend to operate similar to the regular big-name banks, but there are also some differences, for instance profits are meant to be shared more equitably. The situation where the individual is fleeced to serve the collective is seen or understood as being "normal", because of education, indoctrination and schooling. The reality is, in times of crisis, it is the individual that is expected to shoulder a heavier responsibility to save the organs of the system. For example, in times of war, the individual is often expected to put their lives on the line to save the state. For a bank run or financial loss during a natural disaster, the individual is expected to exercise restraint and to shoulder the loss, while the bank or insurance company often asks the state for a bailout. These situations can lead to a sense of disenchantment for the individual who realizes this reality. A conclusion that emerges is that under "normal" circumstances, the organs of the system that are meant to "take care" of the individual may function within what we have been taught to accept as being reasonable parameters. In "not normal" circumstances, however, all bets tend to be off, and the individual would be on their own, as well as often also being expected to support the threatened or no longer functioning system. With this in mind, one may realize the need for exercising personal responsibility, and taking personal initiative to maneuver in ways that adequately meet the individual's needs, and to cater for circumstances where the organs of the system, or the system altogether, are either unable or unwilling to provide the care they are set up to provide.

4.4 Sovereign lifestyle

One of the ways certain individuals who come to the realization that for them, it may not be enough to put their full trust in "the system" to take care of them, is to begin to figure out ways to take their power away from the system. There are degrees of responses to this, ranging from those who take an approach such as the one outlined by Harry Browne in his book *How I found freedom in an unfree world*, where, as I see it, the attitude is to 'check out' or unsubscribe to many of the social expectations on an individual in society. There are others who choose instead to take an approach such as the one outlined by James Dale Davidson and Lord Rees-Mogg, in their book *The Sovereign Individual*. In this latter approach, the individual eschews the trappings of a single state, essentially becoming an internationalist, spreading their 'risk' across different borders and portfolios. Ironically, it is common practice among businesses and business people to spread risk widely, internationally, that is, so as to gain access to better tax breaks, cheaper labour, and what they may perceive to be friendlier governments. A third approach, among those who choose to act due to a sense of disenchantment of one kind or of another, may be to remain connected to "the system" but to select a level of participation that meets their needs.

In other words, to act in a sovereign manner is to begin to take responsibility for yourself, and the degree to which you may act, or not, may depend on the extent to which the individual is aware of the machinations of "the system" and is prepared to take action in the face of that knowledge. For everyone else, to a greater or lesser extent, it is life as usual, in the system. When things go wrong, there is the understanding that change can be brought about by demonstrating to bring about that change, or by being proactive through elections. There also tends to be the belief that the system itself is fine, that it is usually exceptional cases of individuals who bring about fault through the system. Many of these people believe in the news reported on BBC, or on CNN. This is especially the case if it is said by elected officials, the more senior, the more credible. We saw this in varying extents especially in the year 2020, at the height of the Covid-19 pandemic. Various leaders of nations would give addresses, holding the rapt attention of their citizens, as they delivered news on what the collective would do.

Thus, there is a widely held belief that if there is a serious issue to be addressed, that the government would address its people, much in the way that was so characteristically done during the year 2020, where at one point, it was almost unbelievable that the entire planet had come to a standstill. One of my favourite stories during this period, was on a group of elephants in India that had allegedly broken into an alcohol cellar and gotten themselves drunk on corn wine and had fallen asleep in a tea garden. There were animals roaming the streets of many towns and cities. For a time, the entire globe seemed to have come to a standstill because most people were indoors.

Will politicians and world leaders really tell the people of the world if there was a situation completely beyond their control, such as an impending global catastrophe of massive and complete proportions? Well, I do not think so. I recently watched what I thought to be a funny movie titled *Don't Look Up*. This movie, a comedy actually, is star-studded with signature Hollywood names such as Meryl Streep, Leonardo DiCaprio, Cate Blanchett, Mark Rylance, and Jennifer Lawrence. The premise of the movie is that two astronomers (DiCaprio as a professor, and Lawrence as one of his PhD students) discover a comet heading straight for Earth. It is not just any comet. Rather, it is what can be called a 'world-ending' comet. A planet killer. So, understandably, this duo start to freak out. Their first thought is to alert the leader of "the system" in the US, that is, the President of the United States. Herein lies the comedy. In spite of the seriousness of the situation, and even when bigwigs at Harvard, MIT, Stanford, Berkeley and other institutions back this finding, the politicians are either not taking the situation seriously enough as a top priority, or they are looking for a means for personal gain. The duo then try to alert the media, only to be met with derision and scorn as they attempt to get serious with the joking media representatives. In the end, it comes down to two things: one, the politicians decide to do something about it, but only in a way that brings them massive gain an advantage, and two, the truth of the situation only fully dawned on everyone, including those media people who were previously joking, when everyone could now see the comet en route to Earth. At that point, something *unbelievable* happens in the movie. The politicians devise a diabolical ruse to cast those looking up, at the comet, as the 'opposition', and to try to rally people to do the opposite, hence the title of the movie *Don't look up*.

This was funny, but it also brought home a deep truth to me. Which is that people can be mesmerized by their politicians. When it came down to it, in the face of undeniable facts, the politicians chose instead to lie and use propaganda to keep people ignorant, even when the facts were undeniable. Of course, eventually the presence of the comet was too powerful for the ruse to work, so the politicians had to try to assuage the people by executing their solution, the non-optimal one that would bring them most benefit. Anyway, when it all came down to it, and people had lost hope, knowing that they were now only going to live for a short time, some resorted to desperation, alcohol and to wild sexual escapades in an attempt to mentally escape the inescapable situation. The most diabolical part of this movie, which was again presented as a comedy, was that the elite had a backup plan to physically escape this situation that was inescapable for the masses, and this backup plan catered *only* to the elite.

Now, one may say or think that a most ridiculous and extreme situation was picked for this movie, in order to present a hilarious situation of political satire. The situation is quite extreme, to the extent that it is allowable to be funny and for people to laugh at it, because it seems quite far out in reality for something like a world-ending event to be on the horizon, where politicians would either not take it seriously enough to mobilize the strength of the collective in order to best aid its individual members, or will act only in ways that best suit their interests

But what if I were to say to you, the reader, that what is shown in this movie is not only so far from the truth, but in some respects, is representative of a pressing truth, known to governments around the world and yet held from the people they are meant to represent. Similar to one of my favourite documentaries of all time, *911 In Plane Site*, where Dave von Kleist meticulously shows how publicly available footage tell a story, from the point of view of the footage evidence, of what happened on September 11, 2001, that shows the truth, in plain sight, which is completely at odds with the official account. And yet, the footage came from regular news channels, and some major ones at that. In this case of the movie *Don't look up*, we are being shown, in comedy form how the "manipulators" (i.e., politicians and those who support them) and the "artists" (i.e., the media people) would respond if an individual or a group of people attempted to inform mass consciousness of a real-life catastrophe through the organs of the media. The media would laugh about it. You can check out David Icke's treatment at the hands of the media, on this one.

It would appear that as far as in the 1940s and 50s, the US government discovered that there is a natural catastrophe cycle that occurs every 12,000 or so years, with a minor version of this catastrophe happening roughly about every 6,000. By catastrophe, I am not talking about one massive earthquake or a tsunami, or even a category 5+ hurricane. I am talking about something on the scale of the "great flood" of Sumerian and Ubaid times. Something of "Biblical proportions". That level of engagement, which has the potential to reset civilization on surface Earth, wipe out technology, infrastructure, all of that, and send us back to a more basic way of living. The story goes that once the US government was convinced that this event was going to occur, they made classified the one publication that (in their view) most closely describes what is to come. But this was not before this document made its way into publication, outside of their control. The book, written by Chan Thomas, titled *The Adam and Eve Story: A History of Cataclysms*, was classified by the CIA. This book was recently declassified by the CIA. Although the declassified CIA version is heavily redacted, it is possible to find the original online.

Basically, according to my understanding of the situation, it has to do with cycles of the sun, and of the sun releasing something known as a "micronova", or a "superflare". We can think of a micronova as a supernova of a very reduced scale, in which the star remains intact after the event. Apparently, there are periods when the sun goes through this process. Changes in the sun influence changes on Earth. During these times, the electrical activity of the sun increases, and the magnetic field of planet Earth attenuates to zero, leaving the Earth in the field of direct impact from the sun. When this happens, the process may be accompanied by incredible electrical storms, volcanic activity, and earthquakes that generate mile-high tsunamis, not to mention the electromagnetic pulses running through the sky that fry all satellite and electronic devices that have not been prepared to withstand electromagnetic pulses.

So, this is apparently the situation that has been known for over half a century, and that the governments of the world are apparently quietly preparing for. Knowing that if it occurs, the scale of it would be beyond their capacity to "save everyone", we are taken back to the scenarios in section 4.3 of what systems in many modern communities of the world today do. When they fail, they give up on those they depend on and run for cover. Will they tell 'the plebs'? Hell no! Talk about political ponerology!

There is that idea of 'continuity of the species', where governments explored what they would do in the face of a catastrophe such as one during a micronova event. One option is to seek refuge underground or in mountains, and another is to migrate into space. For those who know of the SciFi show "The 100", this is exactly what Earth people did after a nuclear war, because the surface of the Earth was unlivable. Well, if we have one of these micronova events, much of the surface of the Earth may be unlivable, prompting a migration into space, underground or into mountains.

Given that situation, those self-serving politicians would follow options that either save themselves, or make themselves richer. In the movie *Don't look up*, the President of the United States aborted a mission that would have obliterated the impending comet because not doing so would have led to the loss of political support. A top political donor and friend of the US President rejected the workable solution for a tentative one because this latter solution had the potential to make him incredibly wealthier. In both cases, two self-serving individuals put the entire world at risk.

Of course, since it is a movie, there is still that notion of "trust your government to tell the truth". In the movie, even though there is a sinister agenda in place for politicians and donors to benefit, "officialdom" still comes out to make a public statement about impending doom. In real life, however, this will almost likely not be the case. Instead of making this knowledge officially public information, they chose secrecy. The power elite then embarked upon a mission to figure out how humanity can survive. Of course, that survival will be such that they will remain as a power elite. And not without good reason. In fact, people would really panic if there were to be a news broadcast of some impending doom. It has been tried at least twice, in a radio broadcast in 1938, and in a TV broadcast in 1977 known as *Alternative 3*. In both cases, there was panic after the broadcast. *Alternative 3* was a show that was broadcast only once on British TV, where the show attempted to explain an exodus of scientists and technical personnel to the moon and to Mars as part of plan to preserve the human race in a climate change event of massive global proportions that brought life on surface Earth to an end. This one-time broadcast show, *Alternative 3*, has been explained off as a hoax, however for those that know the ways that the "powers that be" operate, they would know that as part of their beliefs, they are required to announce to the consensus mind what it is that they are doing. It does not matter whether people take it seriously or not, or even notice they are being told. This Alternative 3 scenario also fits well with ways that Earth governments would probably think to salvage the human race in the event of a civilization-ending catastrophe such as one that can be brought about by a micronova.

Rather than keep secrets under the premise that the population are incapable of handling the truth of such an impending catastrophe, I would argue that it is better for people to know the truth and deal with any trauma related to impending doom. Yes, people would freak out and there may be all kinds of meltdowns. However, rather than treat citizens like children, it would be better to treat them as adults. When we have self-serving predatory individuals playing the role of 'parent' or 'grandparent' of the state, then instead of having a loving grandmother, we have wolves dressed up as grandmothers, just as it is in the European children's story of Little Red Riding Hood and the big bad wolf. In this story, the big bad wolf gobbles the girl's grandmother, and then pretends to be that grandmother by wearing her clothes. This is a ruse, an attempt to trick the little girl so that she too can be gobbled by the wolf.

Back to the micronova, and to this climate event that is forecast to arrive within the next few decades. The overall point of note, is that what happens with the sun, directly influences what happens on Earth. Therefore, it is the sun, and the Earth, that must be the places of focus to study the changes as they occur. This is our real-life version of the *Don't look up* movie. Rather than look up at a comet, we would in this case be looking up at the sun. That which is right in front of us.

There is at least one individual who seems to have made it his mission to keep looking at the sun and its changes, in order to keep the masses informed of the impending disaster. This individual is Ben Davidson, and his YouTube channel, at the time of writing, is called Suspicious Observers. Ben has been giving daily updates of Earth and solar changes on YouTube, and his website is spaceweather.com. Now, one of the best coverages by this individual that I have come across on the Earth disaster cycle, the history around it, and what is to come, is the YouTube video, titled *Cosmic Disaster | CIA classified*. If, by the time you read this book, YouTube still exists, and/or Ben still has this video on his channel, I highly recommend watching it. He presents the story and the facts to back up the story in a cogent manner that leaves you with information to then decide what to do next.

https://www.youtube.com/watch?v=B_zfMyzXqfI

Ben Davidson is not a movie character but a real person telling a real story. An unreal-sounding story of an impending disaster on Earth, caused by the onslaught of a micronova, coupled with a weakened magnetic field of the Earth, which unleashes catastrophic weather manifestations such as next level earthquakes, mile-high long tsunamis and extremely fast gusts of wind. During this event, which has purportedly happened periodically in Earth's remote past, there will be no electricity (the micronova will take care of that), and life as is known in modern times will come to an abrupt end. A micronova is a much smaller expulsion of matter from the star like the sun, but powerful enough to send a corona mass ejection (CME) toward Earth that triggers these events. What is more. This event appears to be scheduled to occur within the lifetimes of some individuals reading this book.

It is not as dramatic as it was in the movie *Don't look up*, where impending doom was within a much shorter time frame. Yet it is serious enough because the event can happen within the lifetime of today's adults. What is more is that there is a lot of scientific evidence to support the fact that the Earth's magnetic field is rapidly weakening, an event which tends to be a precursor to this solar event. In addition to all the scientific evidence put together by Ben Davidson, I have checked the possibility of this event occurring using my own methods that rely on knowledge of the changes of energies and of the rhythms and cycles of the cosmos. From that exercise (see section 5.5), I have surmised that these catastrophic events appear to be correlated to periods that are the equivalent of the "equinoxes" and "solstices" within the precession of the equinoxes cycle. If correlation indeed does lead to causation in this case, then it would seem that we are in fact at the cusp of one of these catastrophic events, since we are now in what is the equivalent of the "summer solstice" period within the precession of the equinoxes cycle.

So, there you have it. Don't look up, a real-life version. The analogy is apt even in relation to looking up. In this real-life version, looking up does not involve looking at an impending comet, as is the case in the movie. Rather, it involves not pay attention to the sun, and the surrounding galactic environment, and not paying attention to how astronomical changes occurring in the sun and the solar system, including our planet, appear to be pointing to an impending extinction level event. Of course, we are not speaking 100% certainty here. Anything can happen, including entire dimensional changes. However, within the scope of the current data and trends over the last several decades, and if cosmic cycles are to be taken into account, and if the CIA was apparently freaked out enough about this event that they classified a version of the story that is apparently close to accurate, then we can say that it is probably of a high likelihood that such an event is on the horizon, and even that thought is mind-boggling. I entreat you to watch the slightly longer than one hour YouTube video given with the link above. In the end, information is just information. It is up to each individual conscious awareness to decide what they would do, or not do, with it.

Interestingly, former US president Barack Obama signed an executive order on October 13, 2016 titled *Coordinating Efforts To Prepare the Nation For Space Weather Events*. In this document, we can read that "This order defines agency roles and responsibilities and directs agencies to take specific actions to prepare the Nation for the hazardous effects of space weather." What we can also read from this document is that that the hazardous effects of space weather are potentially dangerous enough to severely affect the entire globe. The US therefore needs to prepare for such an event, and to that end, the former US president outlined a strategy that the US would take to cater to such an event. This executive order, coupled with the evidence that is now publicly known about this impending event, through the numerous scientific publications and the efforts of individuals like Ben Davidson, brings to bear its importance, and also of the need for individuals, if they truly think of themselves as sovereign individuals, to not only rely on what their governments would do in such a situation, but to also consider what they too can do to prepare, if they choose to. So, I have chosen to reveal this information to the reader who might not be aware of it, in order to give the reader that extra context to assist in choosing what to do, or not do, regarding this information.

5

THE RING OF THE FIVE SENSES

Ever since we were born, we have been bound to our five senses. In fact, it may even be argued that we were bound to them even before we left the womb. That of course would not matter as much, because the vast majority of us do not remember anything that far back. Just as most do not remember learning to crawl, and to walk, or even struggling to learn our first language. It all happened automatically, it seemed. Our physical bodies, being so adept at learning the basics required to have us reach successive stages of greater self-reliance and self-sufficiency shielded much of these memories from us. That part of the learning was for the physical body's own automatic programs to take the lead, developing us physically and preparing us for a time when our conscious minds could take over. A bit like sleeping. It happens automatically, and a lot of us know how difficult it can be when we try to force ourselves to sleep but do not get anywhere with it. So, it may be a good thing that the physical body runs its genetic, instinctual program during the early childhood years to get us up to scratch.

The result of that preparation, then is a state where we increasingly master the use of our senses, but also become bound by them. That is after all what we know best during a given lifetime. Our bodies have been 'taking care of us', if we admit it to ourselves. Although, for the most part, they have our best interests at heart, our bodies too have a mind of their own. This is why they react of their own accord in times of danger or some perceived imminent threat. This is also why they may register a physiological reaction when they get turned on, even when the conscious mind may be striving to stave the reaction. Our physical bodies are programmed for survival, and that survival includes first and foremost the survival of a given bodily unit, and secondly the survival of the species, through species propagation.

Therefore, if we take for granted that we are spirit beings having a human experience, then we are 'tenants' and our bodies are the 'landlord'. As long as we pay rent (food, water, clothing, shelter, sex where appropriate, etc.), we sustain a healthy, symbiotic relationship with our bodies. Within the comfort of this symbiotic relationship, we could easily become so comfortable as to take for granted the nature of the symbiotic relationship and to incorrectly assume that we are the landlord, rather than the tenant. When that happens, we may identify with our bodies to the extent that its worries become our worries. Its fears become our fears, its reactions become our reactions. Engaging our bodies in unusual experiences, which are experiences outside of realm of habit of our bodies can bring out unusual effects, which include disrupting the identification as landlord by the tenant. The disruption can be on a degree of severity from slight to severe. When put into context, such disruptions can serve as data that can catalyze a re-identification with self as spirit having an experience in a physical body.

In this ring, the ring of the five senses, the spirit is the hero. It embarks on an odyssey, to have experiences that enable it break free of the confines and limitations of the physical body. This physical body, the very home of the spirit during incarnation, can become a routine provider of limiting experiences. Experiences that pertain mostly to the five physical senses, and that make sense from the "common sense" point of view. No rocking the boat. No looking under or behind the veil. As life would have it, however, there are times when experiences the non-physical realms bleed into those in what we would ordinarily call 'normal waking consciousness'. When that happens, it gives the awareness of the spirit a chance to realize that it is more than simply a physical body, or limited only to physical matter existence.

5.1 "Common sense" perception

Have you ever walked down a street and caught sight of an object thinking it was one thing, only to get closer and to find out that it was something else? It often tends to be the case that upon perceiving an object, our brains compare what is perceived to what we may have already stored in our memory. So, our mind's first move when perceiving an object is to attempt to match that object with another that has been experienced and filed away in memory. Have you ever wondered why time seems to have passed by so fast when living a routine, predictable life but then feels much longer when having a string of successive new experiences such as being on vacation in a new place? In the first case, it is as if then we are just living in our memories, proceeding from one memory to the next, when repeating experiences in familiar contexts and surroundings. In the second case, we are making new memories as we have new experiences, so that rather than experience what seems like a time loop being played back over and over again, we are rather "adding more time" to the experience bank.

In any case, the first type of experience where we perceive an object only for our minds to project onto it the object of closest similarity from our memory is very common. This is the scenario that happens when we can fall victim to those images that can be perceived in two different ways. Sometimes our brains play tricks on us, but the function of projecting a memory onto a new perception is a mechanism that can reduce the cognitive load on the mind so that attention and awareness can be freed for other more conscious tasks. Imagine having scenario where our brains have to figure out every single time what it is they are perceiving. That could lead to cognitive overload. And yet this learned behaviour, which is established out of habit, can lead to false perceptions.

Fortunately for us, our brains have and minds have a secondary program in place to figure out what is being perceived in the event that a projected memory results in a false positive. The secondary program that kicks into gear then work to identify the new object in order to categorize it and to include it in the inventory of our minds.

In a similar vein, as members of a community, we engage in interactions with one another through these interactions we generate experiences that lead to norms for common understandings for ways of being and interacting in regard to the context of the community. These common understandings or norms can be called "common sense", because they are commonly shared perceptions of deemed appropriate responses in interactions and experiences. The facet of these "common sense" perceptions that is fascinating is that the mechanisms for creating and changing these perceptions are understandably different from those of the biological programs of our brains which, upon discovering a false positive in an attempt to match a perceived object to a previously recorded item in memory, then proceeds to identify and to create a new inventory.

In interactions that occur among community members, it does not work like that. At some point, the analogy between natural perception mechanisms of our brains, and the common-sense perceptions between individuals in a community fall apart. For one, it is a curious thought to ponder what brings about common-sense perceptions. Although it seems that popular culture must play a role in what constitutes "common sense" perception, it is not so clear how popular culture changes from generation to generation, only that technology seems to be playing a catalyzing role in the change. That there have been propaganda artists in the world for decades is certain. This has been the case ever since the two world wars, and the business of propaganda artists has evolved, from selling war for the state to selling commodities and merchandize for private enterprises. Thus, both state and private enterprise have competed for the compliance of the individual citizen. To this end, technology has played a role and it continues to do so. However, the TV, radio, newspaper and advertising organs of yesteryear are being disrupted today by social media. In private life, outside of state and commercial forces, other factors come into play that influence what constitutes "common sense" perceptions. Some that come to mind are education, religion, and tradition.

Whereas the influences that can bring about common-sense perception are varied and not always clear, the remedy for scenarios where common-sense fails seems to me to be certain across age, race, sex and generational barriers. To me, it seems that the ability to cultivate one's mind and spirit, to be able to think independently and clearly, and to be able to develop one's heart and intuition so as to function consciously and appropriately in a situation where "common-sense" perception fails remains the case even as technology and other pressures change the ways that information is processed in society.

5.2 Concrete knowledge and the real world

For most of us, reality is determined by what we perceive while we are awake. Sleep is often a time to get some physical and mental rest and also in some cases to explore abstract experiences and subconscious desires. The real life is lived in the real world of physical sensory experience. As such, we mostly work hard to succeed in and to participate in the real world. As children, we quickly learn to know things because we perceived them. If we can perceive it, it is part of our reality. If we cannot, then it is not. So, for a while, our childhood awareness could be tricked. Some adults like to have fun with very young children by hiding items in the child's field of perception in order to take the child's attention away from the object. It works for a while, until the child reaches a stage of mental development when the child not only perceives the physical object, but also has a mental representation of it, in memory. At this stage, the child can no longer be so easily tricked, because the reality of the object persists in its memory.

So, if you notice, children, as they are very young, simply perceive. Then they reach a stage where they engage in repetitive behaviour. This is a stage of learning where the child is training its ability to anchor physical objects and physical world experiences in its memory. At this stage, the child has typically not yet developed abstract rational and logical abilities. We are talking really young here, but most if not all of us go through this developmental stage of repetitive behaviour, the purpose of which is to imprint our minds with rudimentary learning skills. These learning skills are important because they activate neural networks that the child can later rely on as it engages in more complex learning and interaction.

We develop our concrete knowledge of the real world through perception and repeated experiences. At this stage, our young minds are sensitive, and sometimes even vulnerable, because we have not yet fully developed those logical and inferential skills that can help affirm or dispel aspects of our experience. At the early stage of our development, our minds are still very flexible and this is why we can learn multiple languages within a space of a few years while very young. Eventually, we begin to mature and to age past the formative years. The foundation we develop at this stage is crucial because as we get older, we rely less on questioning or even second guessing the contents of our physical experiences. We begin to rely more and more on our memory of what is real, based on our perceptions, and also on "common sense" perception and on our rational faculties for determining and responding to the contents of our perceptual experiences.

And so it is, that the habits we so laboriously develop as infants and children then act as an investment we can reap in our more mature years. As we advance in age and in mental maturity, we may also include a range of tools to help us interact with the concrete world. In today's world, at this time of writing, the smartphone has become a ubiquitous tool of choice. It is at once a computer, a communications device, a camera, and much more. Where in past ages, humans relied on their mental faculties and on non-electronic tools to interface with the real world, in this current age, electronics have extended the range of those experiences.

Even after having grown and matured, from infancy into childhood, to young adulthood and finally reaching legal adult age, we still need to learn about the world. We cannot rely only on the repetitive perceptual and memory habits we developed since infancy, nor can we only rely on logical deduction or inference to accept, store, transform or reject the contents of our perceptual experiences. We also learn, through our education, to apply ways of generating and checking new knowledge. Here, I am referring to the ways we learn to think, through philosophy and science, and the ways we learn to test our ideas and knowledge, primarily through science. We learn to do this, out of the awareness that personal perception and "common sense" perception together cover a wide scope of the field of what we need in order to function well in the real world, however these two are not enough, for at least two reasons. First, because they are not completely infallible, meaning that we can on occasion make "errors", so we need to have a backup system for checking and resolving those "errors", especially where an "error" is experienced by a wide range of people and not by a single individual. The second reason is that having a verifiable and a reliable means for generating new knowledge means new experiences can be safely brought into both individual and consensus experience. For example, in our current time, we do not yet have the capacity or the technology to build smartphones or other communication devices that run on nuclear power which never runs out of charge but which nevertheless poses huge medical risks to individuals who use them.

And so it is, that gradually from childhood we get acculturated to the real world. Once we fully mature into adulthood, most of us would have pretty much graduated the "life course" of being prepared to fully participate in the world of sense perception, of the waking state. And yet, on occasion, and in some cases ever so often, we have experiences that, in spite of all our training and preparation from childhood to adulthood, meets a challenge in addressing a circumstance that we perceive but which we struggle to process and to understand. For example, just about everyone who is reading this book would at some point in their lives have had a nightmare while sleeping. These often start at a young age, and may be fewer as adults. As children, we may be told, "oh, don't worry, it was just a dream", which, although such words are reassuring, may not address the core of the issue as to why the nightmare occurred. Saying that it was "just a dream" is meant to reassure the experiencer that the experience was 'not real', and therefore it should not be taken as seriously as a real experience should, especially once the experiencer wakes up. A lot of us with this phrase, that we use then to reassure ourselves when we wake up from a nightmare as an adult.

If you had been one of the lucky ones, you perhaps had a way to address the issue of the nightmare, instead of having it acknowledged and brushed aside by a parent, a guardian or some other individual. Maybe your parent was a psychologist or they had some knowledge about how our minds, including our subconscious minds, process experiences. It is especially salient in a case where the nightmare is in relation to an experience in physical reality that the child (or adult) had, or even observing a disturbing experience another individual had, that had led to some fear or some trauma which was not adequately addressed and healed. That trauma may then resurface in the reality of dreams, to give itself expression in order to bring attention to the fact that the trauma has not been addressed and healed.

So here, the point really is about experiences during the real world that are not adequately understood and processed, brought about by traumatic experiences of some kind that can then lead to the development of fears. Trauma can be defined as serious injury to the body, as from physical violence or accident, or alternatively, severe emotional or mental distress brought about by an experience. Perhaps these are extremes of experience, but fears are a phenomenon we all encounter at some point in our existence. As babies, we are born with few fears. Some babies are more afraid than others of certain things, but it seems just about all babies are afraid of falling, especially from heights, and are afraid of loud noise. There are then a lot of things that we learn to fear, the point here being that even in spite of all our education and the mental measures we take, some experiences may still slip through the cracks. Among these experiences are those that do not fit neatly into the categories of sense experiences that we encounter from childhood to adulthood. As our physical bodies are programmed primarily for survival of the unit, and for propagation of the species, those experiences that threaten these two categories serve as prime candidates for generating fear. It is through knowledge (and sometimes, wisdom) that we understand and then have the capacity to heal and dispel fears.

There are also those experiences that are neither everyday perceptions nor the occasional fear-based response from a nightmare or from watching a horror movie. Consider for instance these situations that are reported to have occurred which, ordinarily, most of us educated in the modern way would not consider 'normal'. These cases, or stories if you will, are from the book *Real Encounters, Different Dimensions, and Otherworldly Beings*, by Brad and Sherry Steiger. This couple have made it their life's purpose to explore unusual phenomena, with Brad having five decades worth of reporting such phenomena, and Sherry having four decades worth of the same. The first case is about a creature that is reported to have come out of the sea:

"On November 16, 2011, around 9:00 P.M., a fisherman named Bob saw something unusual along the embankments of the Sacramento River and called the Paranormal Hotline, conducted by Paul Dale Roberts, to report an encounter with a "Wetlash." ...Bob: My Indian friend calls it a Wetlash. It was the damnedest thing I ever saw. This watery creature came out of the river. It had long ears, must [have] been about 3 ½ feet high. It wore knee-high boots, a strange shirt with an open collar, and the longest tail ever. At the end of his tail, he was holding a fish. The Wetlash caught my eye and looked at me with a strange look and went back into the water immediately." (Steigler & Steigler, 2014, n.p.)

Okay, let's take a moment to discuss this case. For the sake of discussion, let us assume that the event actually occurred and that just as the fisherman had perceived it, you, I, or any other person who functions in a fairly normal way in mundane society could also have perceived the same event in more or less the same way. Firstly, if we are honest to ourselves, we may ask ourselves the question, 'what would I have done, if I were in the fisherman's place?' I can think of a number of reactions, ranging from experiencing a WTF moment, to freaking out, to just blanking out the situation upon perceiving it by telling oneself that it is not real. There may also be some who respond in a reasonably calm way, because they have some prior knowledge with which to address the situation. Remember we discussed earlier that when we perceive an object or a situation, our brains try to identify it by matching it with a memory item in its inventory. Where that process fails, our brains then try to create a new inventory entry for the item just perceived. In the first scenario where the response to perceiving a "Wetlash" is of the freak out or panic variety, the individual is understandably distressed, because in addition to accurately completing a new inventory entry for the scenario just perceived, the individual's physical body defenses (i.e., the 'fight or flight' response) may get activated since, in this case of an animate object, the "Wetlash", the individual has not yet determined whether or not it is a danger to its physical body or even to its survival.

Ironically, activating either a fight or a flight response would erode the chances of an accurate inventory entry, not to mention trigger some unexpected response from the creature. For example, some canines are naturally predisposed to chasing a target running from them. I also remember reading that if hiking in the woods one crosses paths with a bear, an effective strategy is to walk away slowly while facing the bear so as to show that you are not a threat. This strategy may work with other wild creatures as well. Let us consider a second case, also from Steigler and Steigler (2014):

"Virginia told us that a few years back she and her sister were working a Ouija Board when weird occurrences began to happen. At first, it was like footsteps in the hall and on the ceiling. Then there would be loud thuds, like someone wearing boots or heavy shoes. Then things began to get stranger. One night while Virginia was in bed, she began to stare into a dark corner of her room. She was about to close her eyes when she noticed that the shadow began to get darker and darker. She couldn't quite understand what was happening, so she just continued to stare. Then the shadow took up almost the entire corner, and she could see a silhouette of a person. Fear sunk in at this point, and she could feel him staring right through her." (Steigler & Steigler, 2014, n.p.).

Now, the very mention of the phrase "Ouija Board" brings about varying responses. Some swear by it, others are afraid of it, some think it's fake and yet others may not even have heard of it or know what it is. The Ouija Board is a wooden panel with letters and numbers, some symbols and also often some short greeting words. Users interact with the board by spelling out words that are meant to come from the spirit realm. I would emphasize exercising caution when it comes to dabbling in spiritual matters without proper preparation. This is similar to (but not exactly the same as) going into the wilderness at night to hunt, without any wilderness survival skills. The chances of success as a hunter in the wilderness at night are understandably lower for a complete novice than they are for a highly trained expert. In the wilderness, there are creatures that are permanently in a state of survival and that could be dangerous to the uninitiated. In a similar vein, it may not be altogether wise to experiment with the Ouija Board 'just to see whether or not it works'.

Let us examine one more case, perhaps the most unusual one of all the three:

"In 1972, times had grown very hard for the Levesque family of Aurora, Colorado. When Paul, the breadwinner of the large family, was terribly injured at work, his wife, Nancy, was left with the sole responsibility of providing for six children—all under the age of seventeen. "Paul's employer was underinsured, and we had no insurance of our own," Nancy Levesque said. "What money we did receive didn't last long after all the medical bills had been deducted. Paul was left bedridden, and we didn't know at that time if he would ever be able to walk, to say nothing of being gainfully employed, ever again" ... Michael, their seventeen-year-old son, picked up as many small, parttime jobs as possible...But then came the terrible day when Nancy found the money and the note that Michael left behind. "He said that he could not stand being unable to help us more," Nancy said. "Since he was the oldest, he wrote that he was going to strike out on his own and try to get a good job in a larger city...Incredibly, a year passed without word from their son. And then, one night, eighteen months after Michael had left home, Nancy Levesque had her most unusual dream...According to Nancy's account, she was awakened in the dream by an insistent knocking at their back door....Before she could say a word, her visitor spoke in urgent tones: "The boy is sick ... come quick!"...Then, with the boy leading the way, they started to walk "quickly and with a gliding motion."...They hurried through the streets until they reached open country...Nancy and her young escort seemed to travel for hours over mountains, open country, forests. Never once did they halt for drink or food, but kept moving relentlessly forward... "The boy is here," the young Chicano guide said. And then they were inside, and the lad was leading her up a short, steep stairway, covered with dust and cobwebs... "Oh, Mom!" Nancy heard a familiar voice cry out faintly. "You've come!" Her heart beating faster, Nancy rushed forward to discover her son Michael lying on a bare floor in a far corner of the attic. She fell to her knees, clutching her missing son to her breast, noting with alarm that his body was burning hot and that his face was dry and parched with fever. "Oh, Mom," Michael moaned. "I'm so sick! I'm so sick with fever."" (Steigler & Steigler, 2014, n.p.).

The reader would undoubtedly be wondering, 'how did this story end?' Well, I would say that the full story is an extraordinary one worth getting the Steiglers' book just for this. It turns out that Nancy experienced an epic level of fatigue for over a day, after her unusual dream. Two days later, her family received a telegram from a hospital in another US state, indicating that Michael was admitted there, and that he was about to have his foot amputated. His mother Nancy had to borrow some money from her employer to travel to the hospital to see her son. Fortunately, Michael was brought back to full health although he lost his foot. While at the hospital, Nancy shared the dream she had with her son, and even before she completed her account, her son told her the name of the Chicano boy, Alfredo Maqueda. I will leave the rest of the story so as not to spoil it for any who choose to get the book.

What I would like to discuss in regard to this extraordinary experience and story is twofold. First, it should be clear by this point, after these three examples, that the mundane education we receive regarding what constitutes 'the real world' covers much of the phenomena we experience in our daily lives. Yet, it does not cover it all. There are classes of experience that transcend the 'curriculum' of training we receive in our normal daily lives, and are taught to deal with, either through our own personal perceptions and the "common sense" consensus perception of the societies we belong to, or taught through our formal education on how to view the world and to determine the truth of our experiences in it. If the ordinary experiences that we have and that we learn to identify and deal with through informal and formal means of mundane education constitute say, 95% of the possible experiences we can have, related to physical reality, then there is this remaining 5% of a set of non-ordinary or paranormal experiences that are also possible. At one point or another in our lives, without going out there to look for it, our perceptual experiences may cross into this 5% zone. Having some idea of the existence of the types of experiences that constitute this 5% or even of the possibility of them, can augment that 95% of standard education we have received through our formal and informal education in life. This is important so that if ever we find ourselves in such a 5% situation, our brains, when searching through its inventory, can have some reference point with which to address the unusual experience, rather starting from scratch, which could lead to aggression, to fear, or to "crapping out altogether", instead of a sober, reasoned and, where necessary, cautious response to our or another's unusual experience of the 5% zone.

So, that is the first thing I wanted to discuss. The second has to do with the notion of having shared dreams. It has in fact been documented in psychology that two or more people can have a what amounts to a shared dream, where the details of the shared dream and the time that the dream occurred, are the same. This in my view puts a big question mark on what dreams really are, and if they are all "just dreams". Just as not all experiences in mundane existence are of the paranormal variety, could it not be possible, that not all dreams are "just dreams"? Something to ponder. Perhaps the vast majority of dream experiences are "just dreams", but then a small percentage of them may fall into the 5% zone (or whatever small percentage it is for dreams) of the paranormal. This could be the case, if we think of ourselves not just as physical bodies but also as sentient beings with consciousness. In those special cases, an otherwise ordinary experience may be infused with non-ordinary context that can be attributed to an expression of consciousness of one kind or another. What I am suggesting here as a possible explanation is that Nancy, her son Michael, and Alfredo likely had a shared dream or out of body experience. Later in this book, we shall revisit the phenomenon of out of body experiences.

The implications here are fantastic. If indeed there a part of human consciousness that can have "real" experiences (in the sense that they are verifiable) without the physical body present, then that implies that we are more than our physical bodies. Returning to the landlord and tenant analogy spoken of at the very beginning of this chapter, we may identify with the landlord on most occasions, but there may be a minority of occasions during which we may have experiences just as the tenant, and not as the landlord. If we are spirit beings, then our spirits can leave our bodies, have experiences and return, or even meet other spirits that no longer have bodies, and in those rare occasions that the experience of one individual can be cross-referenced with another and verified, that can serve as a learning point both for those who have the experience and for others who learn about it.

Speaking of cross-referencing experiences, as mentioned just a moment ago, there have been records in psychology of such occurrences. The phenomenon as recorded tends to occur between individuals who have a strong emotional bond between them. One example of when shared dreams may occur is between a therapist and a client. Some of this is reported in Anthony Shafton's book *Dream Reader*. Others have also reported shared dreams between family members, lovers and spouses.

To close this section, the main takeaway is that we are sentient beings with consciousness. We often learn the truth of this when we have an individual experience or learn of the individual experience of another that occurs at the boundary between physical and non-physical reality. Having an experience at this boundary is valuable because it is here that we may receive an opportunity to verify the reality of the non-physical experience through physical means.

5.3 Altered states of consciousness

At some point in our lives, we experience a shift in our perception which may be brought about by a physical or chemical event or even a psychological event. In the physical arena, it could be a fainting spell, experienced due to exhaustion or to performing a physical feat without appropriate restraints. It could also be due to an accident. I remember experiencing a head collision with a classmate in the long jump sand pit on sports day while in middle school, which caused me to "see swirling stars", in the spirit with which it is shown in cartoons. In the chemical arena, it could be brought about by experiencing a form of anaesthesia that alters one's perception. One example that comes to mind is the use of laughing gas (nitrous oxide) in dental surgery that sometimes causes individuals to experience altered states of consciousness.

An altered state of consciousness can be defined as "one in which [a given individual] clearly feels a qualitative shift in his [or her] pattern of mental functioning" (Tart, 1969, p. 1). Here the phrase 'pattern of mental functioning' refers to the state of mind and being during normal waking consciousness. So, how most of us function in our daily lives. Any deviation from that normal, brought about by some influence or other, constitutes an altered state of consciousness. For example, if an hour ago, an individual was having a carefree stroll in a grocery store, conducting a regular restock of supplies, that state of consciousness would be an example of what can be termed 'normal'. Now, if after that hour is over, the same individual is now sitting comfortably in a chair, having drunk half a bottle of wine, and feeling a bit tipsy, this second state is an example of an altered state of consciousness. If we think of our consciousness as a compass pointing toward the magnetic north, then one way I like to think of an altered state of consciousness is that it occurs when our compass is pointing away from geographic north.

As common as altered states of consciousness can be, there are certain kinds that tend to be sanctioned in modern societies under approved conditions and other kinds that tend to be frowned upon, or even classified as illegal. This is because once the state of consciousness is altered, it can affect the ability of the mind to function as it ordinarily would in normal waking consciousness. Therefore, carrying out tasks in normal waking consciousness while in an altered state of consciousness can adversely impact efficiency and performance and may even be dangerous to other individuals conducting their lives without being in an altered state of consciousness. For example, in most countries, legal age adults are permitted to consume alcohol under the approved condition of not drinking while driving. Reasonable and moderate consumption of alcohol is not necessarily dangerous to one's health and therefore there is less control of a substance like alcohol by the state. The second class of altered states of consciousness that are frowned upon or even prohibited are those that can be brought about by indulging in certain recreational drugs. We all know examples of these. The danger here is that use of these substances often lead to permanent changes in brain chemistry that can pose serious risks to the mental health of the user. In such cases, the state or nation steps in to protect individuals from themselves by making sale and/or use of such recreational drugs illegal.

There is a third class of substances that are neither dangerous to the individual (or other individuals) if administered correctly, nor do these substances pose possible adverse mental health effects. In fact, in a number demonstrable ways these substances do quite the opposite. Not only can classes of these substances rewire neural networks to heal longstanding problems such as severe addiction brought about by use of some of the illegal recreational drugs, other classes of these substances can bring about experiences of expanded awareness of such magnitude that individuals who use these substances, sometimes even once, may experience life-changing spiritual insights, stimulation of creativity, and improvement in emotional wellbeing leading to improved relationships with self and others. Here, I am referring to an emerging field known as psychedelic medicine.

To be fair, the substances that are now forming the basis of this emerging field of psychedelic medicine have been around for decades, and some even for thousands of years. One example of these substances is LSD, which was first synthesized in 1938 and which saw extensive use in Europe and in the US in the 1950s and 1960s. Another of these substances is ayahuasca, which as been known by indigenous people in the Amazon basin for at least a thousand years. The issue with these psychedelics is that they can have a powerful effect on mind and consciousness, similarly powerful to some of the recreational drugs that have been made illegal because of their dangerous and potential long-term adverse mental health effects. In the United States, dangerous mind-altering substances with no proven medical use get put in a classification known as 'Schedule I Controlled Substance". This is the list that has most of the dangerous illegal recreational drugs. The problem here is that this list also contains substances such as ayahuasca, which has had a history of use by Indigenous people in Amazon for at least a thousand years, and also another psychedelic drug known as ibogaine, which has been used by the Bwiti, an ancient African people, for likely even longer. Ayahuasca has this incredible ability to heal traumas and to bring about extreme expansion of consciousness into heightened states of spiritual awareness, while ibogaine is one of the few substances if not the only known substance on Earth which, when used correctly can permanently *cure* severe addiction to hard narcotics after being administered only once.

So, it would appear that although psychedelic substances have powerful effects on mind and consciousness as narcotics do, they have an opposite and positive effect on mind, consciousness and being. Unlike use of narcotics that can leave an individual severely damaged, use of psychedelics can help free an imprisoned mind to experience expanded mental states and possibly even a greater spiritual reality, while also bringing about powerful healing effects. Psychedelics should ideally not fall under "Schedule I Controlled Substance" because unlike narcotics can provably bring about healing and improvement in wellbeing. This latter point has been the rationale for continued research into the properties as well as the beneficial, medicinal uses of psychedelics. At the time of writing this book, the United States appears to be at a cusp of revising legislation that would decriminalize psychedelics for medicinal and personal use, just as is being the case with the decriminalization of cannabis. Psychedelics have the potential to bring about expanded mind states far greater than the use of cannabis, as shown with LSD, which, by the way, is completely safe *if* used correctly. Legal and correct use of psychedelics has the potential to disrupt the medical industry because widespread use of psychedelics would provide new and efficient means for individuals to attain real healing by addressing root causes and not simply healing by taking symptoms away. There has been a dedicated cadre of scientists who have worked consistently and laboriously to generate scientific evidence of the beneficial medicinal and other uses of psychedelics since they were classified as illegal substances in the US and elsewhere decades ago. One book which features amazing interviews with some of these scientists who have been at the forefront of this development is *Psychedelic Medicine: The Healing Powers of LSD, MDMA, Psilocybin, and Ayahuasca*.

5.4 Being of two worlds

The reality of being a spirit being having a human experience is that we may not realize that in addition to having a physical body, we also have non-physical bodies of different subtleties and that at any given time, our consciousness can be focused either on the physical aspects of ourselves or the non-physical aspect an in some cases in both, simultaneously. Once we come to the awareness that we are more than our physical bodies, especially after we have had our own experiences of altered states during which we were very conscious and aware of what was going on, sometimes even more so than we are during normal waking consciousness, a fundamental change may occur in us. Like Neo taking the "red pill" in the 1999 movie *The Matrix*, we reach a level of knowing where we may no longer remain complacent in thinking that physical reality is all that there really is. The rest is just dreams and imagination.

In other words, there is a certain threshold of experience, often personal experience which, when crossed, leads us to a new way of thinking and being, where life is not necessarily the same way as it was before. This threshold is different from one individual to the next, but the outcome tends to be similar – our worldview changes, expands, in fact. After crossing this threshold, the conviction is no longer from hearsay. It comes from a knowing, based on experience. When this happens, many of us, in the early stages, feel as though we need to choose one world over the other. We may also seek to pull others, usually close friends, family, partners or lovers, into our reality. Let me save you a lot of trouble by telling you this. Don't do it. It does not work. This is not to say do not share your truth with others, especially those that care most about. It is rather to say that do not expect them to fully understand you, or what you have experienced, or where your mind and consciousness are at right now, especially at the onset. And especially, if they have not had their own experiences of awakening, do not expect them to follow you into knowing or realizing the non-physical reality which you have realized, because it may or may not be their time to reach such realizations. There is a timing and a rhythm for everyone.

Rather, I would suggest meeting them where they are at, which is where we probably were at, before having mind or consciousness expanding experiences. This is what it means to live in both worlds. It means finding a way of being grounded, when necessary. It means having the capacity to arrive at sobriety, when necessary. It means remaining focused, keen and fully present in our experiences, whether in physical reality or in non-physical reality. It is kind of a dual mode, that we end up getting used to. At the beginning stages of awakening to the parts of ourselves that pertain to the non-physical, we may not arrive immediately at the space where we are equally comfortable in both physical and non-physical realities. If that happens to be the case in your particular circumstance, remember to be gentle with yourself. And with others around you. Reclaiming our spiritual identity, that expanded part, the tenant, and consciously integrating it with the reality and context of our physical body experiences, the landlord, may take time, but given time and care, it will occur.

5.5 Energy work

"If you do not seek the Great Way to leave the path of delusion, even if you are intelligent and talented, you are not great. A hundred years is like a spark, a lifetime is like a bubble. If you only crave material gain and prominence, without considering the deterioration of your body, I ask you, even if you accumulate a mountain of gold can you buy off impermanence [i.e., can you use your money to prevent your death from occurring?]" – Zhang Boduan, Daoist sage (Cleary, 1987, p. 2)

There is an exercise that people often do when they want to feel their energy bodies but may never have had a qualitative experience of it. It is a simple breathing exercise which entails breathing as we normally would, except that with the in addition to inhaling and exhaling, we also imagine that we are surrounded by a ball of energy. As we breathe in, we imagine the ball contracting, and as we breathe out, we imagine the ball expanding. It helps to do this exercise slowly and mindfully, as it is an exercise that deals with subtle energies. The goal is to activate our auric egg, which is a field of energy around us, that is shaped as an upside-down egg. With some practice, and some luck (the feeling is subtle), as we continue to inhale and to exhale in this manner, we get to feel a slight pressure that pushes inwardly during the inhale round, and that pushes outwardly during the exhale round. It may help to do this exercise while sitting in the yoga posture known as asana, as you are comfortable (full lotus, half, or just cross-legged). If you experience some difficulty sitting in the yoga asana posture, sitting comfortably on a chair or lying on your back would also do just fine. If you do lie on your back, however, ensure that you do not drift into sleep before you have tried the exercise long enough to observe any effects.

I cite this exercise because I think of breathing as forming the basis of all life in manifest existence. This is true from the level of the cosmic breath that creates universes to the level of single cells in our bodies. As we breathe in, we contract our lungs, but also our energy bodies, and as we breathe out, we expand our lungs, and also our energy bodies. When we breathe in, we take in oxygen, and nitrogen when we breathe out, we release carbon dioxide, nitrogen, water vapour, and less oxygen than we breathed in. The oxygen we breathe in ends up in the cells of our bodies, which engage in cellular respiration, releasing carbon dioxide and water. The contents of what we breathe out is the same component that make up fire, or flames. Beyond ourselves, other animals are breathing, trees are breathing, the planet itself is breathing, our solar system is breathing, our galaxy is breathing, our universe is breathing and so on.

At the macro level of the universe, the process of breathing out, is what we can call a big bang, and that 'breath' contains all the life and activity that constitutes the period of existence of that universe. Conversely, process of breathing in, which we can perhaps call a 'big crunch', draws back in all that life, back to the void of nothingness. Interestingly, some ancient cultures, such as the Kemetic (Ancient Egyptian) culture have preserved a record of this in their religious or spiritual text (depending on how we look at it), the Egyptian Book of the Dead, chapter 54, which says, "O Atum, give me the gentle breeze that is in your nose!" (Obenga, 1990, p. 43). This is in reference to the Kemetic tradition of the "cosmic egg", and the beginning of existence when there was only nothing. I discuss concepts of source at length in section 9.3 of this book.

At the level of a galaxy, the process of breathing out would involve periods when a lot of cosmic rays and particles get released from the central stars toward the periphery (a time when the magnetic field of the galaxy is progressively weak), and the process of breathing in would entail a time when the magnetic field of the galaxy gets progressively strong. Similarly, at the solar level, a "breathing out" period would be a time of intense solar outbursts, such as would occur during a micronova (see section 4.4), and "breathing in" period would be a time of increasingly stable and strong solar magnetic field. Likewise, at the level of the planet, "breathing out" would be when the magnetic field is weakest, and breathing in would be when it is strongest. So, just as we can do energy work when breathing, the planet, the solar system, the galaxy and the universe can also do energy work when "breathing".

Now, in terms of energy, it is intriguing to figure out how the levels of energy oscillate with the changes in the cycles and with the rhythm of the cosmos. Ancient Daoist sages, whose philosophy was to follow nature, and the way of the cosmos, were able to figure out the cycles of the rise and fall of energy, in relation to each day, to each month, and to each solar year. These changes reflect the "energetic breathing" of the cosmos. They are useful to know because they tell us what kind of energy is available to use at what times of each period. The theory is based on the principle of change between yin and yang, from periods of lowest yin, and highest yang, to periods of highest yin, and lowest yang. Let us start with the cycle for a solar year, and then apply the same concept for a month and a day.

During a solar year, according to this theory, the period of lowest yang, and highest yin, is during the Winter Solstice of each year. This is evidenced by the fact that in most places of the year, the Winter Solstice also coincides with winter, and with the shortest day of the year. At this moment, yin energy is at its height, and yang is at its minimum. By the theory of change, yin changes to yang, and yang changes to yin. Therefore, starting from the winter solstice, the energy level within the planet slowly begins to rise until it reaches the zenith of yang, and the nadir of yin, during the summer solstice. Along the way, there is a time when the level of yin and yang are equal. This is the time of the spring equinox.

The same principle can be applied at the level of a lunar month. For the lunar month, at new moon, the yin energy level is highest, and yang is lowest. Yang energy then progressively increases until full moon, two weeks later, during which time yang energy is at its height. As such, the full moon is the moon analogue of the sun during the summer solstice. And then from full moon, progressively, yang energy decreases, and yin increases, until the new moon, and then the cycle repeats itself. The same principle can be applied for a day, where the winter solstice is at midnight, and the summer solstice is at noon. For the lunar month, half moon is the analog of the equinoxes. Around 6am, and around 6pm serves the same purpose as 'equinoxes' for the day cycle.

Up to this point is what I learned from my Daoist training. It however occurred to me that the same principle must apply in the much longer galactic cycle of the precession of the equinoxes. These are the large cycles that govern the ages. The ages are those of Aquarius, of Pisces, of Aries, of Taurus and so on. In short, there is an age for each of the signs of the Zodiac, and the precession progresses in the counterclockwise direction, that is, opposite the direction of rotation of the Earth. We are said to be currently in the age of Aquarius, or at the cusp of it, having spent the last close to 2000 years in the age of Pisces. The entire precession takes about 25,920 years, giving each of the 12 ages a duration of roughly 2,160 years. Both of these numbers are approximations, because in reality it takes the Earth a different amount of time to travel through each precession sign constellation.

What I find intriguing is that because the precession is progressing in the opposite direction as the rotation of the Earth, where in the case of a solar year, we have the summer solstice at the beginning of the sign of Leo, during the summer, in the case of the precession of the equinoxes, the equivalent of the summer solstice would instead be at the beginning of the opposite sign to Leo, which is Aquarius. Conversely, the where in the case of the solar year, the winter solstice is at the beginning of the sign of Capricorn, in the case of the precession of the equinoxes, the equivalent of the winter solstice would instead be at the beginning of the opposite sign to Capricorn, which is Cancer.

The reason why I find this to be important is two-fold. First, because we are said to be at the beginning of the age of Aquarius at the current time, so this means we are in the equivalent of the summer solstice period for the precession of the equinoxes. This is the period of maximum yang, in the yin-yang cycle of energy changes that govern the flow of energies within cycles. Maximum yang is when the sun is experiencing its greatest intensity during the summer. Speaking of the said to be impending micronova (see section 4.4), it would make sense that it happens at this time, at the period of "summer solstice" of the precession of the equinoxes.

The second reason why I find this important is that conceptualizing the precession of the equinoxes in terms of the yin-yang changes in energy flow gives a means to model the approximately 12,000- year cycle of the sun that is studied by scientists, and its respective disaster cycle. Disasters happen at the cusps of the yin and yang maxima (the "precession solstices"), and also at the 50-50 points ("precession equinoxes", pun not intended) because those are times of great energy change. However, when modeled with the yin-yang cycle changes, we really can speak just of a 24,000-year cycle (i.e., close to our number of 25,920-year average for the precession of the equinoxes). In this vein, the previous disasters that have happened can be placed at certain positions within the precession cycle, and depending on their position and on the energy change occurring during that period, it would then be possible to speculate on the type of "disaster cycle" change that would happen during that period. I got the disaster information below from what Ben Davidson has published on spaceweather.com.

	"Summer Solstice" (0, 24, 48, …) Current impending disaster Lake Mungo Toba event	
"Autumn Equinox" (18, 42, 66, …) Hilina Pali Laschamp		**"Spring Equinox"** (6, 30, 54, …) Noah/Sumerian
	"Winter Solstice" (12, 36, 60, …) Gothenburg Mono Lake Vostok/Greenland	

6

THE RING OF LIFE AND DEATH

Life and death are like two sides of the same coin. We came from somewhere, in order to end up here in this present time. We have a record of having been born, because our parents and our communities welcome us when we arrive. And then life on Earth happens, during which we go through many experiences. Once our time on Earth for a given incarnation comes to an end, we pass on, and those who know us tend to hold a ceremony to commemorate our departure.

And so, the experiences we have during normal waking consciousness are what we tend to go by when we think about or we decide what life means and what death means. But what if life and death are much more similar than many of us may realize? For all we know, what we call on this side, life, is death, on the other side, and what we call here death, is life on the other side. This could be one way in which life and death are related.

Taking this idea one step further, I would like you to take a moment to imagine a scenario where there are two gateways within a tube or a loop of sorts, one that looks like a doughnut. Imagine further that the gateways within this loop are paced at some distance *within* the loop, one from the other, and not necessarily equidistant. For each portal or gateway within this loop, once traversing the portal, the reality that can be lived and experienced on one side is qualitatively different from that on the other side of the same portal. If then we take for granted that one gateway leads to "life", and another leads to "death", then it could be imagined or thought that, if the situation were turned around, the gateway that leads to "life" could be seen as one that leads to "death" from the alternative perspective, and vice versa.

So, let's just imagine for a moment that we are souls, that come into this Earth life experience. We "enter" into the existences and realities of this loop, and we keep looping around, through the gateways, into life and into death, and then into life, and then into death and around and around, and around, again and again and again. From one end of one portal to another, we are tethered to a physical body. Once we transition through the second portal, we are not tethered to a physical body...until we get back to the other side of the first portal, transition through it again, and then we have a physical body. And on and on and on it goes. In this way, it could be thought that all that happens is simply transitioning from one life to another life. One life has a physical body accompaniment during the duration of that life, and the other one does not.

Of course, it could also be truly said that there is death, since something truly comes to an end. That which comes to an end is the existence of that particular physical body, in almost every case. Almost every case, because, as we shall discuss later on in this book, there is a certain chance to leave the loop altogether, if it can be imagined that we entered into the loop at some point. But otherwise, the existence continues round and around and around, in what has been called reincarnation, each time acquiring a new physical body and gaining new experiences. From this perspective, it is the soul that survives the transition each time, and it is the soul that is ultimately experiencing, therefore at any given point, the soul can be conceptualized as having some memory of the sum total of experiences up to that point.

One individual who made the exploration of lives lived by a soul currently incarnated her central research interest is Helen Wambach, who we first encountered in chapter 3. In that chapter, we examined her work and the evidence around it pertaining to souls prior to entering incarnation. In this section, we shall examine some of the evidence she presents when using hypnotic regression to query souls currently incarnated to learn of the life and death conditions of other lives these souls have had on Earth. Where in chapter 3 we examined evidence from her book *Life before Life* (i.e., life on the non-physical side of the loop), in this chapter we shall examine evidence from *Reliving Past Lives*, another work she wrote that entails recollections of other lifetimes in a physical body. What I find intriguing about this latter work is the effort she took in attempting to verify the data obtained from hypnotically regressed subjects. In chapter 9, for our discussion on epistemology, we emphasize the importance of validity and reliability checks to methods of generating knowledge. Knowing that hypnotic regression is a reliable method, because it consistently works, also including a validity check such as verifying the information, and getting positive results on that, in my view, qualifies this approach as a suitable means of generating new knowledge from non-physical or psychic data. The verification method involves, where possible, cross-referencing data on a historical person obtained during hypnotic regression with records on that person that are available to the public.

In the first example we shall consider, during hypnotic regression, a woman recalled episodes of a lifetime she had in Pennsylvania in the late eighteenth into the nineteenth century. For this lifetime, from the chapter titled *More past lives and more evidence*, Helen Wambach aimed to verify some information from the childhood period of the lifetime that was regressed:

"In attempting to find the data of her birth, I regressed her to 1798. She reported that she was about four years old, and described the small log house she lived in and the view of the countryside. We later discovered that her actual date of birth did indeed correspond with her recall. She was also able to give the year of her death, which she said was 1868" (Wambach, 1978, n.p.)

Here we read a report of an attempt to verify data the hypnotically regressed subject offered during the session. Not only that. We also read that there was some success in cross-referencing psychic and historical data. As the subject is led to further explore this lifetime, an interesting facet of data emerges. Where the regressed subject was in a woman in the current incarnation, the lifetime she was recalling was one where she had been a man:

"As Buchanan, she seemed very articulate and informed, in contrast with the personality she exhibited in earlier lifetimes. Buchanan reported that the purpose of his work was to demonstrate that single-minded devotion to work and high ambition could result in high achievement. But he paid a price for his success. Betty said that as Buchanan she was lonely and had little affection in this life" (Wambach, 1978, n.p.).

The Buchanan referred to her is James Buchanan, 15th President of the United States of America. It is really fascinating, that one trip we make through the incarnation side of the loop may result in a female incarnation, and then, after spending some time on the non-physical side of the loop, going back into incarnation, the next incarnation, or after a few down the line, may be in a male physical body. What is also important to take note of, is that personalities may vary from incarnation to incarnation. In the quote above, we are told that there was a marked difference from Betty's earlier incarnations that appeared during other hypnotic regression sessions and that of Buchanan. From one incarnation to another, interests may be the same, may be similar or may be different. These personalities are however all aspects of ourselves, from the standpoint of our Higher Selves (a subject of the next chapter), even though they may appear different at the level of the personality. We keep our memories from life to life, and that which may appear lost is only so, to the conscious mind of a given incarnation. We find then, in the next quote, that although the subject had no interest in history in her current incarnation as Betty, during hypnosis, she was able to access her memories as Buchanan to give accurate information that was later verified:

"Betty was surprised at her experiences as James Buchanan. She denied any interest in American history and said she had not read anything about Buchanan. It is, of course, possible that she might have been taught something about Buchanan and had this information in her subconscious. But it's quite a feat to be able to produce this kind of information, acquired many years ago, and weave it into a past-life recall with very few errors in dates, names and places. At last, I had a subject reporting a life that could be checked. This is exciting, and the results of our attempts to verify details were also exciting" (Wambach, 1978, n.p.)

As exciting at this may be, some may find it incredulous that an 'ordinary' person could have had an incarnation as a historical person, and none other than one of the Presidents of the US. I suppose this is one of the exciting possibilities for those who venture into the spiritual, to learn more about themselves. When you do, if you have not already, you might just learn some amazing things about yourself as well. For example, at one point in my explorations, I discovered that I have had an incarnation as one of the pharaohs of the very early dynasties of Kemet (Ancient Egypt), one of my few incarnations in this culture, and to give a range of how early for this one, we're looking at 1st to 7th dynasty in this case (don't ask, because I won't tell). I also have a friend who came to learn that he had an incarnation as one of the foremost scientists known to the world, a public and recognizable name. One point is that although we do not remember these lives, partly due to the need to focus on our current incarnations, the memories of these lives are not lost. When we develop our spiritual abilities, we can recover some of these memories, even without external assistance. Hypnotic regression is not the only means to access these memories. For example, another way is to retrieve memories of other incarnational existences is to project one's consciousness out of body and to travel back in time, to the period when a particular incarnation lived. It is then possible to merge with that incarnation and to experience life through their eyes, while obviously not being able to change anything in that time period. So, through these and other means, you may also find out about some of the lives you have lived at other time periods.

Another point of note is that it is not just about discovering your lifetimes as a powerful or a famous person in the public eye. It may turn out that a lot of the incarnations would be what we might term "ordinary". It has to do more so with learning about who you are, as a being, and why you, as your Higher Self, may have made certain choices, incarnated within certain races or during certain time periods. These explorations can give clues into your identity, and may help in the process of integrating your personality selves, the process of becoming more than the single incarnation within a single lifetime.

6.1 God and science save us

The image of life as a loop that repeatedly takes us from one kind of life while in a body to another kind of life while not in a body was discussed in the section just preceding this one. In the modern education available on Earth in a mainstream way, the individual is taught primarily to think scientifically, and to resort to the scientific method as the standard means for gaining knowledge and for learning about the real world. Conversely, one of the main ways that mainstream modern education equips individuals who search for answers to questions about what lies in the non-physical part of life is to find them through religion. Religion on one hand, science on the other.

Fundamental to many, but to not all religions is the notion of a creator, an all-powerful force of creation. From this notion of an all-powerful force of creation comes the idea that this creator can be prayed to. And thus, since time immemorial, peoples in different cultures have been praying to a creator who has also been thought of as a supreme being. In many cases, this supreme being had helpers that aid the creator in creation. These helpers could be thought of as being spirits of one kind or another, and so the belief in spirits and phenomena related to spirit is central to most, if not all religions. And so, religions tend to have a spiritual dimension to them. To me, the distinguishing feature between being religious and being spiritual is that in the former case, adherents are almost always required to accept the central tenets of a given religion on belief or on faith. For example, in the Christian religion, an adherent accepts the existence of God, a supreme being, and also accepts Jesus Christ as her or his personal saviour. In religious Daoism, another example, there is a belief in the three pure ones, a trinity of beings. This is not to say that rationality plays no role in religion. On the contrary, it does. Religious doctrines are known to have a logic consistent within the paradigm of the religion. This logic is built upon the basis of the central tenets, which have to be taken on faith.

Speaking of logic, and rationality, where religions commonly require adherents to hold true a set of foundational beliefs, science requires adherents to strive to establish physical facts based on premises that can be shown to lead to certain consequences. It is important to state here, that science, or rather the scientific method, does not establish cause, although some adherents of science may think it can, or may hold otherwise. Let me explain. Science is based on observation of apparent physical actions. When this happens, then that happens. And when that happens, yet another thing happens. Well, what about the thing behind the thing behind the thing behind...ad infinitum? It would appear that scientific minds have not yet worked it all out, but there are scientific theories that are trying to resolve the infinitesimal layer. This takes us to quantum mechanics, and to related or competing theories. Rather, science appears to be good at selecting a section of the physical action-and-reaction chain, determining patterns about it, and coming up with laws governing the behaviour of the section. Take Newtonian mechanics for example, with its associated laws of motion. These laws are based on observable behaviour which, being repeatable, is therefore amenable to prediction by laws. And yet, what the root cause is, of this observable behaviour, if there is indeed a root cause, appears to still be an open question as far as mainstream science is concerned. There however seems to be strong belief, within mainstream scientific thinking, that physically observable behaviour can ultimately be reduced to the understanding of certain fundamental particles. A discussion of ideas concerning fundamental layers of reality as seen from the standpoints of certain scientific and spiritual philosophies can be found at length in last ring presented in this book.

And so, here we are, in this situation called physical life, where we are born with no apparent knowledge of what came from. And then once we arrive, we become enculturated into the norms of the given society we find ourselves in. Religions have been in human societies for a long time, and in some societies, cultural and religious norms conflate. Scientific thinking of one degree or another has been a part of most Earth societies for millennia. Even in aboriginal and indigenous societies, the manner of scientific thinking, where knowledge studying the mechanics of one action has informed predicting the actions of other actions, has helped these societies survive in their environments. Two examples of these are various forms of scientific knowledge used by horticulturists in farming and by hunters in trapping game. There is evidence of pre-modern scientific knowledge in societies with larger urban areas, such as the use of battery-powered electricity and solar power in Ancient Egypt, textile mills in Mesopotamia, flying machines (vimanas) and nuclear weapons in Ancient India, gunpowder in Ancient China, and telescopes in Arabia. In all these societies, religion and science coexisted, however there can be a challenge in a society where religion and science contradict one another in their teachings about the physical and non-physical realities. This seems to have been the case with the Christian civilizations of Europe, where the standard view of the world as given by the church and which was the official view of reality in the region for centuries was slowly replaced by a scientific worldview. In Europe, religion and science suffered a divorce, somewhere between the medieval period and the European enlightenment. Stemming from that, religion remained as a domain of those who believed in a soul. Science established its place as a domain of the mind (the two domains are not necessarily mutually exclusive, meaning that it is possible to find individuals who are at once both highly scientific and highly religious). And thus, the debate has continued to the present day, where science, predominantly a domain of the mind, seeks to speak on matters of the soul when the version of science that is dominant in the world today and that was largely developed in Europe fundamentally lacks a place for soul in its epistemology, and where Christianity, a domain of the soul, seeks to speak on matters of the mind, when its view of the world includes one which does not match scientific data. This has led us to a situation where, in the modern world, science "saves" us in the physical world, and God "saves" us in the non-physical.

6.2 "New age" paradigms

There is a dissatisfaction among some individuals in modern society who increasingly identify as spiritual and not as religious. The distinction is important, precisely because of what was discussed in the section above. After almost two millennia, Europe, that was originally not a Christian civilization, managed to develop from having become a religious society into becoming a secular society. This meant that religion now took second seat in favour of secular ideas at the basis of which lies the rational orientations that Europeans adopted from Greek civilization.

When the transition was complete, science had taken center hold in becoming the preferred mode for deciding what was correct knowledge in secular European society. The Europeans took science, and then technology, to the next level, and then went out to conquer the world. As a reaction to this action, European society began experiencing an influx of people from their colonies, who now identified with the European country as their "mother country". This trend was taken to an even greater extent in what became the United States of America (the US), because, because now it was everybody that was going there, including Europeans and those who used to be their colonial subjects.

And so, we have a nation, which effectively started a new type of "syncretic civilization", if you will. By that I mean at its onset, and arguably still at the present time, the dominant cultural mode in the US stemmed from European roots. That is, mode of technology, official language, cultural norms, and such. And yet, the US was not "just another European settlement". This is because the US had and still has so many other cultures present and represented in this one nation. I would however opine that the US as a nation, in its earlier stages, continued to draw inspiration from European culture and education. Many of those who would become the educated elite in the US would go to Europe to study, in the UK, in Germany and in France, especially. At the present time, the trend has changed. The US is the place that most people go to from around the world. Very soon, everyone will be going to study in China, and perhaps in India as well, but that is another story.

What I would like to draw attention to, is the idea that by taking on European norms, the US also took on the science that Europe developed in the centuries prior to the US becoming the rising power, and the US further developed this science. Additionally, although there is religious freedom in the US, historically there is also a strong history of Christianity in the US, judging from the manner in which black slaves had to endure conversion, and the fact that Christianity in the US is now a strong current among blacks in the US, and not only among whites. But it still remains a fact that the US is a nation of great diversity, a diversity which includes religious diversity. Therefore, when in the 1960s and the 1970s, the US experienced an explosion of counterculture, a time during which many individuals explored alternative ideas, the US was the perfect place for the birth of what is now known as the "New Age", and what we know of as "New Age paradigms".

In the counterculture era of the 1960s and 1970s, there was much rebellion against the culture of war that the US had embroiled itself in. There had earlier been the Korean war, but in my view, the Vietnam war and its associated military draft stimulated a great pushback from the general US population. As an alternative to war, strife, and death, this was a time that others professed peace, and love. It was the time of the US civil rights movement. It was a time that individuals experimented a great deal with psychedelics, with some amongst this group achieving peak spiritual experiences. It was also a time when segments of the US population experienced an explosion in interest concerning spiritual matters. Being a nation of such great diversity, all of a sudden, the spiritual paradigms of the diverse peoples that make up the US population were of interest to the many, including those with different cultural heritages. In particular, there was born a great interest in yoga and in the spiritual systems of aboriginal and indigenous (shamanic) peoples. Yoga, Buddhism, Sufism, Shamanism, the Great White Brotherhood, you name it, there must have been people who were pushing it at the time. It was as if the European underpinnings of American society was going through an upheaval, and where once there was Christianity, mainly for the white population but also now for the black population, now the white population (I believe this segment of the US population spearheaded the counterculture at the time), now there was a great interest among the counterculture adherents in everything non-Christian, and even in pre-Christian traditions such as druidism and wicca. The New Age movement was thus a response to the inadequacies of religion and science.

This peace and love counterculture movement, coupled with demonstrations against nuclear weapons and the fact (we shall be talking about this shortly) that the detonations of the first nuclear weapons all of a sudden coincided with an upsurge in extraterrestrial visitations, these peace-loving counterculture adherents also started revering and trying to reach out to "space brothers", there was now formed a hodgepodge of alternative influences from different traditions of the spiritualities outside of recent European civilizational influences such as I have described. Thus the "New Age" was born.

One underlying feature of this New Age was the lack of structure and control. The old dogmas were to be toppled, so in their place, people began to pick and choose. A little bit of tarot here, a little bit of feng shui there, some experience with shamanic power animals, and a belief in space brothers and ascended masters. There were also more individuals starting to write about their own experiences, and to share their own thoughts and paradigms. In the face of all this New Age development, the movement began to spread not only in the US but outside its borders as well. The English-speaking world, places such as Canada and the UK, experienced the New Age movement at about the same time as it was occurring in the US, and have had a New Age culture ever since. In the UK, in places such as Glastonbury and Stonehenge, both of which I have visited, there have been festivals over the past few decades that have attracted thousands of people. Stonehenge in particular has celebrated a festival on the summer solstice for many years how. It is a revival of an ancient practice that pre-dates Christianity. My experience of continental Europe is limited when it comes to exploring New Age culture, however I have encountered evidence of alternative health stores, and alternative spirituality sites in different countries in continental Europe and so I would imagine that there is a market for New Age ideas and associated merchandize.

The New Age has been a spiritually refreshing period for some on a spiritual journey in search of a greater understanding of themselves and of the world around them. It became a movement, which spawned its own sub-economy. People would support New Age bookstores, cafes and cooperatives. There began a strong interest in the Native American traditions of spirituality, while others were traveling to places like India and Nepal to find spiritual masters to study with. Not surprisingly, the New Age movement, with its paradigms and its ideas and openness and exploration of personal paths has often drawn the scorn of traditional authorities in academia and even in spirituality. In academia, I have often come across people who write or comment on work that borders on topics also discussed as part of the New

Age movement striving to distinguish such work from New Age works. The very nature of the New Age movement that makes it a celebration of freedom from structure and dogma and an openness to explore has drawn criticism and scorn from those who see this movement as being flakey or non-rigorous. For example, to say that something is New Agey (which has now become a term), such as a book on chakras or yoga or one on holistic health is to brand it as something that is questionable in terms of authenticity. It is however interesting that even the works of established authors in the academic arena or from some spiritual paradigms such as the schools of Tibetan Buddhism end up in New Age bookstores, or in sections of mainstream bookstores marked under mind and body, or spirit and transformation.

One final point that I would like to make about the New Age, in this section, is that with the birth of the movement came greater promotion for alternative belief systems and spiritual systems. Even with the criticism and the scorn, the New Age movement has arguably "opened Pandora's box" for many spiritual seekers who transition through to find what it is they truly seek. For instance, it could be that finding one material in a spiritual bookstore could subsequently lead to discovering an entire spiritual paradigm previously unknown, and that paradigm becoming the mainstay for study. I should also point out that for some people, there is no such system or paradigm. New Age material itself becomes their paradigm, and instead of believing in a conventional mainstream system, they find something else within the New Age paradigm that crossed their paths to believe in. Their faith might not be in God or Allah or in Jesus Christ or Muhammad but rather in the Divine Goddess or in Kwan Yin or in some tutelar spirits. We are each different, and so each must consider their own circumstances in order to know what it is they need to experience. For some, the New Age movement might serve as a means to help them transition from for instance a Judeo-Christian religion to a religion of their ancestral heritage. And that is great and fine. For others, they may choose to treat New Age material itself as a religion, or to transition out of religion altogether, and that too is great and fine.

6.3 Transcending religion

One of the strangest bits of information I have come across on my own journey of awakening is the idea that the story in the

Christian Bible about God creating Adam and Eve is in fact an abridged version of a shocking story that I have since found is at the heart of much of what is going on in our world. The story is about the creation of contemporary humans on Earth by extraterrestrials (ETs). Not only did different ETs contribute to what seemed to be a huge project, some of those ETs also posed as gods. These who posed as gods were different from the one infinite creator, and ideas about the supreme being. The confusion is made even more insidious when I came to learn that the idea of a true creator of manifest reality was usurped by imposter beings, creators in their own right nonetheless, but not who they claim to be, and that when we are born into the world and enculturated into religion and to social norms, we may miss learning about this very important topic.

Why is it important to know about ETs, and about this story that just about every government on Earth (I will get into that shortly) has made it their policy to hide this secret from the masses? The reasons I discovered for this secret are equally shocking. In fact, some of the reasons might annoy or upset some who are reading this book, though it need not. For others, it might inspire them to realize why it is so important, if you are on a path of awakening, to understand yourself and your identity as a spirit being. You have all the power within you, to awaken to the greatest extent you choose to, in this lifetime, and decide on how you would like to channel your spirit energies during your life, to achieve what is important to you as a being.

Let us get into this story which, if you ever learn how to consciously project your non-physical bodies out of your physical body and travel as a soul to other locales on this planet and beyond, you may verify for yourself the truth of it.

"[Shamanic teacher]: Look, how far are you willing to go, in order to become one of us? [Credo]: I am willing to go anywhere. [Shamanic teacher]: Listen, educated man, we are tired of people like you. White men come amongst us to milk our minds and then to kill us. We want to be sure that we can trust you. [Credo]: Great one, I am willing to do anything...; and these were the people, sir, who first told me, about a race of highly intelligent beings which they called the Chitauri, the talkers, a race of creatures which look like reptiles, who have ruled the world for hundreds, if not thousands of years" (Credo Mutwa, interviewed by David Icke in *The Reptilian Agenda*)

This is a story I have learned not only from Credo Mutwa but also from other indigenous people, including the Australian Aboriginal people, and the Indigenous peoples of the Americas. When studying the language and traditions of my own people the Akan of West Africa, I also came to the conclusion that there are records in Akan culture of interaction with ET beings from the far past.

ETs have been visiting Earth since the remotest time until the present time. As I have studied this phenomenon more and more, the conclusion I have come to is that when ETs visit Earth and interact with ordinary people, they frequently have ordinary experiences. For example, an ET would get lost, and find himself or herself at an indigenous person's home. They would ask for directions and then be on their way. Or an ET, or a group of them would crash on a Native American reservation, and they would be taken care of until their situation got better and then they would leave. Similar situations have happened in Africa as well, according to accounts I have read, where an ET or their group would visit an African group, interact with its members and maybe even take one or a few aboard, and then bring them back.

This cannot be said of the experiences I have read of ETs interacting with powerful world governments. Of this second version, it seems the interactions are hostile. The ETs get shot down, and often those that are unfortunately in the crossfire and that get affected by Earth-based weapons, when they crash, they do not always survive. When they do survive, they are taken into custody, and often, horrible things happen to them, even some of those that look human. Things you would not think possible, such as mutilating a human ET while it is still alive. This is not to say that indigenous people did not capture ETs. That is not the point. In fact, there are accounts of medicine men in Africa learning how to capture ETs, however I never read of these ETs getting such severe treatments as those I have read about being caught by some of the powerful governments of the world.

I was soon to also learn that there is a long-standing policy, not only by the US government but by other governments in the world, to keep knowledge of ETs a secret. Because of this policy, the governments routinely lie to their people, and in the US there is even evidence of their government, or specifically the organization known as the Central Intelligence Agency (CIA) adopting what amounts to psychological warfare against their own citizens in order to keep them ignorant of the fact that people from other worlds and in some cases even from other dimensions have been visiting Earth for a very long time, and lately the volume of those visits has gone up. To illustrate the complicity of the CIA in propagating the lie against the people of the US, Victor Marchetti, former special assistant to the Executive Director of the CIA, had this to express on the matter of ETs and disclosure:

"We have, indeed, been contacted – perhaps even been visited – by extraterrestrial beings, and the US government, in collusion with other national powers of the Earth, is determined to keep this information from the general public" (Greer, 2017, n.p.)

So, then I ask myself why? Why would the governments of the world opt to control the information on ETs, so much so that they go out of their way to conduct (in some cases) psychological warfare against their own citizenry. Within academia and militaries, any who work for the US government, if an individual came across the ET or UFO phenomenon in the past, that individual was threatened with severe consequences if they revealed the information they knew. So, why all of this?

I think it is because a good proportion of individuals who make it to the top positions in government and in the private sector, those that see themselves as elite and have a chance to be privy to this kind of information, are of the control freak variety. They are in for personal benefit. Remember what was discussed in section 4.4 in regard to the movie *Don't look up*, and to the book *Political Ponerology*? It is a similar situation here. Those are in positions of power are, for the most part, in it for themselves. Ponerology is an Ancient Greek term that has to do with evil. It is an illusion that politicians always go into government to make a difference. Some do, but according to the research, the majority go in for the control, the power, and the prestige. They are selfish people, and as such they seek first and foremost to personally gain from an advantageous situation. Being controllers, they also seek to control, however in dealing with some of the ETs, they have proven not to be able to entirely control the situation, so they go more toward the benefit angle. There have been companies like Lockheed Martin in the US that have built a lot of technological devices based on ET technology inserts.

So, imagine that the ETs come to Earth, and the representatives of Earth's human population that they get to interact with are these military, business and government types? That causes me to wonder about those specific ET groups that choose to deal with the governments. I suppose if we choose those leaders then we give them the mandate to represent us. I also wonder how many opportunities are missed by these militarized people shooting or attempting to shot down UFOs that come to Earth and chasing the UFOs around with their comparatively primitive technology when it is clear that theirs the Earth's is far inferior in technological advancement. Fortunately, the ET visitors have over the decades interacted not only with military government types but also with individuals.

The thing is that many people inherently trust in their governments. Because of this trust, whatever the people in power say is believed by these people. If then this government comes out to abuse the trust of the citizenry by saying that UFOs do not exist and that they are 'swamp gas', people will believe that. Meanwhile, members of that government would be secretly and fully invested in not only understanding the phenomenon but also figuring out ways to benefit from it. In the US, those that have had the greatest potential to benefit from knowledge about the ET presence are those that have both a foot in government and one in the private sector, according to Greer (2017). Steven Greer, perhaps more than anyone I know, believed he could bring about disclosure by working within the system of the US government. He took his efforts to the greatest extents of government, engaging with US presidents, secretaries of defense, private industry elites and even the UN secretary general at one point. He has not yet been successful in "moving the machine" to make it happen. In the end, what he learned was that people have to take the responsibility for educating themselves. It is not going to happen any other way.

What we get instead is media coverup, and this once again brings to mind Plato's allegory of the cave introduced earlier in this book. In particular, I am referring to the 'manipulator' who employ artists to control the puppets that are projected onto the wall that the chained individuals. In Plato's allegory, the manipulators are not there to propagate the truth. They are there to propagate whatever the controllers want the manipulators to propagate. This is unbelievably admitted by John Swinton, a former managing editor of the New York Times and New York Sun, who can be termed an artist employed by the manipulators:

"The business of the journalist is to destroy the truth; to lie outright; to pervert; to vilify; to fawn at the feet of mammon, and to sell his country and his race for his daily bread. You know it and I know it and what folly is this toasting an independent press? We are the tools and vassals of rich men behind the scenes. We are the jumping jacks, they pull the strings and we dance. Our talents, our possibilities and our lives are all the properties. We are intellectual prostitutes" (Greer, 2017, n.p.)

Now, although this may not necessarily be true for the press everywhere in the world, given that Swinton was managing editor of the New York Times, one of the top, if not the preeminent newspaper in the US, we can assume that at least there was some degree of truth in what he said, at the time he said it, if he said it of sound and honest mind. That, to me, sounds uncannily like the description of the manipulators in Plato's cave. It would also go to show why Steven Spielberg, a film producer, would have access to highly classified information about ETs titled *Close Encounters with the Third Kind*. A retired US Navy commander with a top-secret clearance said:

"I was told by a friend of mine at Wright-Patterson Air Force Base who I've known for years that they had allowed Steven Spielberg to see the microfilm and the Blue Book records on this for *Close Encounters of the Third Kind*. So he [Spielberg] had a pretty high clearance. He had to be associated with some of the ... well, you know who, as far as the control group is concerned." (Greer, 2017, n.p.)

So, why all this secrecy about the ET matter? The basic story is that in the very far past, some ETs had played a role in creating a human prototype on Earth. One negative ET group had started creating humans on Earth. They are the ones behind the story of the Garden of Eden. In their garden, they had a version of what we know now as religion, that was used as a form of mind control, to keep the population of their human workers under control. As part of their religion mind control, these ETs were to be worshiped as 'God', and were to be totally obeyed. No advanced spiritual knowledge was permitted among those who were being influenced by the religion. Those who came into contact with advanced knowledge (i.e., Eve eating of the fruit of good and evil) were to be banished from the garden. That is, the people who gained knowledge, esoteric knowledge, they transcended religion. They became heroes, in the hero's journey. They became free, and went out of the garden, to live and become 'aboriginals' and 'indigenous people', while the rest remained on the ET plantation. This is what Robert Morning Sky calls being a renegade. The story of a few lines in Genesis of the Christian bible is an attempt to capture a much more detailed account of true history from this very ancient period.

In any case, not all the ETs were negative, and not all used religion as a form of mind control. Before long, after this first group had started their experiments, various other ET groups from around the galaxy, some positive, others negative, also came here to also experiment on Earth humans. The collective experiments of these groups resulted in today's diversity of human races living on the surface of Earth. A key and important difference between this new human prototype and ETs living elsewhere in the galaxy is that the Earth human was created with limited genetic code activation. With the condition of limited code activation, the Earth humans could not consciously access memories of existences prior to being born.

Over time, the human population grew exponentially, so that not all humans came into contact with the ETs. The ETs began to retreat and they put hybrids who were their own descendants in power to rule in their stead. These hybrids have been around for thousands of years, going all the way back to the time of the earliest genetic experiments of humans on Earth. Over this period of time, these hybrids, who are part human and part ET (or at least have varying degrees of heritage from ETs who once held sway on Earth) organized themselves into an elite group. They have ruled in the shadows for so long, and in fact these hybrids have always remained in contact with the now minority ET groups that have had a presence on Earth for millennia. This group of hybrids became the "powers that be".

6.4 Metaphysics and spiritual science

We earlier discussed that a key requirement of religion is for an adherent to have belief or faith in the central tenets of a religion. If a key requirement of religion is the notion of belief in the divine, then a key requirement of spirituality, and of spiritual experience, is personal experience of the divine. In the orientation of religion, the adherent learns what the lofty spiritual beings have achieved or are capable of and on the basis of this they worship them and ask for these lofty beings to intercede on their behalf. In the case of spiritual experience, the adherent is inspired by these lofty beings and as such wants to be able to pursue a path similar to what they pursued in order to also be able to reproduce their achievements.

A mundane example would be the image of a highly adept accountant who wows her or his followers with adept mathematical and numeracy skills. The religious among them would be so wowed that they would start to kowtow to this accountant in the hope that the accountant would help them with issues that require mathematical and numeracy skills. The spiritual among them would also admire the accountant, but rather than bow and kowtow to the accountant, would instead be really keen to discover what the curriculum was that the accountant studied to become so good at accounting. What school did they go to, and who did they study with? What were the challenges along the way, and what are any tips for success?

In other words, to put it simply, the religious admirers would look to give their power away, hoping that they can exchange that power giveaway with access to the good graces of the expert accountant so that whenever they needed accounting work, they could have access to the accountant. The spiritual admirers on the other hand would look to be empowered, so that they could themselves become accountants. It would take a period of study, practice, and training. Perhaps they may become as good as the expert accountant, or perhaps not. But whether or not they reach ultimate mastery and expertise, the spiritual admirers would have gained skills in accounting which would hopefully help them in their own accounting endeavours.

Those who study metaphysics and spiritual science, in their efforts to develop their spiritual abilities, awareness and mastery, are more like the spiritual admirers who seek the expert accountant to learn how to themselves gain accounting skills than are they like the religious admirers who only want the expert accountant to do accounting work on their behalf. The study of metaphysics and of spiritual science has some similarities to studying physics and material science. In both cases, the student seeks to gain greater understanding of reality. In both cases, the student accesses a body of work, laid down by practitioners who came before, and who, through their own investigations, made observations and discoveries that contributed to knowledge of reality being studied. In the case of physical reality, observations and discoveries are contributed to the body of knowledge known as material science. In the case of non-physical reality, the same is done as before, only this time contributions are made for metaphysics. Both types of students draw on the processes of logic and inference to organize perceptual data. A main difference is the nature of perceptual data. For spiritual science, data can include spiritual sources whereas for material science, the data is typically from physical reality.

7

THE RING OF THE HIGHER SELF

In our quest to understand who we are, we may at one point learn that there is a version of ourselves that transcends all time and space. This version of ourselves is like a completed record, where each of our incarnations is a track on the record. For those who know or who remember vinyl records from past decades, each track on the record can be likened to a lifetime or an incarnation on Earth. The loop or doughnut idea introduced at the beginning of the previous chapter applies here as well. Imagine that for each time a soul completes one revolution in the loop, consisting of one life in the physical and one life in the non-physical, that constitutes one loop on the vinyl. The sum total of all the loops on the vinyl, and in effect all the lives lived, constitutes the identity of the being.

This being has been called many names, including the Higher Self, the High Self, the I-There (as opposed to I-Here, or the personality self), the Holy Guardian Angel, the Jewel in the Lotus. It is a being that is much more than simply the sum of its incarnations. It is a consciousness, an awareness, a Self, in the making. We, each of the incarnations, are expressions of our Higher Selves. To take the analogy of a vinyl disk a step further, imagine that on a vinyl player, the tip, or the stylus, can be likened to our souls. As the stylus tracks its way along the vinyl disk, our souls also follow their designated paths along the given lifetimes. Together, all the lifetimes a Higher Self experiences on Earth constitute an 'album', which we could call the 'Earth surface human album'.

As such, our Higher Selves are like a music artist. We could think for instance of the hip hop or rap artiste Nas Escobar, as an example. Being an artiste, it is likely that our Higher Selves have produced other albums before their current Earth album. For example, our Higher Selves might have albums corresponding to their time in the Pleiades, in the Orion or in the Sirius star systems. Each of these albums together define the work and the style of the Higher Self, just as we can learn something about Nas by listening to the various rap albums he has released.

7.1 The totally trustworthy parent-spirit

This time around, in incarnation, one of the most valuable bits of knowledge or of remembering that I feel most fortunate to have received, is knowledge of the Higher Self. Many of us who are brought up in religions like to think of God as the being that is watching over us all the time, moment to moment, and is aware of all of what we are doing. Well, if we take for granted the existence of some creator or source consciousness (see chapter 9), then a case may be made that there is a being that at a certain level presides over all of its creation. In certain religions, people are taught to pray to this creator or source consciousness, and from what I have learned from indigenous traditions, it is possible to reach the attention of this source entity, and it is possible to get prayers answered.

And yet, creation is vast, with countless beings at many different levels of existence. Rather than reach out of ourselves to receive help, as discussed at the end of the last chapter, we can also help ourselves. This is what we do when we learn to communicate with our Higher Selves. Our Higher Selves are us, ourselves, only at a different level of awareness and totality. What is also of great importance to know is that not only is the personality self (the soul, or the part that incarnates successively) a part of its Higher Self, meaning that the two are one and the same, also the Higher Self has an active and vested interest in the life, the development and in fact everything that the personality self is engaged in. The Higher Self is like a totally trustworthy parent-spirit, that is always watching over the personality self. Always. The Higher Self knows everything that is going on with each of its aspects, and only things that the Higher Self allows are the things that happens.

In addition to the Higher Self being fully present in the life of the incarnation, albeit as a constant observer, it also has the capacity for a kind of super vision and a kind of super logic that gives exact solutions to the things we want to know and to do. This is because our Higher Selves can see into our past, our present and our future, and, based on our current trajectory in life, it is the being that is among the best if not the best placed to answer our questions and to adequately guide us on our paths. Our Higher Selves are also the ones that manifest the thoughts and desires we express consciously and unconsciously in our lives. Therefore, if we learn to consciously train our ability to hold and to release thoughts, and then focus only on those thoughts we want to have manifested in our lives, these are the thoughts that our Higher Selves will then add energy to, in order for them to manifest in our lives. All of this knowledge about the Higher Self means that through knowing how to work consciously with our Higher Selves, we can mitigate the limitation of being born with limited genetic code activation through which we have suffered a lack of knowledge of our past contexts prior to our current incarnation.

One of the most remarkable occasions I know of in publication, that a Higher Self has made its presence known at the level of incarnated selves is an event that was recorded in the book *The Secret Science behind Miracles* by Max Freedom Long, in the section titled "Case 11: The strangest personality of all appears." In this case, there was a Higher Self that had chosen to alternatively incarnate two personalities (instead of the usual one personality) within the same physical body. The alternation occurred every few years, with the second personality, when it first appeared at age 4 of the first, being at the level of a baby, had to learn from scratch what babies learn in order to survive in the physical world. This situation of alternate incarnational streams from the Higher Self meant that at the physical body age of twenty-eight years old, this female body which was the host to this dual or alternate personality experiment by that Higher Self had two personalities that had lived the same amount of time in the physical body. Each time one personality appeared, it did not remember that it had been away. Even after years had passed, it wanted to pick up right at where it left off, years earlier. To make matters more interesting, the two female personalities were polar opposites of one another. One was quiet and studious, while the other was like a tomboy.

Given this situation, the biological parents of the female body sought help with doctors to find a way to either blend both personalities into one, or to alternatively anchor or lock in the personality of the first girl, the quiet and studious one, whom they preferred, so that her personality would persist without having the situation of alternating from her personality to that of the tomboy. Locking in the quiet and studious personality would also mean locking out the tomboy personality. Through hypnosis, it was possible for the doctors to call in both personalities and converse with them. The personalities were instructed to blend. This was done during the time that the quiet and studious personality was dominant, so that, it was hoped, as the time for the personality of the tomboy to appear, that personality would naturally blend with that of the quiet and studious one in order to have continuity, instead of a break, and a switch. It did not work.

Their attempts failed because when the time arrived, the switch happened as it had been happening in the past. Instead of there being a blend of the tomboy personality into the personality of the quiet and studious one, only the tomboy personality emerged. When asked why the blend had not occurred, the doctors learned that the personalities by themselves could not bring about the blend. At this point, the doctors decided to use hypnosis to drive away the tomboy personality. As they attempted this, the female physical body became as dead, and instead of one or another of the two girl personalities emerging, *a third personality* spoke through. This personality spoke with what is described in the book as a resounding tone, and made statements that were not logical, but "superlogical". The statements were precise, correct, and final, and it was as if they were speaking with an all-knowing God. Statements were made in a gentle but firm voice bent on explaining. This personality had all along been aware of what was going on with the doctors' efforts and it also explained the reasons for its work with the girls. This voice made clear that it was the guardian of the girl personalities, and of the physical body. The situation of the alternating personalities was work that it was doing.

When the doctors realized that they were at a loss to argue with this being, because its responses as statements were perfect in explaining the situation and the need for it to be that way, one of the doctors, out of desperation (because argument was ineffective and useless with this being, it having a superior logic) attempted intimidation and threat. The doctor threatened to continue hypnotizing the girls until the unwanted personality left. To this, the third personality said that nothing of the sort would happen. As an added measure, the third personality also added that if the doctors continued to interfere with the work it was doing, it would take away the girl personalities, and leave them all with a corpse. After that, the conversation was over. Try as they might, they were unable to engage the third personality once again in conversation. All that remained was the silence, and what seemed to be a corpse. And then, after attempting hypnosis once again, the unwanted personality, the tomboy, emerged:

"There was a long silence. Not one in the group doubted for an instant that the wise old personality would fulfil its threat. There had been a conviction of truth and serene power in every word. At last someone ventured to ask another question ... but no answer came. More time passed. Suggestion was made to release the body from hypnosis. Miss Second opened her eyes and smiled. Doctors and parents gave up. They had been confronted as if by God himself. They realized the futility of their efforts." (Long, 1948, n.p.)

This third personality, that was the Higher Self of the two girls. It knew exactly what it was doing, and it had the right to do that experiment, that work, with that physical body. What the doctors were attempting, that is, to banish one of the personalities, constituted an infringement on the work of this particular Higher Self. In such instances, the Higher Self is permitted to directly intervene, as this one did. Ordinarily, the Higher Self works from its level, bringing into action what is required in the life of each incarnation that has a Higher Self. Your Higher Self will never leave you or abandon you. It is always there, always watching and aware. Your Higher Self will not allow anything to happen to you, that it does not agree to. It happens that in this case, because of the circumstances, we were given an opportunity to hear a Higher Self speak directly through a physical body when ordinarily, it would only do so through its extension as the incarnating personality.

7.2 The hierarchy of Higher Selves

The idea I aim to convey here is one of relatedness. We can think of our Higher Selves and their Higher Selves and such, more like different levels of family. In other words, in terms of relatedness, the individual is part of say, a nuclear family, which is part of an extended family, which is part of a clan, which is part of a nation or large grouping of people, which is part of a race.

While the comparison between physical human and Higher Self family is helpful, the comparison is not exact. Rather, it goes to show that there are groups of Higher Selves that belong to the same "family", in the sense that they have the same Higher Self. And that Higher Self belongs to a "family" of beings that also have the same Higher Self. If we recall back to the early portions of this book, the notion of dreams within dreams, this gets us closer to an understanding of how each self is begotten by a Higher Self.

It is perhaps helpful to also think of which subtle levels the Higher Self of a given level of identity resides in. For example, our own Higher Selves reside at a subtler level than the level of our present conscious awareness. It is from this standpoint that we are constantly watched over. The next chapter will have much more about the different kinds of Higher Selves, what subtle levels they reside in, and about dimensions and densities.

7.3 Alignment

After learning about the existence of the Higher Self and what role it plays in the life of a personality self (that is, you and I) during incarnation, the next most important thing I learned about the Higher Self was the need to align with it as I live my life. Now, the desire to align with one's Higher Self is essentially a personal choice. Alignment with the Higher Self, that is, the next level of ourselves immediately within the subtle realms closest to our own, allows the personality self to be guided along its path of development.

There is a presupposition here that each one of us comes into incarnation with some kind of path or plan. It could be as detailed or as cursory as meets the requirements of the Higher Self, which chooses the experiences an incarnation will have based on the developmental and experiential needs of the Higher Self. Remember that if we think of the Higher Self as an artist, then for any given incarnation, the Higher Self may want to express itself in a certain way, just as music artists do in their music, or as poets do in their poems. To align with the Higher Self is for the personality self to work consciously with itself, the Higher Self.

Another way to think about what this alignment achieves, is to consider the personality self from the standpoint of the emotional and mental aspects of our personality selves. In fact, imagine first what life would be like, if we lived, made all our decisions and took all our actions only from the consideration of what the emotional aspect of our personality demands. Pure feeling, no reflection or thinking. Perhaps some of us have experienced something like this at certain stages in our lives. Now, let us introduce the mental aspect of our personality and the idea that our emotions and minds can work together so that we can make better decisions. And now, let us introduce the Higher Self as a whole unit, and the personality self as another unit. With the two working together, this is like adding correct and true vision to the mental and emotional aspects of ourselves.

Thus, aligning with your Higher Self constitutes a form of receiving spiritual guidance. Once you ask your Higher Self for guidance, it is best to follow the guidance received as exact as possible, even if the personality self cannot see the logic of the guidance received. This is where the phrase "totally trustworthy parent-spirit" should remind us of the role the Higher Self plays. It may take some practice to get the personality self to release control and to allow itself to be guided by its Higher Self. With perseverance, however, it is possible to get to a stage of following the guidance 100%, whatever is received whenever guidance is asked for.

So then, how does one align with their Higher Self? This is a natural question to wonder about, after reading this section up to this point. In order to align, the personality self can start by choosing to align with its Higher Self. By the incarnational personality consciously choosing to align with its Higher Self, events will be set in motion by the Higher Self in order to bring information and means into the experience of the personality self that would aid in aligning with the Higher Self.

7.4 Integration

Integration occurs at many levels of our being. Beginning at the level of the personality, we experience successive integration when our hearts, minds and bodies are aligned. In this state, we are reflective. We listen to our hearts, and also to our bodies. We take good care of all three, as our awareness receives and processes the variety of information from each of these aspects of ourselves. For those of us who are also sensitive to energies, we are integrated when we pay attention to these impressions and where necessary, when we act upon the non-physical information they bring into our awareness.

A further stage of integration can be brought about through repeated alignment of the thoughts, emotions, energies and sensations generated at the level of the personality with the vision, wisdom and direction that can be provided by our Higher Selves. It is a two-way process, with the Higher Self ideally taking the lead. Just as our hearts and minds can work together harmoniously, our personality and Higher Self inputs can also work together harmoniously. For the purpose of our experiences here on Earth as souls in the process of becoming, a main goal is to eventually reach integration with our Higher Selves while still physically incarnated. No further level of integration is required for the Earth experience, beyond the stage of personality and Higher Self integration.

We are however not restricted in the potential to integrate with our greater "family" of Higher Self aspects. With each successive integration, we can bring to our level of conscious awareness the subtle energies and inputs of those aspects of ourselves to which we connect and integrate with.

8

THE RING OF THE SEPARATE SELF

When we are born into the physical world as babies, it must be for us like entering into a sea of vibrations. Sensations coming to us from all directions. Gradually, we begin to distinguish between different physical sensations. Sound, touch, smell, taste, and sight. Through our development in the new physical bodies we find ourselves in, we develop a concrete mind, that learns to distinguish between the sensations being registered in our awareness. Gradually, we abstract from a consciousness that is like the universal mind to one that pertains to an individual. We begin to think of ourselves as "I", and by that, we have what some psychologists in the past have called the ego. Ego consciousness learns to view the individual, and specifically the physical body of the individual, as separate from other bodies and objects that are perceivable in the sea of vibrations.

And thus, the ego grows in complexity with the development of the physical body. The physical body is often, but not always, of either the male gender or the female gender. As children, in addition to identifying with our physical bodies, we may also start to identify with one gender or another. This is seen in for instance the types of games we play. Once we approach and then reach puberty, we begin to identify not only with our physicality and with one gender or another, but we increasingly begin to identify with our emotions as well. Some teenagers may also begin to identify with their thoughts and ideas. By the time we have transitioned from our teenage to our adult years, we identify with certain ways of thinking which we progressively develop as we grow and mature from childhood to adulthood. Depending on our upbringing and on influences that enter into our lives, at some stage some of us may also develop and identify with a moral code. This code could originate from a religious upbringing or from a secular one such as the humanist approach. These altogether contribute to what we call our personality. This personality, which is not static, but dynamic and evolving, is what we express in our interactions with the bodies and the objects in the world.

As a result, we form a personality as we incorporate influences coming into our lives during our development. This personality that forms is seen as a unique individual, so much so that even where two people share an identical genetic makeup, as in the case of identical twins, they almost always appear to have different personalities. The expression of this personality happens on the conscious level of normal waking consciousness, as well as on subconscious levels, as is the case when we dream. In the dream world, we find our dream personality expressing itself to a large extent as the waking personality. Now, on occasion, it is possible for elements of the dream personality, such as its appearance, to be different from that of the waking personality. However, judging from my case and from the cases of other individuals I know, for the most part the dream personality regularly conforms with the personality of waking consciousness.

8.1 Physical and spiritual identities

And so, the "self" that we become accustomed to, and which we refer to ourselves as, when interacting with others, is for the most part formed through the experiences we gather and integrate in physical reality during normal waking consciousness. Because this "self" is fundamentally related to our physical body and what it is engaged in, we come to think of ourselves as separate from other physical bodies, and indeed from other physical objects that we perceive. This is also reflected in the pronouns of a language such as the English language: I, you, he, she, it, this, who, what and other examples of these. The use of these pronouns allows our selves to refer to other persons and other selves in a way that can be understood by all parties in a communication event.

As a result of thinking in separate ways while engaged in physical life during normal waking consciousness, we naturally convey a similar mindset to our spiritual selves. This could be because at least one subtle aspect of our selves, our dream bodies reflect our physical selves very much. Yet even this body can be malleable. It is possible, while in the dream body, to change into another creature, say, an animal spirit. This has been called 'shapeshifting', and there are indications that some ETs may even have the ability to perform this function while in the physical body. Shapeshifting in dreams may be an irregular occurrence, so that the next time we dream, we would be back to the regular dream self that is modelled after our physical selves. It is also possible to have a form that, although human, looks different from the physical human form we ordinarily possess while in normal waking consciousness.

Besides our dream bodies, we may learn to have an out of body experience, which involves projecting consciousness beyond the confines of the physical body. Here too, we may think of this projected body as a self that is separate from other projected bodies. Even at the level of our Higher Selves, we may think of our self as a separate entity. And so, the sense of separation persists, from the consciousness of our physical bodies, our emotions, our thoughts, and onto our non-physical or spiritual selves.

8.2 Approaching oneness

In reference to the Higher Self, in chapter 7 we described the image of a vinyl disk as one way to imagine the manner in which the life of the soul in its successive physical incarnations and non-physical existence (the idea of the loops) all compile together into what can be thought of as an album, and that our Higher Selves can be thought of as artistes, who may have released a few albums based on the planetary existences they may have experienced over the course of their time incarnating in physical words in this galaxy.

And now, to take the analogy further. Imagine that there is a part of ourselves that acts in a manner similar to the way the Higher Self acts with us. Just as we have described our Higher Selves as being artistes, we can imagine a scenario where an artiste belongs to or is registered with a music producer, who produces the labels of various artistes. In the gallery of the producer, rather than witnessing examples of vinyl records from a single artiste, imagine seeing scores of vinyl records, each attributable to a different artiste. If the producer has been in the business for a long time, there could be tens of artistes.

In a similar vein to the producer, we could also imagine this level of Higher Self as being a director of movies. If we return to one of our movie examples, *Inception*, the movie about dreams, then the Higher Self of our Higher Selves, as movie director, could be thought of as a director like Christopher Nolan, who directed *Inception*. As a movie director, Christophe Nolan has directed many movies, and *Inception* is one of those many movies.

Featuring in *Inception* are movie stars who, like rap artistes, have a repertoire of movies that they have been in. Therefore, like artistes, our Higher Selves can also be likened to movie stars. Just as there could be tens, or possibly even hundreds of albums produced by a music producer, there could also be tens or even hundreds of movies produced by a movie director. And so, at this level, the Higher Self of our Higher Selves is guiding Higher Selves to generate a great amount of experiences and phenomena indeed. At the level of the Higher Self of our Higher Selves, there are a number of terms that have been used to refer to ourselves at that level of abstraction. One of those terms is the Monad, and another is the Oversoul.

Let us now take the analogy to the furthest extent that I can currently aware of. Beyond the Oversoul or the Monad, at an even subtler level of existence, we may think of a version of our selves that came up with the idea of music or of video recording studios. They invented the genre. It was then taken up, ran with and operationalized in its various flavours. And so, at this level, the version of ourselves could be thought of as a business entrepreneur, or as some engineer inventor whose business or machine model has spawned music producers or movie directors, who in turn have guided many artistes, who in turn have come up with many amazing tracks, or, in the case of movie stars, who have featured in many awesome episodes within a movie or a TV series. And yet, at the end of it all, it down to the lyrics of a song, or the lines of a movie, that we attribute the most memory, excitement, emotion, meaning, or thought. You, I and everyone else who reads this book. We are the lyrics, or those lines, that strike chords in those who study or who simply listen to or watch a given music album or a given movie.

At the very furthest extent of this analogy, there is one more level of abstraction of the self, I am aware of, that can be thought of as the creator of music, or of the creator of video. So, this is a whole different level to that of a business model, or of an engineering machine. When this level of self creates music, it does not necessarily say what this music should be used for. It simply creates music. Or video. This is at the pure level of thought, or theory. That thought or theory can then be taken, and then turned into a certain tangible, or put to use in some applied way. Beyond this level of self, imagine that we move beyond manifest reality altogether.

Now, the analogies I have employed to describe different levels of what we call the self are really just ways to conceptualize aspects of us that are truly best experienced directly to know their nature and extent. The analogies closely approximate a description of some of the purposes of what these different levels of self are set to achieve. They are not complete and exact descriptions of the functions of these selves.

If we consider the various realms of manifest existence, from gross to subtle, or from subtle to gross, this can be a helpful way to get a sense of where each of the selves resides at its own level. I have written about dimensions and densities before, in an earlier book, titled *Out of Body into Life*. In that book, I informed what I wrote about dimensions and densities from what I had learned both through the Law of One material (I discuss more aspects of this material in the next chapter) and also from the theory taught and the practices I learned at the Monroe Institute in Virginia. Basically, in the earlier book, I described densities as consisting of different dimensions. There are also these buffer zones that separate densities. In the Law of One material given by the entity Ra, there is an octave of existence, that consists of seven densities, the eighth leading to a new octave. Thus, first Density includes mineral matter consciousness, second density includes consciousnesses of animals and plants, third density includes Earth human consciousness during incarnation, fourth density includes human consciousness on what has been called the astral plane, or basically if we go back to our thought of the loop, in chapter 6, that would be the part of existence in the loop that is outside of physical incarnation. Fifth density includes the level of consciousness that our Higher Selves have when they actively extend portions of themselves into third and fourth density to acquire learning experiences, sixth density includes the level of our Higher Selves who no longer require extending portions of themselves into third and fourth density to acquire learning experiences (i.e., they are "graduates", or have not yet enrolled, a bit like fourth density consciousnesses waiting to incarnate in third density). And seventh density consciousness includes the level of the consciousness of the Higher Self of our Higher Selves, which has sometimes been called the Monad or the Oversoul. The self at this level is actively "directing" or "producing" experiences at the fifth and sixth density levels. Eighth density consciousness includes levels of consciousness of those Oversouls who have "graduated" from active direction or production of Higher Self experiences within star systems of a given galaxy. They may "retire", move on to other experiences, or become consultants, assisting other beings on behalf of the consciousnesses that create experiences within a galaxy. So, some of the guardian beings, entities and groups, may also be operating from a level such as eighth density.

Okay, so that takes us through the level of experience within a galaxy. To recap, our physical and etheric body awareness operate in first and second density, where the conscious mind and awareness is like a "higher self" to the physical and etheric body awareness. Conscious human awareness at third density, and astral awareness at fourth density have a Higher Self whose awareness is stationed at the fifth density level. This being, and the "astral" version of itself, at sixth density, have a "Higher Self", the Monad, at the seventh density level of awareness. And the pattern can continue upward.

So, one might wonder if the pattern ever comes to an end. My current answer to that question is that I do not know. What I have come to learn, however, is that just as our personality selves can naturally be associated with life at the level of the planet Earth, or at a planetary, level our Higher Selves can be associated with life at the level of the solar system, or of a star system, and our Monadic selves can be associated with life at the level of the Milky Way, or of an entire galaxy. My consciousness exploration, some of what I did while I was at the Monroe Institute, as well as on my own while not taking programs there, has allowed my consciousness to be projected beyond the realm of influence of our planet, of our solar system and indeed of our galaxy. Just as we have multidimensional vehicles (e.g., physical, etheric, astral, etc.), planet Earth (including other planets), the solar system (including other star systems) and the Milky Way (including other galaxies) also have the equivalent of multidimensional vehicles. Putting things into perspective, this is so that "space" is never really empty, but rather holds fields of life, of different grades of subtlety. As a natural birthright, our human multidimensional vehicles can interface with those of the planetary, stellar and galactic bodies through which subjective experiences registered on our consciousnesses can give us direct experience of the life fields associated with these bodies. Some esoteric materials have called these life fields "spheres", stemming from the fact that the approximate shape of a sphere seems to abound in nature when it comes to the shape that heavenly bodies assume.

For example, there is thought to be a cloud of planetesimals, that is, small objects in the solar system made of dust or ice that could be the size of asteroids or comets. The cloud is known as the Oort, and it is thought to surround our solar system. Current conceptions are that this cloud encloses the solar system, creating a spherelike structure, such as shown in the picture below:

When the Oort cloud is included in the structure of the solar system, it gives it the appearance of a planet-like object. In fact, if we think now about pictures of the Inner Earth that show an inner sun-like structure, then it is almost as if the Earth is a miniscule version of the solar system, just at a different density level. One level of life within the Earth, existing as a "solar system", would be at first density (i.e., the mineral, iron core etc.). Then the etheric realities within the Earth's consciousness would be at second density. It is a place that we can sometimes visit in our dream experiences. We exist on third density, which is still within the realm of the Earth, and we can experience various existences (what I understand to be dimensions), between the surface of the Earth and the Van Allen belts, that house non-corporeal consciousnesses. Some of these areas are inhabited by elemental beings, and other areas by discarnate humans.

In a similar vein, of we think of the Oort cloud as the "crust" of a "planet" which has the sun and solar system at its core, then life existing on this planet would function at the level of fifth density, and the "astral" region around this planet would function at the level of sixth density. These notions might be a bit confusing for individuals not used to thinking about the concept of densities, or who may not be aware of this concept from works such as the Law of One teachings. Just to further the comparison by correspondences one more layer, just as we may think of our solar system as a planet of sorts, it can also be imagined that the Milky Way galaxy, at some density level, may also be thought of as having spherical properties, giving it the look of a planet of sorts. That being the case, life on the "crust" of that planet would function at the seventh density level, and beyond that, into the "astral" region of the space between galaxies would be a life field corresponding to eighth density. During previous out of body journeys, I have interacted with entities at the planetary and solar cores, and during one program at The Monroe Institute, I also interacted with beings at the core of the Milky Way galaxy.

I shall leave the comparison by correspondences here, only to remark that one other material I have studied which I delve into more in the next chapter, are the CDT-plate materials that Ashayana Deane shared with the world (see section 9.3). In these materials, the concepts of dimension and density are similar to but also a bit different from those in the Law of One materials shared by the entity Ra. In the CDT-plate materials, what the Law of One materials call densities, are effectively called dimensions. The CDT-plate materials also make use of the term "density" however I find that they do so from the standpoint of the various aggregations of self. For example, what the Law of One materials would refer to as densities one, two, and three, the CDT-plate materials would call each one a dimension (i.e., dimensions one, two, and three) and together, they term these three as density one. This is because from the perspective of the CDT-plate materials, their use of the term density references the station of awareness of an aggregate self. In other words, density one corresponds to the station of awareness of the personality self. Dimensions four, five and six constitute density two, which also corresponds to the station of awareness of the Higher Self, and dimensions seven, eight and nine constitute density three and correspond with the Oversoul self.

And so, the main takeaway from knowing about these different abstractions of self is at least three-fold. First, it is the sense that within manifest reality, there are levels or abstractions of self that operate at different scales. There is operation at the planetary scale, corresponding to the personality self, there is operation at the scale of a solar or stellar system that corresponds to the Higher Self (sometimes called the Soul), there is operation at the galactic scale that corresponds to the Monadic or Oversoul level, and beyond. So, that is the first takeaway. The second takeaway, and this one I find quite amazing, is that even at the level of the personality, with awareness and consciousness stationed at the planetary level, it is possible to align with, or tune into the aspects of ourselves at more expansive levels of abstraction. The third takeaway, a natural consequence of the second, and one which I find even more amazing, is a realization that thinking of ourselves as separate from everything else, is ignoring or being ignorant of the fact that as the concept of self, as described in this section, advances to more and more expansive levels of abstraction, the more expansion notion of self allows us to realize we are connected to what we may see as 'other selves' when in fact those other selves, at a certain level of abstraction of self, are ourselves. And so, the concept of separation, ultimately, appears to be an illusion. Of course, there are other selves that are closer in self-abstraction to our incarnate selves (e.g., where two personality selves have different Higher Selves that are however of the same Monad). This way of thinking about selves at different levels of abstraction gives a way to reach an understanding that ultimately, we are all one.

This information is being released primarily for those spiritually oriented individuals who either know some or all of it already, and would be interested in hearing about it from another perspective, mine, or for those spiritually oriented individuals for whom this information could assist one way or another in their process of awakening. For some, this information may mainly be an intellectual possibility of what might lie out there to one day experience. I would like to point out that it is in fact possible for one part of yourself to see another part of yourself at a subtler level of existence. What I am alluding to here, is that when consciousness is projected out of body, it is possible to travel to the subtle realms where the body of the Higher Self resides, and to have a subjective experience of this self, from outside of it. It is even possible to travel to an even subtler realm to perceive the luminous body of the Higher Self of our Higher Selves. Through some forms of meditation, it is also possible to enter into the awareness and presence of our Higher Selves, and to have subjective experiences in what can be thought of as the body of the Higher Self. I have witnessed all three events. These are some ways that the knowledge of the Higher Selves can be ascertained, and has been ascertained, by various individuals, as they activate, develop, and use their spiritual abilities in other to gain knowledge within non-physical realms.

8.3 The universal self

Coming to the realization that we are all one, even while still embodying the level of consciousness of the incarnate self is a wonderous thing. The consciousness of the concrete mind of the incarnate self may see separation, however there is a part of us that transcends mind and body. It is a part that transcends life and death, a part that is always in the background and always watching, observing. This part is our original, primordial nature, and it exists throughout all our selves. It is also this part that can identify with other selves and with all that exists in manifest reality. This part has been given different names, such as the Inner Self, or the Wise Old Self. Those who sometimes call themselves Old Souls, sometimes refer to this self. It is a part of us that we share with all our selves at different levels of abstraction. It is a piece of the All, that is also in us.

When we learn to acknowledge and to integrate this part of us, this awareness or consciousness, and let it be the leader of the mind, the heart, and the body, we can progressively also align with those other aspects of ourselves at different levels of abstraction, all of which also have this awareness. It is an awareness that never dies, and through this awareness, we can see ourselves in others, even where we have different Higher Selves, different Monads and so on. This part of us knows that it is whole. Because it is part of the All, it is the All. It understands that the All expresses through the Divine Love that is manifest existence. By embracing the Inner Self, we embrace that love-vibration that brought everything into existence. This love can be expressed inwardly our outwardly. Inwardly, love of self, and outwardly, love of other, because other is self, and self is other. Through this awareness, it becomes understood, that when we serve ourselves, we serve others, and when we serve others, we serve ourselves.

When we realize that all that we interact with is part of the One, it can be a realization that frequently brings joy, both when we give and when we receive. We give freely, and we receive freely, knowing that that which comes, and that which goes, are all part of the in-flow and the out-flow of the One. We can express gratitude more easily in this knowledge. It necessitates a certain humility, and simultaneously a certain joy, to see self in all things, knowing that when it is all reduced to the pure level of awareness, all that appears to be, are simply different flavours of the One. When this realization becomes a permanent part of awareness, it can stimulate a drive to reach for balance and harmony with all, as well as in some cases a deep reference for the different flavours and the need to respect each in a process of expressing the truth of the One.

8.4 Healing polarities

At the infinite level, there is only One. From unity awareness we emerged, and to unity awareness we return, through ages of trials and tribulations, grappling with different forms of polarity expression. Polarity is simply a means through which the All experiences itself. Without any distinctions, the undifferentiated whole may not have a mirror through which to understand its own reflection. Because of the need for contrast, the creator forces realized that a great way to learn is by pretending that there is actually separation within the All. Through separation and difference, the All can inspire movement within itself in order to learn about itself. Thus, polarity experiences came into being.

Therefore, polarity situations were set up for learning, and the polarities tend to work in pairs of opposites. For example, on one hand there may be chaos, and on the other hand there may be order. On one hand there may be masculine, and on the other hand there may be feminine. On one hand, there may be those who align strongly with a love of self, and on the other hand there may be those who align just as strongly, but with the love of others. On one hand, there may be those who are much more predisposed to giving, and on the other hand there may be those who are much more predisposed to taking. On one hand, there may be those devoted to promoting and preserving life, while on the other hand, there may be those who are devoted to condemning and taking life (or promoting and preserving death). And on and on it goes.

The idea, is that in order to learn about a particular dynamic, for example the dynamic of giving and of taking, the All can choose aspects of itself to take up positions. One group provides experiences that pertain to giving while the other group provides experiences that pertain to taking. A tricky part of this learning condition, however, is that in order to arrive at an understanding of the dynamic of giving and taking, the parts of All that engage in this learning activity must ideally experience both sides of this polarity divide. Now, from this example, we can extrapolate to many, many, many examples of dynamics that fall on one or of the other side of what can be called a polarity dynamic. Add to that the innumerable aspects of the All, that are experiencing these dynamics at different levels of existence, and we can get an image of a very complex undertaking indeed.

Due to the powerful lessons involved in learning about one or another aspect of polarity, it seems to also be the case that self tends to get addicted to one or another flavour of the polarity experience. For example, an aspect of self may spend numerous ages exploring what it means to be of service to other selves and through this long learning process, becomes to the idea of the idea that this is one position on the polarity divide. The other position can be equally addictive, and at any given time, the self, especially while incarnated, is grappling with numerous levels of polarity, one of which is even the gender of the physical body. The resultant effect of all of these polarity experiences is that the self that is caught up in the learning experiences may lose touch with its original nature, which is one that is one that is non-dual, and non-polarity based. The original self is whole, in all ways, but the learning experiences within polarity can be blinding to that fact.

And so, not surprisingly, some spiritual schools and practices have developed ways to heal the predisposition of self to get stuck in one or another of the polarity experience spectrum. One that I can think of, is the doctrine of the "middle way", an important idea in Buddhism that is touched upon more in section 9.3, and similar ideas in Samkhya, an ancient Hindu system of philosophy also discussed in the same section. But here, I would like to focus on what I deem to be a wonderful method given in the Law of One teachings, on how to successively heal the distortion of polarity in order to slowly regain wholeness. Ra suggests that whenever we encounter a concept, or engage with an experience, if we process one aspect of the polarity divide, in our minds, we should simultaneously process its opposite. For example, the opposite of teaching is learning, and the opposite of learning is teaching. This is one example that Ra likes to cite, that of teach/learn, and learn/teach. In order to activate this exercise of simultaneously processing a concept and its polarity opposite, a pre-requisite that

Ra notes, is that the one doing this exercise should strive first and foremost to be able to reach a silence of mind. The idea with this polarity exercise is to examine the self, and whenever a polarity concept is encountered within us, we examine its opposite. Not only that. We should then embrace and accept both expressions of a polarity dynamic. Once we work on ourselves in this way, accepting all aspects of ourselves, we then extend the same exercise beyond ourselves, when interacting with other selves, in a bid to accept all aspects of themselves as well.

Again, I find this method of encountering and processing polarity-based ideas and experiences to have the same essence as striving to follow a non-dual or "middle way" path. The goal is to arrive at balance and harmony, to become whole again, and to regain our natural state prior to becoming mired in the learning experiences brought about by delving into polarity dynamics.

9

THE RING PASS-NOT

This is the final ring discussed in this book. The idea is that experience beyond this ring leads to the ineffable. Within this ring is the first layer of the "dream that is manifest reality". To awaken while within this dream, is to know that you are still dreaming, but then if you were to wake up from this dream, the reality that would be experienced would be unlike any that can be experienced in the nested "dreams within dreams" of manifest reality.

All the six rings that were discussed before this one, can be thought of as levels of awareness that constitute nested dreams within dreams. Yet the awareness and consciousness gained from awakening to the reality within each of the six rings helps encounter the reality of the seventh. The process can be cumulative, from successive ring to successive ring, although not necessarily so. Each one of us is different, and since the progression to greater awareness in consciousness is not necessarily a linear process, each can be triggered to their own awakening in different ways.

The ring pass-not is the ring to the level of the infinite. Approaching the infinite, it may help to already be whole, to have already approached unity consciousness or at least, an intellectual understanding of unity consciousness. Unity consciousness is where, as discussed in chapter 8, it becomes apparent to one's consciousness that in actuality, all is One. You can look at yourself at anything, as anything, and in anything. It is also where separation is understood, and incorporated within unity. Unity consciousness is not to say that separation does not exist. Rather, it is an understanding that while separation is a means through which the infinite experiences itself, it is ultimately an illusion.

It is possible to hold the consciousness of simultaneously being separate and unified. At the ultimate level, there is neither unity nor separation. There is just one infinite.

In this final chapter, we attempt to talk about that which can only be talked about in a way that makes sense to the concrete mind, but which must really be experienced and realized, in order to understand it and to awaken to the reality of it.

9.0 Prelude

This final ring effectively takes us to the beginning of this book, to its purpose, which is to discuss some of the big questions that have been on the mind of humanity since the dawn of the ages. In order to do that, we consider aspects of ontology, epistemology, and philosophy, and their relations to science and spirituality. We do this from the standpoint of positions that peoples and cultures on Earth, across a span of different geographies and a range of time periods (very ancient to post-modern) have adopted. The rationale for this approach lies in the idea that since these big questions have been plaguing humans on Earth for millennia, there must be records and accounts of them that have guided different families of humanity in different places over the ages. By examining some of these thoughts that have reached us at the present time, it may be possible to make correlations, connections, of identical, similar or in some cases narrowly to widely differing positions. For that reason, the first part of this ring will delve into just what these five terms are, or in some case mean, and to contextualize them in relation to the peoples, cultures, time periods of various families of our one big humanity. The goal of the first part of this final ring is to contextualize discussions that come in later sections, so as to make available some information with which to frame a comparative presentation of the approaches that different systems of knowledge of Earth's peoples have adopted in their quest to provide answers to some of the big questions we have been addressing in this book.

On ontology

Imagine for a moment the case of an individual who is perfectly able to see but who at some point in life either chooses to be, or is made to be blindfolded. Now, in place of eyes to allow for sight, this individual takes a stick to feel around where to go to, just as a blind person does. And so, this person goes about their business. Imagine also that over a period of time, the individual becomes so used to maneuvering with the blindfold that they even forget that they have it on. In the place of their eyes, the "feeling stick" becomes the means through which to get around. Of course, with the feeling stick, its reach is more limited than that of natural sight. The blindfolded individual may be walking at the very edge of a precipice and not even know it. All they may feel is that there is a gap on the way. Or it could be a gap that can be jumped, but not in the condition of walking around blindfolded.

And then, one day, events lead to the blindfold coming off. At first, it may take a moment for the individual to ascertain their environment, after having been blindfolded for so long. And then, if unlucky, the individual may be upset or even terrified as to how far they have wandered close to a precipice while blindfolded. If lucky on the other hand, they may be elated to have arrived at a great place, even in the condition of being blindfolded. Or they may simply be neither. However, with the ability to see once again, the individual can now decide where they want to go, without it depending on luck, and then apply mind and body to reach the desired destination.

This story is one that presents my view of the world is, at the present time. I see the world as an individual who is blindfolded, and who is wandering through existence based on chance and on where the "feeling stick" leads. The blindfold and the stick are reflective of the ontology that the world as a blindfolded individual has adopted. Ontology is a branch of philosophy that pertains to questions about being, existence, and reality. It is a subject that is reflective of the underlying premise that informs an individual or a society's idea of what existence is. In the modern world at the present time of writing, it appears to me that the dominant mode of thought, that which we may call 'scientific materialism', presents a view of existence and reality as one that consists essentially of physical matter and nothing more. This dominant viewpoint governs the formal, in modern secular society. That means, the manner in which for instance formal medicine, formal law, formal industrial production, and such, are conducted, is one where the subject of concern is seen as being of an inherently physical nature. The non-physical, that is, the spiritual, is not accorded a place in formal processes of modern secular society. For example, evidence from a spiritual source is ordinarily inadmissible in most modern secular courts, unless the evidence is provable through some generally accepted method from material science.

This situation, I find to be akin to an individual capable of sight, who has either chosen to, or has been made to take on a blindfold, as described in the earlier part of this section. The blindfold is the worldview, the means through which to understand the world. In today's world view in most secular contexts in societies around the world, a version of science where spirit or at least non-physical phenomena is frowned upon, or removed altogether, as I began to discuss earlier in section 6.1. I describe the situation of the world's secular societies taking up material science as its dominant mode of operation as a blindfold because that has not always been the case in history. This is a recent development, brought about by scientific progress made in Europe a few centuries earlier, which empowered European colonial masters to essentially take over the world with their ideas and their way. Over the course of the past century and a half, at least, improvements have been made to this version of science that is mostly keen to consider what is physical and not much else. In the next sections immediately after this one, we will consider an ontology that takes us back to questions and to topics discussed at the beginning of this book.

The big dream

Now that we are in the final chapter of this book, we not only leave Plato's cave, as the freed prisoner who is out in the natural world and reveling in the light of the sun. We also float above ground, out into outer space, or we sit and meditate, to go inward, into inner space, and beyond, to the source of all life.

We return to the idea of dreams within dreams, which we addressed in chapter 2. Recall that this idea of dreams within dreams was the basis of the movie *Inception*. In chapter 2, we were briefly introduced to each of the rings. Within the context of dreams within dreams, we can think of the awareness of ring one as a dream contained within ring two, two contained within three, three contained within four, four within five, five within six, and six within seven. Ring seven then, can be thought of as the dream that contains all the other dreams. It is the big dream, the dream of the creator of manifest reality. Awakening from the dream of the creator of manifest reality leads to a level of consciousness beyond what we can imagine while within manifest reality.

Awakening

While it may be fascinating to ponder the possibility of awakening beyond the big dream, a more immediately present matter at hand is to contemplate what it means to awaken within the big dream itself. In the previous chapter, we talked about the Universal Self, a level of awareness which, when reached, is tantamount to being one with all of creation. Our process of awakening for ring seven, and for that matter for all the other rings since they are within this one, includes understanding and realizing what existence entails within the big dream. In this chapter, we shall reach into understandings of the condition of existence at the subtlest levels within manifest reality. After having realized what this level spiritually entails from the previous chapter, we now delve into ideas and teachings of beginnings. In this chapter, we shall examine some of concepts of source, and of creation, from ancient to modern times. On one hand are teachings from a science that empowers us to reach beyond materialism. These teachings are helpful and necessary because it shows that there can be a technical understanding of the outer reality of space-time that is true to the multidimensional nature of manifest reality. On the other hand, there are teachings from metaphysics and spirituality that empower us to understand our experiences when we reach into the inner reality of time-space in a qualitative way. These latter teachings are also true to the multidimensional nature of manifest reality.

Empowerment

And so, awakening and empowerment go hand-in-hand. We empower ourselves with knowledge an also with the conviction, desire, and motivation to practice the ideas that empower us. We learn to become a soul that thinks, that feels, that draws on its spiritual abilities and qualities, and that is fully engaged in the act of living and being in the manifest reality. Becoming a representative of creator-source while still living and being incarnated in the physical. Thus, a part of empowerment involves practice of a chosen path. It is good to develop the thinking faculty to be philosophical and inquiring about life. It is great and, in my view, even better to practice that philosophy. Whether that philosophy is scientific or spiritual or both. I personally advocate for developing knowing and understanding of both science and spirituality.

The practice of science is not only in the doing of experiments. Rather, it is first and foremost in the sense of cultivating an inquiring mind that, if needed can draw upon its faculties of perception, inference and vision or correct witness, to help penetrate an investigation of interest. The data used for this process might be gathered by yourself, firsthand, or it might be gathered by others. The data might also be of a physical or of a non-physical nature. And so, the idea here is to empower self to the extent of being able to, when necessary, think scientifically, so that scientific theories or discoveries are not merely taken as givens, which, when done, promotes science close to the realms of belief, which borders on religion. Therefore, an inquiring mind which develops its ability to examine and understand scientific information, when necessary, can be a crucial part of our empowerment.

Likewise, part of spiritual empowerment is to not only to know about and understand spiritual philosophies, but also to develop abilities to experience the truth of those philosophies based on the spiritual qualities we possess that allow us to directly engage with manifest reality in a multidimensional and even in a multi-density way. In this regard, what is implied here, is the need to develop one's spiritual perception in one's own way, small, large or anything in between. This is a way to develop our own personal power to know things based on empowering ourselves to do so, and not only from second-hand information obtained from others. There are cases where our first contact with information would be second-hand, however as multidimensional beings, we have the potential know just about anything, within what we can perceive both physically and spiritually, and within what our Higher Selves and guidance would deem we can know. So, this not to say that at any given time, you can delve into all the secrets of the universe, or into everyone's dark, private secrets. Rather, that there is a potential there, for us to grab hold of, that can empower us far beyond what we can only access through our five physical senses.

Thus, it is, that we can develop our spiritual, mental, emotional, energetic and physical aspects, in order to attain more and more of our potential. It is also not to say that it will necessarily be easy. Some of this development will take work. Some of it would be like a workout. Just as going to the gym can be quite a workout, but can also lead to desired benefits, developing our energetic, psychic, mental or even spiritual abilities may entail something similar to a workout as well. For example, it took me almost 3 years of continuous effort before I was able to learn to consciously project my consciousness for soul travel. I know of others for whom it took 6 months. So, everyone is different. When I delve into non-scientific and scientific theories, as well as spiritual philosophies, it is the equivalent of a mental workout for me. Perhaps for others, it may not necessarily be so. When I have sat to do meditation and to move my energy during my Daoist practices, that was very much like a workout. The practices are not necessarily easy, but they come with their benefits. Physically, I maintain a workout regime that is often hard work but is conducive for my particular circumstances. And it is not all about just "working out". I also resort to other tools like herbs, sound therapies etc., and even to allopathic methods for diagnosis of the physical body as and when needed.

The point of these opinions, and examples, is to encourage a "hands-on" attitude to bringing about your own awakening and enlightenment. In a reality that encourages free will and choice, we have potentially a large degree of leeway to determine the extent to which we can actualize the potential we set ourselves to attain, before we come into each incarnation. The Earth incarnational experience is one of the most challenging out there in this galaxy, not only because of the memory constraints but also because of the degree of opposition that may be experienced from family, peers and society at large, and also at times the lack of support to progress and advance on the path to awakening. A lot of the time, it may be left to ourselves, to make it happen.

Transcendence

To transcend is to overcome the limitations set forth by the challenges of incarnation in a physical body on Earth, and to progressively integrate all levels of one's identities, physical, energetic, emotional, mental and especially spiritual, progressively becoming more aware, awake and conscious within the big dream. Awakening is not a one-time affair. It happens in successive stages. What exists beyond the big dream, is for each to discover for themselves.

On epistemology

We can define epistemology as that branch of philosophy that examines the nature of knowledge, its presuppositions and foundations, and its extent and validity. Philosophy itself is a broad ranging subject. It is the subject of questioning and thinking, of inquiring into causes and principles underlying reality. In philosophy, the mere asking of 'why' may not be enough. Rather, it is that asking, as a means of reaching greater understanding in order to unravel the secrets underlying the nature of reality. Often, the process of unraveling these secrets leads to gaining greater knowledge, which can lead to gaining greater wisdom. Therefore, philosophy intersects with many other areas of specific study. Epistemology goes beyond just having unraveled the knowledge. It is the study of the foundations of that knowledge, to determine for instance what the means for determining truths are, within a knowledge system. Therein lies the need to check for validity and reliability of the means for arriving at knowledge.

Pre-modern

There have been a great variety of civilizations and peoples over the ages leading up to modern times. We can call this prior period the pre-modern time. Of this pre-modern time, we can divide the period into largely two categories. One category consists of spoken of civilizations of the archaic time, for which there are scant physical artifacts or written records of their existence. These include the ante-diluvian cultures that are said to have come to an end in cataclysms. Because of the paucity of easily available physical records from those times, it is difficult to know what systems of epistemology they used. There are indeed some exceptions or cases where records have survived that give a glimpse of these cultures. Examples of these are accounts of Atlantis given in Plato's writings, and accounts of 'the culture of the Mahabharata' given in that epic. Some of these accounts seem fantastic to modern reckoning because they detail examples of technologies that may come as a surprise, given that for the most part the progression of civilization from pre-modern to modern times known within mainstream knowledge has involved an advancement from less scientifically and technically inclined societies in time periods of past ages to the more technically inclined period of the current time.

The second category consists of societies and civilizations for which we have some largely available records. These records are either physical artifacts, such as stone monuments, and preserved texts, or a survived culture that is still vibrant and evolving. Of the latter, there is often a record of the culture through its language, observances and traditions. Some of these cultures were briefly touched upon in section 6.1. Of those cultures that we have physical records for, we also tend to have written records of their intellectual, secular, and spiritual lives. For instance, in Ancient India, there are texts such as the Mahabharata that speak of an ancient time and a life that is clearly different from the current time. We learn of the ancient sage Vyasa, who is said to have authored the *Mahabharata* and to have also compiled the Vedas. The Vedas give insight into the epistemology of the culture of the Hindu people. Likewise, for the Maya of Central America, there have survived codices kept at museums in Dresden, Madrid, Mexico City, and Paris. In these codices, we learn of the epistemology of the Maya people. Over on the African continent, the Ancient Egyptian culture left writings in the form of the Pyramid and Coffin texts as well as *the Book of Rising Forth into the Light*, all of which can educate us on the epistemology of the people in those ancient times. In Europe, the *Eddas* of the Icelandic people allow us to gain insight into the epistemology of a Scandinavian people.

It was not always through written texts that we learn about the intellectual and spiritual culture of a people. All over Africa, oral tradition has held an important place in the transmission of knowledge from one generation to the next. In modern times, due to a strong emphasis on written culture, oral traditions are frowned upon. I think that one of the main reasons why modern scholarship frowns upon oral tradition is because there may be a lack of understanding about the culture. The main criticism I have come across regarding oral culture is that, not being written, it is subject to arbitrary change, and therefore not necessarily reliable. As mentioned above, epistemology involves not only gaining knowledge but also being aware of the ways that the validity and reliability of the knowledge gaining process is guaranteed. It is often through a real practitioner or expert of a given knowledge system that we can learn some of its ways. When it comes to the gaining and the transmission of oral knowledge, one such expert was the late Zulu Sanusi, Vusamazulu Credo Mutwa, who was the high spiritual leader of the Zulu people and was also a great leader for many medicine people from groups across Southern Africa. Something like the Pope for Christians, or the Grand Imam of al-Azhar, among Muslim people. According to Credo Mutwa, one of the ways African secret societies trained their members was to urge them to commit transmitted oral lore to memory, and to repeat it again and again. Below is a quote from his book Indaba, my Children, about this:

"A particular story was put across to him in such a way as to imprint a vivid picture in his mind that could never fade. But to make assurance doubly sure, he was required to retell the story a hundred times on a hundred different occasions while subjected to the vilest torture, to ensure that nothing at all could divert his attention. For example a High Brother would, from time to time, apply a red hot knife to his body and if he lost the thread of the story he had to start again" (Mutwa, 1999, p. 556)

This kind of practice that incorporates torture or trauma into experiences is a powerful way to bypass short term memory and to directly access long-term memory, as research in brain science has been able to show. That this is one of the ways the African initiates trained is something I find really interesting. They were basically imprinting the knowledge directly into themselves, to become like living computers. I would imagine that this technique is something that is not very well known among the naysayers of oral tradition. Yet, it is known that our minds are extremely powerful, and with persistence and repetition, we can memorize unbelievable amounts of information. Today, we know of individuals who can memorize the digits of the transcendental number pi, to tens of thousands of digits. That is seen as an amazing thing, not strange. It is not only the memorizing of facts such as the numbers of pi that our brains can do unaided. Our brains can also analyze, theorize, and synthesize information to an extreme extent, all mentally, and still get correct results, without having to externalize the process on paper or on a computer. This is the way the Indian mathematician Srinivasa Ramanujan produced some of the most beautiful mathematics. He did all of it in his head, during meditation and chanting mantras, only writing his results on paper. It took some of the world's top mathematicians many years to do the step-by-step process of the Western method to reach the proofs of his otherworldly equations. This is a similar thing to what these indigenous people in Africa have been doing for thousands of years. Talk about epistemology, in the sense of ensuring validity and reliability of knowledge, when you have to apply a red-hot knife to your body in an effort to check if that would derail your concentration while in the process of recitation. So, before we jump to conclusions about something we may not fully understand the reasons behind, like oral traditions, and how it has suited a people for millennia, it is usually wise to withhold judgement. Similar to Ramanujan, another individual who was able to do phenomenal things with his mind, this time in physics, creating and testing complete inventions all in his mind and making sure that they were fully functional before building anything, was the inventor Nikola Tesla, of whom much more is said later in this chapter.

Modern

Modern epistemology is very much influenced by the scientific method, which is a process involving observing phenomena and testing hypotheses to ascertain their truth, through experimentation, analysis and synthesis. Whether it is the humanities, the natural sciences, or the social sciences, making claims based on observed physical data, and testing those claims with specific instruments and methods is the way that knowledge generation and checking has been occurring in most places in the secular world over the last few centuries. The measure of truth, is when an experiment or a test is seen to be reliable because it gives the same results when carried out by different individuals. An experiment or a test is also valid when it accurately measures that which it is meant to measure. So then, it is possible to have reliable tests that are not valid (i.e., they are reliably repeatable, but they do not measure the phenomenon they are said to measure), or that are valid but are not reliable (i.e., they accurately measure the phenomenon that they are meant to measure, however for one reason or another, they are not repeatable – for example an experiment or a test that works perfectly on one occasion, but does not work at all on another occasion).

This way of thinking, that is, coming up with methods that are both valid and reliable, and that are demonstrably based on observable physical data, then undergirds the processes of knowledge generation within most subjects in modern scholarship – those found in humanities and the sciences of different kinds. Of course, within each subject, there will be specifics as to what constitutes data, what constitutes instruments (if those are used), what are the modes of observation, and so on. These differences lead to traditions for knowledge generation and participation in different disciples. On the most basic level, most of these disciplines and arguably all the mainstream ones have one thing in common. The research that happens in these domains are all, to one extent or another, based on physical data.

What is also really interesting is that this method, the scientific method, being just a method, can bring about reliable and valid results when applied to data that is not physical. So here, we have domains or knowledge and research that pertain to non-physical phenomena, yet use research methods common to those domains that deal with physical phenomena. Here, I refer to parapsychological research, into areas such as extrasensory perception (ESP), remote viewing being one of these research phenomena that I discuss in section 9.3. I think the use of conventional research methodologies for non-physical data is still an area that has a long way to go before it gains acceptance in the mainstream scientific community. For example, the book titled *Varieties of Anomalous Experience*, which deals with psychic phenomena studied in a conventional research way, and which was published under the auspices of the American Psychological Association (APA), has in my view received minority attention in mainstream academia.

On philosophy

Philosophy has been called the king of all subjects, or perhaps we should refer to it as the queen of all subjects, if we consider that it has birthed many a discipline. This is a subject known for its tradition of asking probing questions into the nature of phenomena in reality. Some of these questions have led to the formation of entire disciplines. For this reason, there are a number of disciplines that, having been born out of philosophy, include philosophical aspects in the discipline, and so intersect with philosophy. For example, religion is one of those subjects that intersects with philosophy at a certain level. I was marveled after learning that Christian priests at some seminaries also take up courses in philosophy. If we think that the question, 'how did the world come to be?' is a philosophical one, then a related question, 'Did God create the world', can be investigated and presented in a philosophical manner. Another subject born out of philosophy is natural science. Here, a philosophical question that has been posed for millennia, is 'what is matter made up of?' We know now that among other ancients, there were various Greek schools that pondered this question and that one individual known as Democritus postulated that matter comprises these small indivisible particles known as atoms. Within the disciple of natural science, and specifically of physics, a philosophical question related to the one just posed is, 'is matter made up of particles, or of waves?', a question that can be explored philosophically as well as, in this case, experimentally, and mathematically. So, philosophy is quite the subject, and naturally, being a discipline that poses questions, it is a subject that can be found in the knowledge systems of diverse people the world over. In sections that follow, we shall introduce a bit of these knowledge systems, and say something about them in relation to philosophy.

Eastern

There are systems of thought from regions of the world that are geographically East of the West, and have therefore been termed 'Eastern' within modern scholarship, which itself is highly influenced by Western thought. In truth, there is no 'East' or 'West'. We are all one planet. To term one region as the 'East', is a point of view reflected from another point of view. The latter point of view is one in which the British, and their empire, saw themselves as being the center of the Earth. That being the case, Britain (i.e., today's United Kingdom), advanced a system of geographical reference where longitude zero went right through their capital city, London, and Greenwich, to be exact, which is part of Greater London. The Greenwich meridian, as it has been thereafter known, was accorded longitude zero. Those cultures west of longitude zero, such as those in the Americas (c.f., the "West Indies") were ascribed "the West" (i.e., west of empire, the British empire that is), and those cultures east of longitude zero, and east of empire (c.f. the "East Indies") were ascribed "the East". This nomenclature also goes to show how important India was to the British Empire, as seen in all the roles the British East India company played in building the British empire. Mind you, it could just be that the British made their system of global reference, for themselves, and then everybody else adopted it. So, no judgement here. Rather, just stating a fact, that longitude zero, as it is now a standard reference across the globe, goes through Greater London.

In time, the terms "East" and "West" came to be associated with Asian centers of culture ("the East") and European centers of culture ("the West"). These were not just any cultures. Those Asian cultures that came to be dubbed "Eastern" were those that European culture deemed as rivals in terms of empire building, of intellectual strength and of impact in the world. We can see this as a politics of cultural ideas, where some exist and have great reign and spheres of influence, while others exist but may be more limited in their reach. For example, the West sees Julius Caesar as a great emperor of Rome that influenced much of the known world. Likewise, the West sees Genghis Khan as a great emperor of the Mongols who also influenced much of the known world. In the intellectual arena, the West sees Greek intellectual philosophy, especially the ideas of Plato and Aristotle, as highly influential in the birth and development of what has today become known as the modern intellectual tradition and have been influential in the prior two millennia. Likewise, the West sees the intellectual philosophies in India that developed along with the spiritual practices of Yoga of Buddhism as highly influential across much of Asia for over two millennia, and increasingly influential in the West in recent times.

This section is however about Eastern philosophy. Of these, there is much to say. Let us consider examples from two regions. Beginning with India, we find there, that traditionally, the idea of divinity has featured strongly in Hindu culture, as evidenced by many of the deities who make up the Hindu pantheon of gods. Because of this featuring of deity, we find also that philosophy features very much in the arena of religion and spirituality. What I find fascinating is that not all of these deities are thought to be spirits. Some were corporeal, and they walked among the people. Some of these deities must have been non-corporeal spirit beings and others must have been extraterrestrials of the ancient astronaut variety who interacted with the ancient people of India. That aside, one Hindu school of thought that can be called philosophy in its own right, is that of Samkhya. It is a fascinating philosophy that influenced the practice of Yoga and that I argue (later in this chapter) that it also very likely influenced early Buddhist thought. In Samkhya, there is acknowledgement of spirit, but not acknowledgement of deity. It is a school of thought meant to train individuals into becoming "thinking souls". Aside from Samkhya, there are various other examples of philosophy within religious and spiritual contexts, including philosophical aspects within the Vedas and also within Vedanta, a spiritual system that holds that manifest reality, which is ultimately an illusion, stems from a supreme being in the Hindu pantheon known as Brahma. Both the Vedas and Vedanta have a place for divinity and deities within their systems.

Elsewhere in Asia, this time in China, we find too that divinity has played an important and enduring role in Chinese philosophical thought. Among these, are thoughts of the creation of the world by Pan Ku, which shall be discussed in the section on concepts of source. In the arena of spiritual philosophies, Laozi's *Dao De Jing* stands out as an extremely profound treatise into the nature of reality. Laozi's poetic treatise is about principles of the Way, which manifests through all of reality, including in the lives and doings of humanity. Besides Laozi, within secular life, arguably the most influential philosopher to come out of China is Kongzi (Confucius). Comparable in some ways to Ancient Greece's Socrates, Kongzi's philosophy touches many arenas of mundane life. He is known to have delivered his wisdom in the form of aphorisms, which are short, pithy sayings that hold great truth.

Indigenous

One way that indigenous philosophy is similar to that from Asia, specifically from China, is in the use of aphorisms to convey thoughts and wise sayings. Uniformly across sub-Saharan Africa, similar to Kongzi's philosophy in China, it is through the use of proverbs that thoughts about all aspects of life are expressed. Among my own people, the Akan of West Africa, there is a strong connection between philosophy, epistemology and ontology connected to the idea of spirit. For traditional Akan society, it is understood that the ability to be philosophical is derived from the spirit. Gyekye (1987) informs us that:

"Akan thinkers in fact hold that nyansa (or adwen, its possible equivalent), understood as the capacity for philosophical thinking, is a mental faculty that is inborn; it is not acquired...the basis of the assertion that nyansa is inborn is the Akan belief that it is the spirit (sunsum) of a person that makes nyansa possible (sunsum no na ema nyansa), and that thinking is in fact a function of the spirit (adwen no wo sunsum no mu)" (pp. 61 - 62)

This quote suggests that in Akan epistemology, it is understood that the being having the experience is a spirit. Evidence of this is in the two Akan proverbs Gyekye quotes. The first Akan proverb "sunsum no na ema nyansa" which Gyekye quotes can be translated as "it is the spirit that gives wisdom", and the second Akan proverb he quotes, "adwen no wo sunsum no mu" may be translated as "the wisdom is within the spirit". So here, we find one example of an African people for which their philosophy is embedded in aphorisms, similar to the case of Konzi's philosophy in China.

There is another way in which African philosophical thought is similar to that of the philosophies of the East, in particular some of the philosophies of the Hindu cultures of India. This is in the role that religion, and in particular the divinities and non-corporeal entities play in African worldview. Again, the Akan are one example of an African people, among many, for whom, traditionally, religious life intertwines closely with a philosophy of existence. Reverting to Gyekye (1987), we learn that:

"Quite often the impulse of philosophical reflection finds its expression in religious life and thought. A philosophical idea may be found concealed in a religious perspective or expressed in religious language. This is the case with Akan ontology, that is, the doctrine of being. For the religious language, attitudes and practices of the Akans provide a great deal of insight into their conception of reality, that is, the sorts of entities considered to be real or to exist." (p. 68)

Here, Gyekye (1987) makes the comment above in relation to the manner in which Akans refer to different divinities during their act of traditional prayer. For the Akan people, these divinities are real, in the sense that they are called upon from the world of spirit to assist Akans alive and living in the physical world. Thus, spirit plays an important role in the Akan conception of reality. It is however not to say that spirit is the only concept that plays a role in Akan life and thought. That would be an incorrect assumption. Rather, it is that Akan traditional thought primarily thinks of reality as first originating at the level of spirit, and through spirit, physical reality emerges. Gyekye (1987) once again educates us on the Akan position:

"Akan ontology, as shown in Chapter 5, admits both visible (material, perceivable) and invisible (immaterial, unperceivable, spiritual) entities, although ontological primacy, in my view, is given to the invisible. In Akan conceptions what exists is primarily spiritual" (p. 166).

Gyekye (1987) is essentially arguing once again that in Akan ontology, primacy is given first and foremost to the existence of spirit, although there is clear acknowledgement of the existence of the physical. I find this interesting because it aligns with what I term in this chapter a "top-down" orientation to thinking about the origin of existence. In the top-down orientation, existence proceeds from the subtle to the gross, from the non-physical to the physical. It starts with a non-physical entity such as a creator, and an emptiness of existence, and from this level proceeds the creation of form. In the Akan view, the spiritual exists *before* the physical, which is why the spiritual has primacy.

We learn even more about the indigenous African philosophical perspective from Credo Mutwa, who writes not of a particular group such as the Akan, or the Zulu, his people, but of the Bantu in general. Of the Bantu, he tells us that:

"The word *Bantu* is plural, and its singular is *Muntu*, and it is this noun that is of the greatest interest. The prefix 'Mu' denotes the agent ('Ba' being the plural), like the 'er' in the English 'teacher'. The *ntu* is a contraction of the word *ntu-tu-tu*, which is an onomatopaeic word to describe the steps of a creature walking on two instead of four legs…Thus the word muntu means more than just a 'human being' or 'man'. It means 'he who walks erect', or, to denote the agent, the 'two-legger'…These tribes belong to the basic stock of all such tribes who identify with the prefix *Ba*. They are the Ba-Mileke, Ba-Mbara, Ba-Kongo, Ba-Ganda, Ba-Hutu, Ba-Luba, Ba-Tonga, Ba-Saka, Ba-Tswana, Ba-Kgalaka, Ba-Venda, Ba-Pedi, Ba-Sutu and Ba-Chopi" (Mutwa, 1999, pp. 557 – 558)

Similar to the Akan conceptions shared earlier, we learn from Credo Mutwa also that spirit is an important part of the conception of the Bantu people. Of this concept, he shares an experience he had during a secret initiation where he was psychically guided by a female High One, an initiate of a secret order, to see a human soul, in the presence of other High Ones who witnessed the initiation:

"I strain my eyes to see through the shimmering haze that covers the plain. I strain my soul to interpret one of those floating spheres clearly and miss no detail. Each sphere is about the size of a man's head, transparent and perfectly round" (Mutwa, 1999, pp. 566 – 567)

Thus, he shares his vision of some orbs he perceived while under the guidance of the female initiate. These orbs represent human souls. The takeaway here is that the concept of soul, or spirit, is central enough to the Bantu way of thinking that it constituted an important part of his initiation with a secret Bantu order.

Moving on from Africa, let us proceed to Polynesia, another culture of indigenous people who have a philosophy tied to spirituality. Particularly in Hawaii, and perhaps elsewhere among Polynesian peoples of the Pacific, there is a knowledge system known as Huna, of which the word 'kahuna' is related. Learning about how the kahunas, practitioners of Huna, can be found in many fields of knowledge, I am reminded of the notion of the 'Great Belief', that Credo Mutwa explained, which is the collection of knowledge of the Bantu people, presided over by a High Custodian in each African group, and consisting of people of various branches of this knowledge, who apply the principles of the Great Belief within their specific knowledge branch. In particular, the concept of the aumakua, is of great interest, because it underscores yet another group of indigenous people, this time the Polynesians of Hawaii (and perhaps others) whose ontology, epistemology, and philosophy incorporates spirit at a fundamental level. The aumakua is a term that encompasses expression of spirit, whether as ancestral energies, or as nature spirit or totemic energies, or even the energies of the Higher Self. It is an important concept in the philosophy and world view of the Hawaiian Polynesians, since this concept emerges in the different branches of knowledge practiced by the kahunas.

Western

Contemporary Western philosophy has largely grown out of the philosophical tradition of Ancient Greece, but the Ancient Greek basis also served as a point of departure for European thought to develop ideas beyond those that were introduced almost two millennia earlier. Ancient Greece had many schools of philosophy. In Europe, from medieval times into the enlightenment period and then to the modern era, there was a gradual development of philosophy in the sense that different approaches emerged. There were the rationalists, the likes of Rene Descartes, and there were the empiricists, such as John Locke and David Hume. A few were in both camps. Rationalists view the acquisition of knowledge primarily through the application of logic and reason. Empiricists on the other hand view the acquisition of knowledge primarily through information obtained from the five physical senses.

I discuss Western philosophy in the context of science and spirituality at greater length in section 9.3 of this chapter. There, we shall go into why rationalism and empiricism have been such successes in European thought, and also touch upon metaphysics.

On logic, mathematics, and science

Throughout known history, most cultures of the world have represented ideas abstractly in the form of numbers, patterns and shapes that express relationships. In this section, we shall explore some of the abstractions that have been known to be associated with certain cultures of past times. It would be made clear that just about every culture in the past has had a form of science and mathematics. We shall start with those of ancient time.

Antediluvian

In his book The *Last Days of Atlantis*, Jon Peniel, a present-day High Priest of an Atlantean order that has survived to this day, gives us a description of a view of Atlantis close to the very end of its reign. From this account, it would seem that in the final days, Atlantis was deeply steeped in polarity struggles. Peniel belongs to one faction known as the Children of the Law of One, who it seems resonate with the positive polarity. Their opponents, the Sons of Belial, resonate with the negative polarity. In regard to science and technology, this book is interesting in that it mentions the kinds of technology that each group used. This is how Peniel (1997) describes some of it:

"For many years now there had been two entirely different types of power generation plants in Atlantis. This came to be as the result of disputes between the Children of the Law of One and the Sons of Belial. Originally, all we had were the same type of passive generation plants that the Brotherhood still uses. But that kind of plant doesn't generate as much power as the Belialian kind. Because the Belialians are energy ravenous and wasteful, they demanded greater amounts of energy to suit their extravagant lifestyles." (p. 32)

He then goes on to describe the two types of power generation commonly used by each group at the time. For example, the "lightsiders", the Children of the Law of One, used a version of power generation that we would call today a "zero-point device" (ZPD) or zero-point energy module. This approach tapped into Earth's electromagnetic field, using a device called an "ark" together with pyramid and crystal technology to focus Earth's electromagnetic energy into a form of electrical energy that could be transmitted through the airwaves, like radio waves. Those with receivers would receive the energy and have it converted back to electricity that can be used at home. This form of energy transmission was totally clean and harmless to the Earth, and it was in harmony with the universal flow. Brings to mind some of the electricity generation and transmission work that Nikola Tesla was said to have been pursuing before his efforts came to an abrupt end when J. P. Morgan and his government cronies intervened to confiscate all his equipment and his work.

For the "darksiders" on the other hand, this form of electricity generation was not so powerful, so it was not enough for their needs. This faction instead petitioned the Atlantean government to allow the building of a complex system of electricity generation that involved the use of solar lasers to bore into the Earth in order to reach the magma layer. This was done in order to set up a geothermal energy generation system through which vastly more energy could be obtained than was the case with the passive methods. Although this method generated much more power, that advantage also came at a risk, which was that boring into the planet could cause geological destabilization.

Anyway, the power generation issue was one of the key sticking points between these two factions. Some readers who learn about these seemingly fantastic technological feats may shake their heads in disbelief, as to the notion that there may once have existed civilizations on Earth that had technologies on par or in some cases even more advanced than what is available today. This is because of at least three reasons I can think of. First, most of us are born without any memory of past existences, so, until we start to look around and beyond the 'common sense' consensus notions, we typically only know what we are taught to know in formal and in informal settings of mainstream knowledge. Second, the prevailing explanation for today's advances is that humanity has progressed steadily from the caveman era to the present, leaving the impression that this a case of linear advancement rather than a case of cyclical advancement. Instead, it would seem that surface Earth civilizations and cultures are prone to the condition of cyclical advancement, where advanced cultures come and go over large periods of time separated by powerful geological upheavals often of global proportions.

The third reason I can think of is the argument that well if places like India had such advanced technology, why is it that we do not see their flying machines throughout history, into the present time? There are a number of reasons for this, that I can think of. First of all, there are indications of advanced technology in India in its ancient literary tradition. For example, the Mahabharata speaks of flying machines and of an explosion that is akin to the detonation of a nuclear device. In the Ramayana, another ancient Hindu epic, there is mention of flying machines, as well as fantastic weapons unlike any we know of conventionally today. So, where is the evidence of all of these things? Well, in regard to the possibility of a nuclear device having been exploded in India in ancient times, I remember reading about how a three square-mile area close to Jodhpur in Rajasthan, India, registered radiation. At this site, scientists apparently unearthed an ancient city of about half a million people which had been destroyed in an atomic explosion of about the magnitude that occurred in the cities in Japan in 1945. Dating the event, it is measured to have occurred between 8,000 and 12,000 years ago. This would be during the intermediate period after the final demise of Atlantis, and before the 'great flood' of Sumerian times. It also appears that the area in Rajasthan even today still registers radiation levels so high that it is common for birth defects to occur. So, where is all of this advanced technology? Well, secondly, it seems the Earth has also suffered periodic upheavals of global proportions. The most recent of these upheavals occurred about 6,000 years ago, which would be a couple of millennia after the Rajasthan event. 2,000 years is a long time for things to change. Add a global upheaval to that and things could have been reset to the much lower levels of technology that followed the event.

If it is surprising that there were flying machines in Ancient India, then the surprise might be even greater to learn that there were flying machines in Atlantis as well, times even more ancient, according to accounts. Not only that. They were a common way people got around in Atlantis, just as people use cars today. There is much evidence pointing to the truth that there have been ancient advanced civilizations that preceded the civilization of this current time. Unfortunately, this truth is not taught as part of history and geography in the mainstream schooling system. The cycles had changed, and the time of those 'high civilizations' was over. There still remain the equivalent of "caveman" people in the world today. Just check which peoples, in Africa, in the Amazon, Sumatra, Andaman and Nicobar, and related places, some of which are still classified as "uncontacted peoples", would have little or nothing to do with modern ways. They would probably survive the demise of this current civilization and would be around when the next cycle of technologically advanced civilizations come around.

Indigenous

The science and mathematics of indigenous cultures can be found embedded in the arts and the works that they produce. Connecting with ontology and epistemology, it is also in works that have some connection with spirit, that we may find intriguing patterns that are mathematical. In many places across traditional Africa, for instance, there are different artisans whose work involves pottery, bricklaying and the design of homes, who decorate their finished products with ornate designs of geometric, sometimes even fractal complexity. Some of these geometric and fractal shapes have an interest among academics who study them to for example inform coding in computer science. It brings to mind the notion of an 'organic mathematics' or of an 'organic science', the kinds which are studied through cellular automata and the approaches that physicist Stephen Wolfram is promoting. Similarly, in the arena of weaving, we find geometric shapes and designs that may code surprising mathematics, such as the Fibonacci sequence found in the weaving of Kente, a type of cloth used by the Akan and Ewe peoples of West Africa. Beyond Africa, among Native American and Polynesian peoples (as examples), there is again found these ornate geometric patterns embedded in woven materials, with some of these patterns similar and in some cases identical to examples found in Africa.

I make the connection with spirit because these artisans, be they building designers or weavers, tend to incorporate spirit in their work. This could take the form of prayers or offerings to spirit during the process of building a home or weaving a section of cloth. The consecrations also include equipment that is prepared in such a way that the work done on it is sanctioned by spirit. This could be, for example, consecrating a weaving loom before setting to work on it. Even the fascinating geometric designs used on some of the buildings may be brought into this world from the spirit world, as we learn in Somé (1995). When it comes to forms of geomancy, a type of divination done with sand by people all over West Africa, again we find some incredible mathematics and computer science, in that the computational processes that underlie the divination have connects with actual mathematics and algorithms. Divination is another area where there are connections between Africa and Asia. The process of conducting a divination, be it a sand divination among the Dogon people, or the Ifa divination among the Yoruba, there is one thing that is similar to for instance divination with the I Ching, which is common in China and across much of Asia. That is, that the underlying computation is binary, and as such it can be modelled by binary mathematics and computing. The I Ching, in particular the Hetu and Luo Shu squares embed mathematics such as magic squares and even connections to group theory, that applies to the trigrams.

And so, the main point here is that, for a great part, among indigenous people, we can say that their science and mathematics is embedded in their tools for living, integrated in fact, rather than theory being studied separately and of its own accord.

Medieval

The ancient, post-diluvian world was replete with mathematical and scientific achievements. There were the mathematicians and engineers in Mesopotamia, who used fractions as well as what we know today as algebra. They had quadratic and cubic equations, and also used what is known today as the Pythagoras theorem. The Ancient Egyptians were known more for their engineering feats and practical inventions, although they were also quite adept at the use of geometry. During the Ancient Greek era, Euclid was the most well-known mathematician, whose works are still studied in schools and in academia today. The most well-known physicist to be associated with Ancient Greece was probably Aristotle. In Ancient India, already in the fifth century, mathematicians were developing some of what is known today as modern mathematics. The mathematician Brahmagupta, who was born at the end of the sixth century. He was a full-scale mathematician, advancing ideas in algebra, arithmetic, number theory, geometry and particularly in trigonometry. Having also been an astronomer, he contributed to this field as well.

In medieval times, a lot of the science and mathematics occurred in Arabia. For example, the Persian mathematician Muhammad ibn Musa al-Khwarizmi (or al-Khwarizmi for short), after whom the word 'algorithm' is named, was born at the end of the 8th century. Similar to Brahmagupta in India, al-Khwarizmi made contributions to algebra, to arithmetic, to astronomy, and to trigonometry, among other areas. In fact, medieval scholars in the Islamic world made many contributions to mathematics and science, which were later taken up by scholars in Europe. For instance, the word 'algebra' is said to have been adopted into common usage due to an influential work that al-Khwarizmi wrote. Most of us know the word alchemy. It is actually derived from an Arabic word relating to Khem, a name for Ancient Egypt, where the practice of what is today known as 'alchemy' (i.e., of Khem) must have flourished an age before. The word alchemy then influenced the naming of the scientific discipline that is now known as chemistry. The Arabian world also influenced medieval Europe in its knowledge of astronomy, judging by the number of star names in common usage today that have Arabic or Arabic-influenced names.

Modern

The modern era has witnessed an explosion in mathematics, science and engineering. Perhaps the most influential scientific work that ushered in the modern age was Isaac Newton's Principia Mathematica, a treatise on natural laws, and the mathematics that govern them. Newton's work set in motion an entire paradigm of scientific thinking, what is now known as classical mechanics. Newton's efforts were built upon by other powerful scientific minds of the era, such as the German philosopher and mathematician Gottfried Wilhelm Leibniz. Together with Newton, Leibniz is seen as the founder of calculus, which has since become a central mathematical language of physics and of other disciplines in engineering and science.

Over the next few hundred years, classical mechanics, which is now known as Newtonian mechanics to distinguish it from quantum mechanics and relativity, prevailed as an established paradigm of thinking about and doing science. During this period, perhaps the biggest impact made in physics since Newton published is groundbreaking work were the treatises on electricity and magnetism published by physicist and mathematician James Clerk Maxwell. Maxwell's work has been so influential that it has survived the modern era into the postmodern era, which we shall delve into shortly. Then, at the turn of the twentieth century, Albert Einstein brought forth his paradigm disrupting work on the theory of relativity. For the first time in about four hundred years, a theory emerged that had the capacity to shift Newton's ideas from center stage. Einstein's work also contributed to the development of quantum mechanics, with others like Werner Heisenberg. We have now arrived at the modern era, where quantum mechanics, together with the theory of magnetism and electricity, are commonly resorted to when explaining phenomena occurring at atomic and molecular levels.

Newtonian mechanics still remains useful for modeling phenomena concerning large bodies.

Post-modern

The post-modern era is still being developed. More than any other well-known character, Nikola Tesla can perhaps be singled out as having ushered in the post-modern era of physics. It may not be widely acknowledged today, but perhaps in the centuries to come, it will. Tesla's achievement lies in the fact that although he appeared to begin his investigations within conventional physics, his work led him to discover aspects of Maxwell's theory of electricity that went beyond what he had previously worked on involving alternating currents. In short, Tesla's discovery broke the boundary between the physical and the non-physical.

On spirituality

One key difference between religion and spirituality is the notion of practice that empowers humans to engage with spiritual aspects, either within the scope of the human multidimensional nature, or within the spirit realms of nature. Sometimes, both are engaged. As humans, our multidimensional nature includes spiritual elements. When we learn to engage these and use them in ways that help bring wanted changes to us or to others we know, then we are being spiritual. Such use can be to gain more knowledge, or it can be to bring about a wanted action. For example, use of human spiritual (in this case, clairvoyant) abilities could help learn about the state of inner health of self or others. Human spiritual abilities can also conceptualize a thought and then project it in such a way that it would manifest a desired action. These are but two examples.

Apart from engaging our own spiritual faculties, with the knowledge to do so, we can also engage with spirit entities in nature. This has been a natural way to practice spirituality among just about every culture on Earth, during pre-modern times. The idea of having a spirit do a job that we could potentially do, using our own spiritual faculties, brings to mind the runners of ancient cultures who would carry a message from one village or town to another. The same message could be carried by a person being pulled by horse carriage, or even in a third scenario where the messenger is riding the horse her or himself. Here, the horse can be likened to the abilities brought to bear by the nature spirit. Made relevant to spiritual situations, the first example of the runner doing the running from village to village would be like a human using their own spiritual faculties. The second where the human messenger catches a ride in a horse carriage operated by another controlling the horses would be like one human going to another, a spiritual specialist such as a medicine person, for spiritual consultation of some kind, and the third, where the messenger personally rides the horse would be a situation where the person seeking spiritual means is also a medicine person, or is a person that has some spirits working with them, even where they may not offer spiritual services to others.

I would say that throughout the pre-modern cultures we have had on Earth, at least one of these three versions of spiritual practices has featured in the culture. There are for instance in Asia and elsewhere in the world, those Buddhists who primarily use their own spiritual abilities in their spiritual work, or the various cultures around the world that made offerings to their spiritual ancestors as a form of seeking spiritual aid. This would be the scenario of the runner doing the running. Then there are those cultures who had members that either knew how to for instance make offerings to nature spirits or go out into the wild searching for a vision through which to gain some knowledge or power. These individuals would be like the messenger who mounts a horse and together they ride from village to village. Among the many examples of this second kind of spiritual engagement are those who gain power by ingesting some food, or taking a spirit bath or encountering spirits in dreams or in nature and then working with them. The third category, are those cultures where members would go to a generally recognized spiritual expert or specialist, such as a medicine man or medicine woman, or a shaman.

In the discussion that follows for this section, I shall draw on these three types of scenarios to frame the kinds of spiritual practices that existed in the cultures and societies to be discussed.

Eastern

In the East, that is, parts of Asia that are South, East, and Southeast, we mostly find the first and the third orientations. In other words, much of this region subscribes to the spiritual practice where the individual uses their own spiritual faculties in spiritual activities. This is due to the strong presence of the yoga culture within Hinduism, Buddhism, and Jainism. Buddhism in particular has spread widely across much of Southeast and East Asia, and within this spiritual practice, there is an emphasis on the individual working toward attaining liberation. Winters (1994) reminds us that "Buddhism is primarily a path, not a philosophy" (p. 10). Similar to Daoism, which offers a way, the important point here is the idea of both theory and practice in one. There is the notion that in order to reach enlightenment, an individual needs to use its mind, body, energy and spirit together as an instrument and the means to achieve the goal. Sikhism is also a fascinating spiritual tradition which advances a moral philosophy based on justice and on the seeking of truth.

In addition to the first orientation of humans using their own spiritual faculties, we find also in the East the third kind of spiritual engagement, where people go to a medicine man or a temple to consult with the representative of a deity or of an entity in order to bring about spiritual changes. Again, in India, there are traditionally many Hindu temples. There are temples for Ganesh, temples for Hanuman, temples for Parvati, for Shiva and so on. People go to these temples to pray and to consult the temple specialists to seek the assistance of the spiritual entities on their behalf. Likewise, there are those who consult with shamanic specialists all over the region (South, East, and Southeast). Shamanism, the term itself, derives from the practice of Mongolian peoples of Asia, and is also common in many parts of Asia including central Asia (Kazakhstan, Kyrgyzstan, Tajikistan, and neighbouring areas).

Indigenous

Among indigenous peoples, it seems to me that the second and third orientations are traditionally prevalent. Much of what can be found in terms of the spirituality of indigenous peoples involves usually advanced understandings and applications of knowledge interacting with spirits. Of the second orientation, there are individuals among for example some Native American groups of the plains area who would go out into the wilderness searching for power. Through interaction with spirit, they would get a vision, or direction to find an object of power, which they then bring back to their community. The vision quest is reminiscent of the hero's journey discussed in the earlier chapters of this book. In West Africa, there are also cases of individuals who are guided by spirit to find objects of power in the wilderness. The object could be a stone, a crystal, a feather or some other natural object connected with spirit. In the case of these individuals in Africa, they would often bring the object back to their societies and then become medicine people for their community, on behalf of the spirit they brought from the wild.

And thus, the third orientation or scenario of spirituality is also very common in the indigenous world. For this scenario, there are individuals who are knowledgeable in particular aspects of spirit, who then bring their knowledge to the rest of their communities. These individuals are often specialists in one discipline of spiritual application or another. For instance, they could be diviners, or herbalists, or dream specialists, or makers of talismans, or priests and priestesses who periodically share their physical bodies with the nature spirit or deity they work with, that speaks through them. Traditionally, these individuals work in a cultural paradigm where the existence and function of spirits is acknowledged, accepted, and promoted. That is, it may be common knowledge within the community that such and such a tree houses a certain kind of spirit, such and such a mountain is the home of an ancient gnome, or such and such a water body is a place where 'Mami Wata', an elemental being of the water element, would manifest on occasion. Because of this, their work has also been traditionally encouraged by the members of their communities who share the same world view as the 'spiritual technician' and who see this individual as one who is more specialized in knowledge and experience than they are, thereby being more qualified to help them on spiritual matters.

In fact, before the advent of Christianity, and then Islam, much of the indigenous world practiced one form or another of spirituality involving or interacting with nature spirits. This was true in Africa, in Asia, in the Americas, in Europe and in the Pacific. The organized and more powerful Abrahamic religions reversed this trend, and in some cases, incorporated attitudes from indigenous spirituality in their religion. For example, the veneration of saints in the Catholic church very much resembles veneration of ancestors. The Catholics offer incense and wine in their mass, and these are also somewhat used in indigenous practices. Indigenous practices in Africa and pre-modern Europe made offerings of alcohol to the spirits. Catholics believe that the wine they drink is transfigured into the blood of Christ. Many African spiritual practices use actual blood of animals as offerings to spirit. Not quite the same, but there is use of blood in both. Asian practices use incense a lot, and so do some African practices. Incense is one of the ingredients that is used to summon the water elemental 'Mami Wata'.

Another interesting dynamic, this time in Africa, are the similarities in spiritual practices between the Nile Valley cultures of Ancient Egypt and Ancient Nubia, and those of currently existing African groups in West Africa and beyond. Some of the similarities can be seen in the practice of libation in both groups and also the practice of what can be called elemental magic. Similar to those cultures in Mesopotamia, the people of Kemet, Ancient Egypt, had a firm understanding of spirituality involving the classical elements (fire, air, water, and earth) and this same tradition can be found to a profound extent among groups West of the Nile valley region. Malidoma Somé has written about some of these traditions from his initiation. There are several other groups in the region that to this day practice unbelievable spiritual feats such as sitting in a burning fire and not being harmed. The spiritual mysteries of Africa are still very much alive.

Western

In the West, we find some interesting dynamics. When it comes to the three scenarios of spirituality, it appears that the third scenario has traditionally been most prevalent. Before Christianity accompanied the Roman invasion of Europe, much of the region had traditional spiritual practices that very much mirrored the nature spirit practices found among indigenous people the world over. Pre-Roman Europe had spiritual traditions that, after Christianity became established, were termed paganism. There were druids in the Celtic societies of Europe, and there were those Germanic and Scandinavian peoples whose spiritual world included deities such as Odin and Freya, and who had knowledge of the faeries and the gnomes. In that regard, early Europe practiced a nature-based spirituality that mirrored other nature-based spiritual and shamanic approaches of different indigenous peoples around the world. Today, some people of the European and Western world are engaged in a revival of their spiritual roots, in what has become known as Neo-paganism, that includes aspects of druidism, shamanism and wicca. This movement is a spiritual "San ko fa" (go back and retrieve, in the Akan language) movement of sorts, that those Western peoples who aim to reconnect with European spiritual roots.

The West has also incorporated aspects of Ancient Egyptian spirituality into its traditions, so that now, there are Western esoteric schools that trace back to Kemet. Among these are the Hermetic Gnostics and the Rosicrucian order. I also sometimes find it tricky placing Mesopotamian influences within Western esoteric traditions. Perhaps the Middle East needs to be in a group on its own, however there have been significant inclusions of Mesopotamian influence in Western traditions. Starting with Ancient Greece, Mesopotamian and Egyptian ideas made some influences. It is perhaps mostly in Western esoteric orders that the spirituality of Mesopotamia shows itself most strongly.

In the Middle East, all three orientations of spiritual activity existed. Some areas had one form more so than others. For example, before Islam, there was a preponderance of the third kind of spiritual practice, where members of a community would consult with a spiritual specialist. These were the domains and the realms of what is known as ceremonial magic, a kind of formal occult practice that applies specific procedures when dealing with clearly classified spirits of the four elements (fire, air, water, and earth). The practices and traditions of ceremonial magic are ancient indeed, going back to ante-diluvian times, periods such as in Atlantis, and, since the "great flood", has been practiced in Mesopotamia (e.g., the great Chaldean and Turanian magicians), in Assyrian lands, and among the Hebrew people. Among the Hebrew people, we can think of Solomon, and Solomonic magic, which is highly ceremonial. Here, we can also think of the story of Aladdin (i.e., Al-Aden, or the Gulf of Aden) and the lamp, where we find formal rules put in place to bind a nature spirit of the air element, tethered to a lamp, to the service of any individual owning the lamp. This brings up also the notion of the djinn (i.e., the "genie" of the lamp, of which the word "genius" is derived). In Arabian culture, the djinn are nature spirits of the elements, as mentioned moments earlier. Even today, with the great dominance of Islam within this region, there is still an understanding of, and the practice of magic involving djinn.

9.1 All manifestation is illusion

There is an intriguing thought that has made its way into a number of systems of thought, and even into science and spirituality. It is this idea that nothing exists of itself. The way this idea is arrived at, is to play a kind of mental game, where an object is taken and then recursively queried about its components, and the components of those components, and so on, until one arrives at the fact that, really and truly, the object is not really "there". Rather, it is our mind that makes it seem as if the object is there. If it is indeed our minds that "construct" objects and gives them solidity, based on whatever quality mind has for doing that, then it could be that each one of us is continuously walking through the illusion we term physical reality.

Take a spoon for example. What is it made of? Well, we can say that if it is a metal spoon, then it is made of the specific metal in question. So, that could be gold or silver, maybe iron. More commonly, it would be made of stainless steel, itself made of iron, carbon, aluminium, nickel, titanium and other components. If we were to take one of those components, say carbon, then we may again ask the same question, 'what is it made of?' to which we could say that carbon is an atom made up of some fundamental particles, such as electrons, protons and neutrons. And if we ask the succeeding question of what are those fundamental particles made up of, well, then we would be running into some uncertainty, as the arena of fundamental physics is still not completely unresolved.

Even upon admitting that, if we were to scale back a moment and consider the atom itself, as it is typically shown, we find that there is the central part, that is called the nucleus, and then there is a region around the nucleus where in complete atoms (i.e., those that are not ions), the electrons are said to exist. Now, you would notice that there is much "space" between the nucleus and where the electrons are thought to reside. In modern particle physics theory, electrons are not given specific orbits, as was the case in the time of Neils Bohr. Rather, the election is thought to reside in a region of probability around the nucleus. Enter the notion of an electron cloud. Even if we go with the notion of an electron cloud, it would seem that much of the atom, as it is conceptualized is "empty", because the majority of mass of the atom is at the nucleus, with the peripheral area, or probable area, being occupied by a charge of comparatively negligible mass.

And so, even without resolving the quandaries of quantum mechanics, we can think of objects that exist as nuclei and lots of space around them. What is in this space? Now, that is an interesting question that I think is worth pondering. To help us ponder that question, if we consider a rough approximation of the atom, but at a much larger scale, we would then be speaking of a solar system. Or even of a galaxy. There is the central core, the sun, and the periphery. In the case of a solar system, the "space" between the star and the planets is occupied by plasma. The sun has one form of plasma, the hot or the very hot kind, incredibly hot, and the space between the sun and the other stellar bodies also has plasma, but of a cooler kind. So, there are hot plasmas, and there are cold plasmas. This is not so much a theory than a physical fact. Hot and cold, yang and yin, fire and ice, these two opposing energies are fundamental in nature, and will be delved into some more in section 9.3.

So, much of the solar system is made of plasma, and in fact, much of the galaxy is made of plasma, of one kind or another, with some estimates at 99.9% of the universe consisting of plasma, according to at last one scientist associated with NASA, Dr. Dennis Gallagher. What exactly is plasma then? It is a form of energy in motion. It can be heat, and at very high intensities, it has electric properties. Sometimes, it is by looking at the larger scale cosmos, and studying it, that we can understand the smaller scale world of humans. As above, so below. This is an ancient Kemetic saying that underscores the fractal and holographic nature of reality. Astrology works under this principle. It is by studying larger patterns of the cosmos that we can understand how the same energies affect us at the level of humanity.

And so, what if we can roughly model the atom by the solar system or even by the galaxy? Then it would mean that just as most of the universe is plasma, or energy, most of the space between the nucleus and its outer extent is energy. Just as the sun and the central galactic stars are sources of light and energy for the periphery that orbits them, perhaps the nucleus of each atom is the source of "light" and "energy" for unit that is known as the atom. Perhaps scientists might even find one day that the nucleus of each atom is a sort of fission-fusion generator that generates heat, light, and energy amidst the sea of energy it finds itself in, that consists of its periphery.

All that "empty space" between the nucleus and where the electrons are meant to be is simply energy. If that is the case, then, just as outer "space" is not empty, the spaces between nuclei and periphery of atoms is not empty. It is filled with energy. Similarly, atoms do not touch one another, because they have energy fields. As two atoms closely approach one another, their energy between them increases exponentially, a condition that is governed by a concept known as the inverse square law. Once again, if we think about space, solar systems to not touch one another but rather there is "space" between them, a space we can reason is not empty but filled with plasma energy of one kind or another.

All of this is leading to the idea that for our spoon, much of it is simply energy, consisting of relatively small energy generation units. In the case of stainless steel, these energy generation units would be the nuclei of the constituents of stainless steel, which include aluminium, or carbon, or nickel, or iron or titanium and so on. These nuclei are surrounded by a sea of energy, that we can think of as the "space" between the nucleus and its electrons, and indeed even between different nuclei, where the "space" would be even greater. Just as stars generate heat, energy and vibrations through their stella ejecta and ionic particles, the nucleus of each atom generates energy, particles, perhaps even photons, which are light, and much energy and vibration.

So, all that exist around us are a sea of energy and "stars" upon "stars" upon "stars". Some so huge (like the sun) we would not be able to see the whole thing if we were standing next to it, and some so small (like the nucleus of an atom) we would not be able to see it with our physical eyes even if we tried. And thus, the little child in the 1999 movie *The Matrix* who told Neo, "there is no spoon" may have been right! There is no "spoon"! There is no "stainless steel". There is no "carbon", there is just energy, and units of generation within that energy, which interact with the energy around them, taking in and releasing energy in an endless process that mimics breathing. If we can imagine that there is no spoon, following this line of reasoning, then the same line of reasoning can be applied to any other physical object.

9.2 Exiting creation

If we return once again to the child in *The Matrix* movie that told Neo that "there is no spoon", we may recall also that he effectively told Neo it was impossible for him to try to bend the spoon from without. That it was Neo that had to bend, and not the spoon. I think that little bit of advice holds a world of truth in it. Once we realize that much of reality is energy, of one sort or another, it helps to know another truism that is taught in esoteric schools, or in teachings about the power of the mind. That truism, is that "energy follows thought". Quite simply, what we think, can affect the energy around us. This energy is in a constant state of flux. The ancient Daoists talk about the only constant in existence being change. Change is the motion within existence, within the All. This change, an ever-flowing flux of energy, responds to thought.

We may not realize it, but it can be said that we hold the version of the world we experience in our minds. It is a curious kind of situation, where one informs the other. In other words, we learn since childhood, to think of the world in a certain way, and then, once that becomes habit, we essentially hold that image of the world, subconsciously. Our minds then imprint the structure in that version of the world onto the energy around is, and then it becomes our world. What that means, is that the energy around us conforms to structure of the world that we learn to hold in our minds. Here, we are properly referring to the physical world. But remember, "there is no spoon!" There is in reality no "physical world" around us. All that there really is, is a sea of energy, within which are innumerable "stars", that we can call atomic nuclei at the microscopic level. Our brains have the ability to take in vibrations from our physical senses, and turn those vibrations into images and 3D holographic realities.

In addition to the energy that is all around us, there is awareness. There is consciousness. It is not easy for me to describe or explain what this thing called awareness is, other than to say that it is like thought energy. And that this awareness pervades the energy, and can shape it. Therefore, if we 'bend' the way we think, that will in turn have an effect on the energy in which the awareness is embedded, because energy follows thought. As the boy says to Neo in *The Matrix*, it is Neo that has to bend. Neo must bend his way of thinking, and when that happens, the reality outside Neo would change. The inner can influence the outer. And it is in the bending and changing of our ways of thinking that we can change the realities we create and experience. Our awareness can be caught very deeply in energies that are heavy. If we raise the quality of our thoughts, we can also raise the quality of the energies we interact with. If this process is taken to the furthest extent, where we feature a most subtle quality in our minds, or even access the state of no thought at all, in a state of absolute, total and utter silence and stillness, just as oil mixed with water slowly rises to the top to float, we, our awareness, can successively reach the subtlest states of energy, and even reach a state where it is possible to exit the outer existence altogether. This is a way to exit creation.

9.3 The unspeakable

The concepts we speak of in this section can in truth not really be spoken of. What we attempt, instead, is to approximate the concepts by discussing them in a way that the finite mind can grasp. In grasping these concepts, the mind is given a platform from which the spirit can leap into the beyond, where no words are necessary and only a knowing that can be grasped directly, is experienced.

Concepts of source

Since time immemorial, humanity has pondered the question of whether there was first cause, a creator, or some intelligent or purposeful agent through whose agency manifest existence came into being. This can be seen in the cosmogonies, legends, and spiritual doctrines of people the world over. Even where the idea of a divine hand is rejected the idea of some first beginning is acknowledged and explored. Throughout history, these concepts of source have accompanied religious or spiritual doctrines because source has been thought of as having a creator, or of having something to do with a creator. One with qualities that can be attributed to spirit. In the recent past, of the last few centuries, scientific and philosophical thought has veered away from knowledge that can be gained from spirit. This has in turn influenced the ways the concepts of source are taught in contemporary times. In sections that follow, we examine the role that spirit can play in understanding knowledge that can lead to correct solutions.

The need to emphasize correct witness

If you do not have a fixed destination that you are working toward, you cannot travel to a predestined one. This is akin to the scenario of the individual with the ability to see but who nevertheless walks around blindfolded, as presented at the beginning of chapter 9. The context of choosing to be blindfolded in spite of being able to see is similar to epistemologies that are guided by their minds without the guidance of the spirit, through correct witness. Correct witness is the ability to arrive at an accurate answer or solution without having to have first worked it out through deduction or inference. As an illustration, imagine being stuck in a labyrinth or a maze which has dead ends and drops off a cliff. Correct witness is the ability to rise above the entire landscape of the labyrinth, having a view along and across it, and seeing the way out. With correct witness having accurately and correctly determined the way out, logic can then be used to piece together a path, one that leads from the current position within the maze to the predetermined exit. As such, correct witness views a problem scenario not from within the paradigm and thinking of the problem but from an outside view that encompasses the entire problem space.

Correct witness, which in some other paradigms has been called "seeing", is one of three modes of gaining knowledge mentioned postulated by Samkhya and explained in the work known as the Samkhya Karika. It is a way of gaining knowledge that has been known for a long time. Regarding the notion of the three modes of knowledge discussed in the Samkhya Karika, which are perception, inference and correct witness, materialist science has no place for the third, because that invariably involves spirit. The mind cannot "see". It can infer based on information that it receives. Materialist is very much fixed on inferences, so this version of science that is the status quo in modern times across most secular societies is continually guided by processes that involve inference, even as this version of science has the ability to and can choose to incorporate processes that involve correct witness. It is like the blindfolded person whose eyes work but who has been given a blind man's stick to feel around in order to find a way forward.

Correct witness can be achieved as examples through one's own spiritual agency, or through information provided by some "revealed" texts of high spiritual authority and authenticity. These texts are revealed because they are obtained by humans, in the human world, by an entity or agency that is external to a human and is of a spiritual nature. A quintessential example from Christianity is what is known as the "Ten Commandments". In several philosophical and spiritual paradigms in Asia (e.g., Bön, Buddhism, Daoism and Hinduism), it is commonly understood that guiding spiritual texts and treatises from high-ranking spiritual entities can be revealed to humans through spiritual means. These are not just spiritual texts. Some of these can also guide scientific thinking.

Now, this is not to say that there are no revealed texts out there in the West that can guide scientific inquiry. It is that mainstream Western mainstream education has discouraged revelation as an appropriate source of gaining wisdom. There are excellent examples of revealed texts within the West. Three of such examples are the *CDT-plate teachings*, the *Law of One teachings*, and the views expressed by the spiritual personalities in *The Magic Bag*, all of whom are remarkable individuals that once lived on Earth. These three are high quality materials, and very high level. They are each discussed in this section of chapter 9.

Infinite energy and infinite intelligence

One source material that emerged in the West and that provides much advanced scientific and spiritual information worthy of note are the Law of One books, given to humanity by an entity known as Ra. It was first made available starting in 1981, and has stood the test of time. This is material that was transmitted via telepathy from an extraterrestrial group known as Ra to a group of humans on Earth. The transmissions were received primarily by a woman named Carla Rueckert and a man named Don Elkins. The woman served as a medium through which the telepathic messages were received. The man served as the questioner. There was a third individual involved with the group named James Allen McCarty According to him, "Our research group uses what I prefer to call "tuned trance telepathy" to communicate with an extraterrestrial race called Ra." (The Law of One, Book I, p. 5).

The entity Ra is said to be a sixth density consciousness. It belongs to a group, a confederation, in fact, of beings and worlds that act as beings and guides for evolving races and worlds, on behalf of the one Infinite Creator. At the beginning of each communication session, Ra always started with the phrase "I am Ra". This was done to distinguish Ra as the consciousness speaking through Carla Rueckert. For example, when Ra spoke of the confederation, this is what we learn, "I am Ra. I am one of the members of the Confederation of Planets in the Service of the Infinite Creator. There are approximately fifty-three civilizations, comprising approximately five hundred planetary consciousness complexes in this Confederation." (The Law of One, Book I, p. 102). What the entity Ra is saying in this quote above is that there are a group of highly advanced beings, who are collectively referred to as "guardians". The confederation that the entity Ra belongs to, is one of the many groups and organizations within this galaxy and others that play a role as guardians on behalf of the infinite creator. They are advanced because these races have achieved the highest extents of development in terms of both scientific and spiritual advancement. In many cases, the entire race of the members of a guardian group has ascended to a higher density than the one we currently live in. Not only that. They are guardians in the sense that they have also aligned their progress and advancement with the purpose of the infinite creator of this manifest reality. As a result of this, they work in the service of the infinite creator to maintain the created reality and also to assist other races along their own path of evolution and self-determination. In a reality where there is much polarity, negative and positive, the guardians represent balance, and are in service to all sentient beings, assisting beings that choose paths and orientations along the polarity spectrum to find their own way. The entity Ra, thus, is a member of this group of beings known as guardians.

At the end of each session, the entity Ra would end in a similar way, by declaring who it was, and then saying it was leaving the group in the love and the light of the Creator. Here is one example of what Ra communicates at the end of a session, "I am Ra. I leave you in the love and the light of the one Infinite Intelligence which is the Creator." (The Law of One, Book I, p. 93). As such, in the Law of One teachings, the concept of creator is of one being that is infinite and also intelligent. This infinite intelligence makes available infinite energy to all aspects of itself within creation. This energy that pervades all of creation is an energy that can be described as one of love. This brings to mind the saying "God is love". In relation to infinite energy and infinite intelligence, or intelligent infinity, this is what the entity Ra has to say:

"I am Ra. Awareness led to the focus of infinity into infinite energy. You have called this by various vibrational sound complexes, the most common to your ears being "Logos" or "Love." The Creator is the focusing of infinity as an aware or conscious principle called by us as closely as we can create understanding/learning in your language, intelligent infinity." (The Law of One, Book I, p. 138).

So, to summarize, in the Law of One teachings, the concept of creator is one of intelligent infinity. This infinite awareness also creates infinite energy, which is what some have called "divine love".

The partiki of the universe

As we have just discussed infinite energy in the previous section, we can continue into this section to discuss concepts of source from the point of view of the materials known as the Emerald Covenant CDT-Plate Translations, which form the basis of the Voyagers books made available to the world by Ashayana Deane, and from which we get the notion of partiki and its related terms discussed in this book. To learn more about this material that is the basis of Keylontic Science, let us have a read through the following quote:

"The information contained within the Voyagers Series Books...and related materials produced through the 3 legitimate GA [i.e., Guardian Alliance] Speakers, represents translation of ancient records. These ancient records exist in physical form as a set 12 Silver-metallic discs called the Cloister-Dora-Teura-Plate Libraries "CDT-Plates." The 12 CDT-Plates are holographic recording, storage and transmission devices that hold massive amounts of data in encrypted electromagnetic scalar-standing-wave form. Translation of data from the CDT-Plate Libraries is accomplished through initiation of specific frequency transmissions, through which the discs activate to release the stored data in the chosen form of holographic, audio, visual or digital translation. The 12 CDT-Plates were manufactured from a form of striated-selenite-quartz crystal organic to the Density-2 planet Sirius B, surrounding a radioactive isotopic core, encased in a "hybrid-metal" silver alloy compound organic to Earth." (Deane, 2001, p. xxii)

These plates remind me of copper scrolls held by David Sanipass (Lonebear), a Native American (Algonquian) individual of the Mi'kmaq band. David has in his possession some copper scrolls that employ a form of technology requiring touch and sound vibration to activate a holographic display that gives access to a vast library of information. I almost met David a couple of years ago when he was in London, England, hosting a public event and while I was in the city at the time. It was a shame to miss it. At any rate, the point here is that there are some amazing technologies in the possession of individuals and groups on this planet. In the case of the CDT-plates, they were created by a group of guardians, similar but different to the Ra group mentioned in the previous section. While the Ra group are associated with the planet Venus in this solar system, but from a very long time ago (i.e., the race that Ra belongs to already ascended into the subtler spiritual realms, sixth density to be exact, a very long time ago), the guardians responsible for creating the CDT-plates are associated with the Pleiades and Sirius star systems. Both star systems have played key roles in our human ancestry and heritage. The original ancient humans, our ancestors, were a form of guardian. They were planetary guardians, responsible for maintaining and assisting the evolution of various lifeforms on our planet. Human types have been guardians in many star systems. As a gift to the Earth human, after the polarity-based ETs arrived (c.f., Orion reptilians and grays and 'Galactic Federation' humans) and started doing their genetic engineering, the relatives of the Earth guardian group in the Pleiades and Sirius systems created these 12 CDT-plates to keep a record of the guardian human heritage on Earth.

The CDT-plates are essentially an ultra-advanced data repository or library of information about the manifest reality. They contain information on creation mechanics the founder-creator group used, universal unified field physics, theory and application of the Law of One, spiritual science and ascension-merkaba mechanics. The plates have been on Earth for almost 250,000 years. They are guarded and protected by a group of guardians on Earth, and on occasion parts of their contents are released and shared in a public way. The most recent release occurred with the work Ashayana Deane did, and shared publicly. This release was sanctioned because we are at a time of cosmic change on Earth. Planet Earth is ascending into a higher density, and with it, the life existences within its boundaries. Information on ancient human history, unified field physics and ascension mechanics may be of assistance to many beings who are incarnated on Earth at the present time, and who choose to take the opportunity to ascend with the planet. Remember that ultimately, if you are born of an Earth human heritage, then you are part of the family of the original angelic human that was a guardian on Earth and that had 12 strands of DNA activated. This is notwithstanding all the genetic engineering that has occurred with Earth humanity, with its resultant races. So, that was the rationale for releasing information from the CDT-plates in the most recent occurrence over the past two or so decades.

Before we get into discussing concepts related to source, there is one interesting aspect that I would like to expound upon. In the preface to Voyagers II, the second book of the Voyagers series, the revelation of this material from the CDT-plates is compared with what in Indian philosophy is known as "shruti". Shruti are texts that come from high spiritual sources which act as authorities onto themselves. They are a form of revelation. Texts and scripture that can aid in achieving or operationalizing correct witness (see section below, titled Samkhya postulates three modes for gaining knowledge). Correct witness can be gained through the faculty of one's own Inner Self or from the Inner Selves of others. In the story above about the individual whose blindfolds are removes, to allow for sight. Texts termed as shruti help attain the third mode of knowledge, which is correct witness. These texts are revealed from a high spiritual authority. In India, examples of texts that are considered to be on the level of shruti are the Vedic texts, which are seen as having the highest spiritual authority within Hindu tradition. I had read the Voyages books many times over the past two decades, however it was not until I had read the Samkhya Karika (Wilson, 1835) and specifically Gaudapada's commentary for stanza 5, that the notion of shruti came into my awareness.

And now, let us discuss the material itself, and how concepts from it pertain to the notion of source. We are told in Voyagers II that "Partiki are units of electro-tonal energy-identity that emanate from a central cosmic source called the Yunasai" (Deane, 2002, p. 453). Electro-tonal refers to two qualities that these partiki have. They are electrical in nature, and they also have a sound or vibrational nature. It can be said that all that exists in nature has a unique vibration. With that vibration comes an associated sound. It is as if all of manifest reality is making music. The idea of the music of the spheres. Speaking of which, NASA has these sounds known as "Symphonies of the Planets" from recordings of sounds emanating from planets that the Voyager probe made as it journeyed past these heavenly bodies in our solar system. It is not like any human symphony, but a symphony nonetheless. There are various sounds on Earth as well, with some hauntingly beautiful sounds from creatures living deep in the ocean. And of course, on the planet, there is sound everywhere. Not only from people and animals, but from the wind, from rain, from fire, earthquake, objects rubbing on each other in friction and so on. Humans also emanate sounds. For those readers who engage in meditation or other spiritual practices or who may simply be attuned to their own vibrations, it is possible to listen to the various sounds emanating from various parts of your physical and non-physical vehicles, while in a state of stillness.

One final topic of discussion in this section in the meaning of the word "Yunasai". Since we are dwelling on concepts of source. Yunasai is the notion of source in this paradigm. From Voyagers

II, we learn that "The Guardians refer to this Central Source as the Yunasai and it is the sentient, creative identity-in-energy through and within which the cosmos and its parts manifest." (Deane, 2002, pp. 451 - 452). In other words, the Yunasai, in the teachings derived from the CDT-plates, is the same idea as infinite intelligence, and the creator, from the Law of One teachings, and also as the "Overlords" from the teachings in the Magic Bag from the Inner Circle, which is the topic of the next section.

The Creators and the Inner Circle

Now that we have discussed the guardians a bit, and the teachings they have shared with Earth humans, let us talk about the Creator group itself, and their teachings, which they too have shared with Earth humans. In the Law of One teachings, the guardians (Ra entity) state that the creator beings responsible for this galaxy are located in the octave above our own, that is, the eighth density. Their representatives in this solar system are located in the rings of the planet Saturn, as a group known as the Council of Saturn. They are the final arbitrators of whatever goes on in this solar system. This same group, the Council of Saturn, is sometimes referred to as the Council of Nine, because when members of the Council of Saturn sit in session, there are nine of their group that are represented. It does not mean that the entire Council of Saturn is made up only of the nine members who make up a Council of Nine at any given session. Of the Council of Saturn, the entity Ra has this to say:

"I am Ra. The members of the Council are representatives from the Confederation and from those vibratory levels of your inner planes bearing responsibility for your third density. The names are not important because there are no names. Your mind/body/spirit complexes request names and so, in many cases, the vibratory sound complexes which are consonant with the vibratory distortions of each entity are used. However, the name concept is not part of the Council. If names are requested, we will attempt them. However, not all have chosen names. In number, the Council that sits in constant session, though varying in its members by means of balancing, which takes place, what you would call irregularly, is nine. That is the Session Council." (The Law of One, Book I, pp. 106 – 106).

Within the same conversation, the entity Ra indicates that the two 'semi-undistorted forms' (that is the term used by Ra) of material available to the public on Earth that are representative of this Council of Nine, were released by two individuals. One of these individuals was a man named Andrija Puharich, a medical doctor and scientific investigator of parapsychological phenomena. Parapsychology involves the study of extrasensory perception phenomena, such as telepathy, where one mind can demonstrably communicate a thought to another, and psychokinesis, where one or more individuals can cause objective changes to the condition of objects, which by that, means the objects can be moved, or bent, and that action would not be a result of mass hypnosis but could for instance be captured on video. Puharich worked a great deal with an Israeli man known as Uri Geller, who has for decades demonstrated psi-ability feats such as telepathy and psychokinesis to diverse audiences ranging from Israeli military personnel to school children. It was revealed in Puharch's book *Uri: a journal of the mystery of Uri Geller* (Puharich, 1975) that a lot of the power and the feats that Uri demonstrated were made possible through group known as 'the Nine' (i.e., the Council of Nine). Puharich worked not only with Geller but also with other individuals who also had unique abilities. One of these was Dr. Vinod, a sage and scholar from India who also had mediumistic abilities. In one of his sessions with Puharich, the council spoke through Dr. Vinod, and this is what Puharich reported that they said:

"M calling: We are Nine Principles and Forces, personalities if working in complete mutual implication. We are forces, and the nature of our work is to accentuate the positive, the evolutional, and the teleological aspects of existence. By teleology I do not mean the teleology of human derivation in a multidimensional concept of existence. Teleology will be understood in terms of a different ontology. To be simple, we accentuate certain directions as will fulfill the destiny of creation." (Puharich, 1975, n.p.)

In simple terms, a member of the Council of Nine, M, whom I speculate could be the personality known as M was affirming that the purpose of this Council of Nine that are aspects of the creator is to fulfill the destiny of creation by catalyzing positive evolution and an increase in the awareness of existence. The part about the nine principles and forces is interesting because it aligns with the idea in the Law of One material that the council are in reality representative of principles. Their members are more associated with a principle than with a given name.

Apart from Andrija Puharich, the second semi-undistorted form of material out in the public domain in relation the Council of Nine associated with the Council of Saturn is a book that was dictated via clairaudience to an individual called Mark Probert. Clairaudience, like clairvoyance, is a psychic ability wherein nonphysical ideas and impressions can be registered through the psychic equivalent of the sense of sound. Basically, an individual adept in clairaudience can hear sounds from a spiritual source that others may not hear. Dictation began in 1947 and continued for a period of 5 years. The version I read was published in 1963.

The Inner Circle are incarnational aspects of the Council of Saturn. At the time they made contact with Mark Probert, they were said to be 15 in number. Their membership ranges from humans that lived a very long time ago, such as Yada Di Shi'ite (pronounced she-he'tee), the High Priest of a civilization that existed hundreds of thousands of years ago to for instance Professor Alfred Luntz, a member of this group who was born in 1812 and who died in 1893. Among the members of the group that dictated the book are Lao Tse, author of the Dao De Jing. Interestingly, Lao Tse explains what the Magic bag is, close to the beginning of the book, in the following quote, ""The Magic Bag" – What do we mean by this? What is the "bag"? The bag is consciousness, and in this bag is all" (Probert, 1963, p. ix). Other members of the group dictated segments of the Magic Bag include the Maharaja Natcha Tramaliki, a man of English and Hindu heritage born in 1848 who trained as a medical doctor but later gave up that path to become a wandering sage, Ben Casi, Kay Ting, and Lo Sun Yat, all three of whom nothing is said about in the book about their personal history, Ramon Natalli, born in 1598 into the Royal House of Astronomy in Rome, Arakashi, who was born in 1398 and who lived as a holy man in the Punjab region of India, and Dr. Sukuto Nikkioi, a Japanese medical doctor who spent many years working in India and who later abandoned medicine for his stronger interest in learning about the nature of man and of manifest existence.

It would seem that there are different Councils of Nine written about in different books. It appears to me that the Council of Nine spoken of in the book *The Only Planet of Choice* by Phyllis V. Schlemmer is not to be the same Council of Saturn in this solar system, with its nine session members known as the Council of Nine. This is because in Schlemmer's book, the spokesman for that Council of Nine, a being known as Tom states that "The members of the Council of Nine are not, and have never been, in physical form" (Schlemmer, 1994, n.p.). In other words, this Council of Nine has never had incarnational aspects. The Council of Nine spoken of in the Law of One material, however, has had incarnational aspects on Earth at different time periods. These aspects are the voices that spoke through Mark Probert in the various seances that lasted years, and certain members of their group are also the voices that clairaudiently dictated the book *The Magic Bag* to Probert.

What I like most about the material in the Magic Bag is that it provides perspectives of these nine aspects of the creator that are at once both unified and varied. The views are not so varied, however, to create a collection of thoughts that are confusing and discordant. Rather, the need to be able to think for oneself, and to express an opinion, is held up as a high ideal among the Inner Circle members. Even as incarnational aspects of the creator, these beings do not pretend to be know-it-alls. Rather, they value variety and perspective. The Inner Circle members proclaim the following position:

"We of the Inner Circle feel it indispensable for you to know that all that is written within these pages are not put forth with the thought that they should be taken as indisputable facts or ultimate truths but merely as aspects of truth as seen from our particular point of observation. All of us subscribe to the doctrine of variability, and if we so confess our beliefs we must adhere to them, at least until such time as we may find something that will seem closer to the truth." (Probert, 1963, p. vii)

In the Magic Bag, where the members are referred to as 'Controls', the following is made clear as well:

"...it should be noted that the Controls specifically disclaim any pretense to omniscience— "You will get nothing but opinions on all the planes." —and are very cautious and reserved in making predictions, saying in effect, "We have more means of information than you do, and can see a little further and more clearly, but we are always subject to error from unforseen decisions on your plane as well as by other natural limitations." (Probert, 1963, p. xvi).

These two quotes underscore the importance of realizing that information comes from a lens or a perspective. The perspectives are at once highly intellectual, highly philosophical, highly scientific, and highly spiritual, not to mention interesting and even with elements of humour in some cases. As such, the Magic

Bag, gives us perspectives from nine beings who in my view qualify to be thought of as 'thinking souls', a condition which is a goal or desired outcome of Kapila, the author of the Samkhya Karika, for those who read it. Obviously, we are not discussing the Samkhya Karika here, however when I learned that to be a goal of that material, I thought it to be a worthwhile goal. It is also clear to me that there are some points of view that appear to be held in common across a number of the perspectives that were shared by members of this Inner Circle group. For instance, a number of them shared perspectives that concurred on the idea that motion as an important factor in the manifest reality. But there varying and differing opinions as well, opinions that in my view are almost universally very nicely expressed.

It also fascinates me that this group comprising the Magic Bag appear to represent a number of races on our planet. There is a black looking representative (Yada Di Shi'ite), a Hebrew or Middle Eastern representative (Ben Casi), Occidental representatives (Maharaja Natcha Tramaliki, Professor Alfred Luntz and Ramon Natalli), and Oriental representatives (Lao Tse, Arakashi, Kay Ting, Lo Sun Yat, and Dr. Sukuto Nikkioi). The Maharaja Natcha Tramaliki also belongs to the Oriental group. Some of these discarnate entities had the ability to manifest prominently in sight for Mark Probert to produce detailed drawings of them. Photographs of these drawings were taken and included in the book as portraits of these discarnate as they appeared to him clairvoyantly.

Having just written all of this, I am surprised that the Magic Bag has not made as much of a 'splash' among adherents and readers as for instance the Law of One material has. The Magic Bag conversations have been around a while longer, the book having been published in 1963 (the Law of One Books started being put together in 1981). There could be a number of factors that influenced this lack of widespread reach, including possibly the manner in which the book was distributed or even the feeling of the time. Perhaps the messages in the book or even the entire project including the seances, as delivered from the 1940s into the 1960s did not catch on as much. In any case, I am grateful that the Mark Probert was mentioned in the Law of One books (Book I, session 7), otherwise I too may have missed out.

In the previous section, I mentioned the notion of shruti in regard to the CDT-plate translations that ended up as the Voyager books and related materials. The word shruti is from the Hindu tradition and it is often used to refer to the Vedas as texts revealed to mankind that has a high spiritual authority in and of itself. The author of the preface in Voyager II compared that book to shruti and to a large degree, I agree. However, I would opine that even though the Inner Circle members advise caution and discretion with their materials, I think some of what they reveal falls under shruti of the highest order. For example, I have read nowhere else, an account of cosmogony, that is, the creation of the universe, that spoke from the perspective of the creators themselves. The closest I have found are accounts of creation where the perspective is from the unmanifest, that then becomes manifest. In three examples, the Kemetic (i.e., Ancient Egyptian), the Hindu and the Shamanic-Daoist, we shall examine accounts that are somewhat related in that they all relate to the notion of the "cosmic egg" and all include both the creator and the created. After these three, we shall also examine two other accounts, one from the Stanzas of Dzyan, an ancient text of a secret Himalayan brotherhood, and another from the secret initiation knowledge of the late Zulu High Sanusi Credo Mutwa. In these two latter examples, the account starts from pre-creation and nothingness, and then something happens which leads to creation. Let us start with the Kemetic, Hindu, and Shamanic-Daoist perspectives, and then we shall proceed to the last two.

The Kemetic version is taken from the *Book of Emerging Forth into the Light*, which is now commonly known as the Egyptian Book of the Dead due to early translations of the Medu Neter (the Ancient Egyptian language). The version cited below is translated from the French version found in Obenga (1990):

"O Atum, give me the gentle breeze that is in your nose!
I am that Egg that was in the belly of the great jargon-maker
And I keep watch of this great entity that Geb separated from the Earth
If I live, she lives
May I become again young and live
And breathe the breeze
I am the one who separated what was reunited
I have circulated around
I am the morning of time, and the great power, Seth"
(From the Book of the Dead, chapter 54)

Livre des Morts : chapitre 54.

Source: Obenga (1990, p. 43)

In the above citation, there are a number of notable points which will be apparent when comparing this version to versions in India and China. The second line is really important, because it brings attention to gestation in the primordial womb, before Heaven and Earth were separated. That which is kept watch over, is Heaven. It is important also to pay attention to the notion of breath, and of breathing, also in relation to the separation of Geb (Earth) from Shu (air). This is one of the greatest secrets of existence. Encoded in understanding the breath, is the understanding of all life, from the macrocosmic level of the universe, to the microcosmic level of atoms, molecules, and cells. It is the breath from Atum that would give life to the entire universe, have it reborn, or become young again. Gaining a better understanding of the secret of the breath can lead to a better understanding of the pulse of life in manifest existence. I devote some thoughts to the discussion of breath, to cycles and to rhythm, in section 5.3 of Chapter 5, titled Altered states of consciousness. Interestingly, Obenga (1990) notes that the idea of the cosmic egg was not unique to Ancient Egypt. Within West Africa (at least), there are several examples of cultures whose spiritual practice includes the "cosmic egg" concept. Three cultures he cites are the Bambara, a Mande people of Mali, the Fali people of Cameroun, and the Abouré, an Akan people of Côte-d'Ivoire. There are sure to be other examples within West Africa and beyond.

The next example is also a rather fascinating account of cosmogony. This one is known as the Hiraṇyagarbha Prājāpatya and it is from Mandala 10 of the Rig Veda. The Vedas are *the* shruti of Hindu culture. The account below is from Jamison & Brereton (2014):

1. The golden embryo evolved in the beginning. Born the lord of what came to be, he alone existed.
He supports the earth and the heaven here— Who is the god to whom we should do homage with our oblation?
2. Who is the giver of breath, the giver of strength; whose command all honor, whose command the gods honor; whose shadow is immortality, whose shadow is death— Who is the god
to whom we should do homage with our oblation?
3. Who became king of the breathing, blinking, moving world—just he alone by his greatness;
who is lord of the two-footed and four-footed creatures here— Who is the god to whom we should do homage with our oblation?
4. Whose are these snow-covered mountains [=the Himalayas] in their greatness; whose is the sea together with the world-stream, they say; whose are these directions, whose (their) two arms [=the zenith and nadir?]— Who is the god to whom we should do homage with our oblation?
(Jamison & Brereton, 2014, pp. 1593 – 1594)

This is an excerpt of the first 4 of 10 verses. Now, the reader might notice some incredible similarities between this account and the Ancient Egyptian account. Both accounts speak of an egg or a womb, and both have a single being in the entire existence. Also fascinating are the similarities in regard to the breath, and to the mention of Heaven and Earth. In the Kemetic version the ultimate being, Atum, is mentioned at the start, however in the Vedic, the question that keeps being posed, is "who is the god to whom we should do homage with our oblation?" By verse 10, we are told who this god is, "O Prajāpati! No one other than you has encompassed all these things that have been born" (Jamison & Brereton, 2014, p. 1594). Thus, Prajāpati in the Vedic version is the equivalent of Atum in the Kemetic version. Prajāpati is said to be another name for Brahma, a Supreme Being in Hindu spiritual philosophy. We shall discuss Brahma in other parts of this chapter in relation to the Hindu spiritual philosophies of Samkhya and Vedanta.

Now, let us advance to the third example, which holds some resemblance to the first two. The legend of Pan Ku can be found written in various forms. This version is from Werner (1922):

"It was Time's morning
When P'an Ku lived;
There was no sand, no sea
Nor rolling billows

Earth there was none
No lofty Heaven;
No spot of living green;
Only a deep profound"
(Werner, 1922, p. 78)

And so here too, we find associations with a primordial beginning, when there was only one being existed. Here, the being is named as P'an Ku, whereas in the Kemetic and Vedic versions, we are not given a name for the being but rather given a name for the name of two Supreme Beings, Atum and Prajāpati. Although the account given above of P'an Ku is relatively shorter compared to the quoted Kemetic and Vedic versions, it is in commentary about P'an Ku given in Werner (1922) that we learn even more about this being:

"The most conspicuous figure in Chinese cosmogony is P'an Ku. He it was, who chiseled the universe out of Chaos. According to Chinese ideas, he was the offspring of the original dual powers of Nature, the *yin* and the *yang* (to be considered presently), which, having in some incomprehensible way produced him, set him the task of giving form to Chaos, and "making the heavens and the earth". Some accounts describe him as the actual creator of the universe – "the ancestor of Heaven and the earth and all that live and move and have their being." 'P'an' means 'the shell of an egg' and 'Ku' 'to secure,' 'solid,' referring to P'an Ku being hatched out of Chaos and to his settling the arrangement of the causes to which his origin was due" (Werner, 1922, p. 76).

Okay, so this commentary that elaborates on P'an Ku is very helpful for a number of reasons. First, it establishes the link between the Kemetic, Vedic and Shamanic-Daoist versions in regard to the notion of a "cosmic egg". It would appear that the traditions and teachings of the ancient cultures concur on this point. It is possible that all three traditions have a common origin since they are so similar. My initial suspicion, and speculation, is that this teaching may have been part of an ancient Lemurian tradition, since all three cultures (Kemetic, Vedic, and Daoist) are said to have been "daughter cultures" of this once-great culture that spanned the globe (Churchward, 1931).

As it would be the case, one aspect of this Chinese version of the "cosmic egg" story that I find really intriguing, and that is different from the Kemetic and Vedic versions is the notion that not only was P'an Ku the creator or fashioner of the universe but that once the job of creation was done, P'an Ku then incarnated into creation. In Werner (1922), we learn that:

"When P'an Ku had completed his work in the primitive Chaos, his spirit left its mortal envelope and found itself tossed about in empty space without any fixed support. 'I must', it said, 'get reborn in visible form; until I can go through a new birth, I shall remain empty and unsettled'" (Werner, 1922, p. 129).

The excerpt above tells us that the creator then entered its own creation in other to participate in it. I find this to be interesting because I see the members of the Inner Circle, those minds who contributed perspectives in the Magic Bag, as being in a similar situation. They are aspects of Creator-Source of this universe, that then ended up entering their creation to participate in it. No wonder that they would have the advanced knowledge of creation from the creators themselves, knowledge which I have not found in any other accounts from ancient cultures and the present time. We will get into their version of cosmogony to learn just why it is so different from other extant accounts, but before that, we still have two more examples to consider.

Now that we have discussed versions of cosmogony that have in one way or another to do with the idea of a "cosmic egg", let us consider excerpts of one version of cosmogony from an ancient text known as the *Stanzas of Dzyan*, a book said to be from Atlantean times, and that was first popularized in Helena Petrova Blavatsky's *The Secret Doctrine* book series which quotes from it and discusses it. The excerpt of the other version comes from Vusamazulu Credo Mutwa's book Indaba, my Children. First, the Stanzas of Dzyan excerpt:

"The eternal parent wrapped in her ever-invisible robes had slumbered once again for seven eternities
Time was not, for it lay asleep in the infinite bosom of duration
Universal mind was not, for there were no Ah-Hi to contain it

The seven ways to bliss were not, the great causes of mystery were not, for there was no one to produce and get ensnared by them
Darkness alone filled the boundless all, for father, mother and son were once more one, and the son had not awakened yet for the new wheel, and his pilgrimage thereon
Stanzas of Dzyan (See references section for online link)

This, to me is a beautifully poetic account. Again, these are only the first few verses of a much longer telling, but it is enough to help us arrive at the point I would like to draw attention to here, which is that this account also starts from the creation itself. No indication as to why the creation came about, or to how it did come about. Mind you, this is a very ancient version we are reading here. If it is in fact true that the Stanzas of Dzyan are from Atlantean times, then this story is tens of thousands of years old. At any rate, it still gives us some points for comparison with the other versions in the examples already presented. There is the concept of time, of the nothingness, of the primordial trinity, and of the creation existing as the seven ways to bliss (i.e., the mysteries of the number seven, that include the seven chakras, and the seven planes or densities of existence, the eighth being the next octave, etc.), and the idea of a trinity, which has not appeared in other versions until this one.

Now, we are ready for the final example, before we get back to the actual work and teachings of the Inner Circle. This version of cosmogony below was given to the late Vusamazulu Credo Mutwa during his initiations in the secret orders of Africa. This is one of my absolute favourite versions. Few can tell stories like Credo Mutwa did. One observation I have made with this version is that it has some uncanny similarities with a part of the version that Yada di Shi'ite of the Inner Circle gives, that pertains both to the nothingness that existed before creation and to the actual process of creation. What Mutwa's version does not have, as published, are the thoughts of the creators, and the reasons why the creation was set in motion. As a result, I have wondered if Credo Mutwa knew more but chose not to reveal that part of the story. Here is an excerpt of his version:

"No stars were there - no sun
Neither moon nor earth–
Nothing existed but darkness itself–
A darkness everywhere
Nothing existed but nothingness
A Nothingness neither hot nor cold

Dead nor alive–
A Nothingness far worse than nothing
And frightening in its utter nothingness

For how long this nothingness lasted,
No one will ever know;
And why there was nothing but Nothing is something
We must never try to learn
[Sorry Baba, I am breaking the trend in regard to these last two sentences -my emphasis]

Nothing had been floating
For no one knows how long
Upon the invisible waters of Time–
That mighty River with
Neither source nor mouth,
Which was–
Which is
And ever shall be

Then one day-
Or is it right to say 'one day'?–
The River Time desired Nothingness
Like a flesh-and-blood male beast
And as a result of this strangest mating
Of Time and Nothingness,
A most tiny nigh invisible spark
Of living Fire was born

This tiny, so tiny spark of Fire could think
And grew conscious of its lonely state;
No one nor nothing could hear its cries
In the lonely depths of utter Nothingness–
Like forlorn a babe,
Lost and in despair,
In a cold dark forest"
(Mutwa, 1999, pp. 5 – 6)

So, there it is, an excerpt of Credo Mutwa's version. This version goes on for page after page, several pages more, in his book. However, it is enough to have an excerpt to illustrate the main points I have been touching upon with these examples, which are that (1): they all tend to talk about the creation from the standpoint of what was not there before, and then what came, or was to come, and (2) there was nothing, or in some cases, one being or consciousness that floated within the nothingness, before it started doing something. Credo Mutwa's account also mentions the notion of time, which also appeared in a number of the previous examples. Where his account differs from the other examples and bears similarity to the account from the Inner Circle is on two points: (a) his mention of desire, and (b) the idea of the tiny spark of fire that grew in consciousness to engulf the extent of the nothingness (you can read more about this in the rest of the account). This last point about the spark is very important, because it speaks to the actual mechanism of creation, which is elaborated upon in much greater detail in the Inner Circle account. Now, let us return to the Magic Bag.

The Magic Bag takes it to a whole other level, where we are taken into the mindset of the creators themselves, and into the mechanism of creation itself, which gives incredible information into both science and metaphysics or spiritualty. Specifically, the account given by Yada Di Shi'ite details what I believe is a key to reaching a unified understanding of the two disciplines. This account also introduces a group of beings that the Inner Circle calls 'the Overlords', who are creator-level beings. These Overlords work with a second set of beings known as 'the High Archangels'. Events occurring between the Overlords and the High Arch-Angels led the former to collaborate with the latter in setting forth events that led to the creation of manifest reality. Let us begin.

As with the other examples above, of cosmogony, the Inner Circle begin their discussion of the subject with the topic of the void:

"The space you now see and seem to feel to be outside yourself was once a black void that stretched out into all, an endless eternity. There was neither wind nor elements of any kind whatsoever. All was in utter quiescence, of a kind which no human can even faintly comprehend. And yet, within that incomprehensible void there was a vast world of life and ceaseless activity that far surpassed in beauty and grandeur anything Earth-people have ever known." (Probert, 1963, p. 5)

For a while now, I have come to the conclusion that space is not empty. I first came to this knowing through dream and out of body experiences where awareness experienced "space" as containing matter and energy. The Inner Circle is saying here that at the time of the beginning, there was really a void, which contained life, the like of which we cannot understand from a human perspective. What then, was this world like? Well, we are told, "This world I speak of is Man's True Consciousness" (p. 5). I find this to be really valuable insight. In the Buddhist and Daoist spiritual paradigms, there is the notion that humanity, or mankind if you will, attains liberation not merely by thinking or by philosophizing, but rather through a process of cultivating stillness and being, that enables conscious awareness to penetrate the subtlest levels, culminating in the achievement of unity consciousness with nothingness. Perhaps, this is what the Inner Circle is alluding to. Let us continue. Now, the account introduces the Overlords and the High Archangels:

"The sin, or evil, of life on any plane is not in the act of the spirit in making form and substance and entering therein, but in the spirit's willing desire to sink itself so deep into the form that it loses all consciousness of Itself. Now, this was what the Over-Lords discovered the High Archangels of the Low Etheric were secretly working to do, and thereupon sent a messenger to the Low Etheric, forbidding the High Archangels to go further with their experiment in lowering the vibratory rate of their world, warning them that such an act would automatically throw everyone who entered into the Low Etheric into an entirely new dimension of thought which would eventually cause him untold misery." (p. 6)

So, it would seem, that in the etheric worlds of the Overlords and of the High Archangels, the latter were conspiring to create, without having first consulted with the former. It would also seem that the former have supervisory authority over the latter, and therefore, upon discovering the schemes of the latter, felt compelled to intervene. Continuing:

"The Over-Lords knew also that the High Archangels had not yet discovered the method of changing inner motion to outer motion, but that they eventually would... There is a generally upheld law that one plane of consciousness shall not actively interfere into the desired doings of another plane of consciousness, whether it be higher or lower...once a true creative desire is set into motion by one on a lower plane, someone on the plane above his must aid and abet him to the best of his ability to bring that which is desired into manifestation...So it was that the Over-Lords were only abiding by a law they themselves had originated when they decided to aid the High Archangels in creating the new world they so desired." (pp. 7 – 8)

Let us take a step back and consider a few things. First, we have been introduced to two groups of beings, on one hand, a group that is referred to as the Overlords, and on the other hand another group that is referred to as the High Archangels. Okay, so, at this stage, all we know about these beings is that at a certain stage in existence, when the void of the universe was just that, a void, with no manifest reality, there were these two groups of beings. We are not told by the Inner Circle who created these two groups of beings or whether they were self-created or anything like that. So, there are some limits here, to what is being revealed. Having admitted that much, I would add as well that this account still stands apart from all others so far that I have been able to access, in the amount of detail it goes into about those that created the manifest reality that can be experienced. Third, it is admitted in the quote above that the new world to be created would be a collaborative endeavour between the Overlords and the High Archangels.

The one clue that the quote above gives, that is truly revealing, is the part about changing inner motion into outer motion. This brings to mind two other concepts, from the Law of One teachings. These are the notions of time-space, and of space-time. At a very basic level, time-space is the world we experience in our dreams during sleep, and space-time is the world we experience in the physical world while awake. I have this suspicion that at the time of utter emptiness, of the void, life was blooming and blossoming in time-space existence, which would be where the etheric worlds of the Overlords and the High Archangels would be located. Space-time was a void, but time-space was teeming with life. As a general note, in space-time, we can travel from point A to point B, in space, within a given time, whereas in time-space, we can travel from point A to point B, in time, within a given space. Moving on, to the moment of creation itself:

"Suddenly the two energies rushed with tremendous speed and force into one another. For the barest tick of time nothing happened. The next, lightning, the brilliance being of appalling magnitude and intensity...while the Over-Lords watched with growing interest the violent churning of the heat and cold energies...At the same time, the terrific vibrating waves of sound created an ever-widening magnetic field that drove the heat and cold waves together...The first form of electricity was of the static or friction kind created by the tremendous vibratory motion of the heat and cold waves when they attempted to combine." (pp. 11 – 12)

Here, in this first act of creation by the Overlords on behalf of the High Archangels, we can observe principles of creation at play. There are two forces, one being heat and the other being cold.

Upon meeting, they create electricity (lightning), which is the spark of life that was mentioned in Credo Mutwa's account earlier. There are other processes going on here as well. There are also magnetic fields and vibratory energies, and radiant energy, which is electricity that can travel on vibrations. Altogether, this account by the Inner Circle, is the most scientifically inclined that I have yet come across, yet it is not only science at play here, because there are also deep spiritual principles being enacted in this described episode as well. Later in this chapter, we shall revisit these scientific and spiritual principles at simultaneously at play in this episode of creation but for now, we shall bring this part to a close.

Ontology and epistemology meet philosophy

It is natural that ontology and epistemology would intersect with philosophy. Philosophy being the general subject of enquiry, and in particular of thinking about the fundamental nature of things, and ontology being the same, except specialized to the instances of being and existence, it can be said then that ontology falls under philosophy as a subset of philosophical enquiry. Epistemology, being those means by which the world view expressed by an ontology is explored and investigated to acquire knowledge, intersects with philosophy insofar as inquiring into what the means are for ensuring valid and reliable knowledge within the worldview of the given ontology. Thus, all three intersect. In the parts that immediately follow, the discussions center particularly around issues of epistemology. In particular, the discussions are framed within three suggested means for gaining knowledge, given by an ancient Hindu philosophy known as Samkhya, within a treatise of this philosophy known as the Samkhya Karika. The Samkhya Karika qualifies as a "revealed text", having originated from the consciousness of a being known as Kapila, one of seven ancient sages of India and who is thought to be an incarnation of Brahma, an aspect of the Hindu trinity. Within this trinity, Brahma is seen as the creator. For a revealed text, it is extremely dense in logic. I found it fitting that a revealed text would emphasize the importance of revelation.

Samkhya postulates three modes of gaining knowledge

In the Samkhya Karika, specifically in the edition translated from Sanskrit into Latin by Colebrooke, and from Latin into English by

Colebrooke (1837), we are given the fourth postulate of the work, which states:

"Perception, inference and right affirmation are admitted to be threefold proof; for they (are by all acknowledged, and comprise every mode of demonstration" (p. 18)

I was struck by learning of these three modes of gaining knowledge, because I realized that every human being has the potential to access knowledge through these three means. Perception brings information to our awareness. At the most basic level, we perceive through our five physical senses. We can perceive sounds, sights, we can taste and smell things and we can also have tactile sensations of objects, substances and textures when we touch them. Through these physical perceptions, it becomes possible to learn about the world.

Beyond our physical senses, there is also the possibility of perceiving with non-physical senses. The ability to perceive with non-physical senses presupposes the existence of non-physical aspects or bodies of the human being. One example of a non-physical sense is the notion of clairvoyance, which is when perceptions far beyond the range of what our physical eyes can register can be brought to our awareness. The idea is that rather than physical light reaching the eyes with sensory information, another form of energy brings information to our awareness. This energy impresses upon our non-physical bodies, thereby registering information that generates a form of perception. This is analogous to the manner in which light impresses upon our eyes, registering information which then leads to perception of physical phenomena.

Just as clairvoyance can be thought of as a non-physical equivalent of sight, one can imagine that there are also said to be non-physical equivalents of other forms of sense perception as well. For example, clairaudience is a non-physical relative of the sense of hearing whereas is clairsentience relates to the sense of touch. These non-physical 'senses' are often described as being subtle. It is because the information obtained from them arrives through non-physical means, such as energy, as was mentioned earlier. This energy, sometimes termed subtle energy, tends to be felt more strongly by some than by others. In modern societies, individuals are typically not formally trained to notice and develop awareness of subtle energies, as is the case for the training at home, in the community and at in formal education that engages our physical senses since birth. As such, there is a wide range of abilities among individuals when it comes to understanding subtle energies and the non-physical senses they might register on.

In any case, perception involves information that registers on our senses. Once that information registers, we then process it. There are a number of ways our awareness processes information. Think of all the sense data that arrives in our awareness, and the fact that we only dwell on a fraction of that information. At any given moment, there is sensory information from our physical bodies, such as our heartbeats. There is also sensory information of things we perceive in our environment, such as the objects in our peripheral vision. For most of us, in order to function optimally, our awareness pays little attention to much of persistent sensory data, our heartbeats and peripheral vision data as examples. There are however other sensory data that more strongly demands our attention. One example could be if we accidentally injure ourselves.

Besides the unsolicited information that comes into our awareness, we also often seek out specific information within our environments. This tends to occur when we focus our attention in search of specific information that we aim to see or hear or feel, as examples. So, the point is that the process of perception can be passive as well as active.

This brings us to an active process of awareness that is facilitated by mind. In postulate or stanza four above of the Samkhya Karika, inference is given as a second mode through which to gain knowledge. To infer is to reason from facts and premises in order to arrive at conclusions based on them. Inference involves thinking, based on what is known or what is assumed to be known. In the absence of direct perception, inference can serve as a means for reaching conclusions, even for data that was not personally collected through one's own five physical senses. For example, if we learn of a fact derived from a trusted source, such as a weather forecast, that there is a very high probability that there will be rain the following day, one can infer from this data that it would be a good idea to carry protective gear such as a raincoat or an umbrella. Between the data indicating that it is highly likely to rain and the inference that it is a good idea to carry rain protection is the reasoning that if it is highly likely to rain, then it is also highly likely that if one is out and about, then one may be subject to rain. Being subject to rain involves getting wet, which can be inconvenient when one is stuck under a shelter waiting for the rain to pass, or undesirable when one has to travel in the rain but wants to keep clean and warm while also avoiding illness. Therefore, in order to avoid these two scenarios, one should carry rain protect, such as a raincoat or an umbrella, to lessen inconvenient or undesirable effects of possible rainfall.

For many of us will not occur consciously because we may take for granted that the logical thing to do in the event of possible rainfall is to carry a raincoat or an umbrella. The point here is that our minds can enable us to make inferences based on data we have not collected ourselves through our own perceptive processes. Inference thus serves as a means through which to extend the reach of what can be taken as known, beyond the reach of our five physical senses. Inference is a process of mind, and as such it serves as a kind of "sixth sense" that helps guide our decisions based on data that comes to us from the world.

If perception can be thought of as a process of body (physical, or non-physical), and inference can be thought of as a process of mind, then the third means that the Samkhya Karika gives us for gaining knowledge, right affirmation, can be thought of as a process of spirit. In stanza five of the Samkhya Karika, we are told, among other things, that "Right affirmation is true revelation" (p.21), however it is in the following stanza, the sixth one, that distinctions between perception, inference and right affirmation are given. I shall quote it in its entirety for us to discuss it:

"Sensible objects become known by perception; but it is by inference (or reasoning) that acquaintance with things transcending the senses is obtained: and a truth with is neither to be directly perceived, nor to be inferred from reasoning, is deduced from revelation" (p. 25)

From this stanza, we can learn that the third mode for gaining knowledge that the Samkhya Karika teaches comes about not through a sensory process, or through a rational or logical process, but through a process of spirit that is one of revelation. For this, we can think of our awareness experiencing discernment, enlightenment, insight, penetration, revelation. Think about receiving a vision, during a vision quest that Native Americans went. In Africa, visions and revelations from and by spirit have been the order of day since ancient times. In Asia, there has been a long tradition of receiving holy texts from beings of high spiritual rank. There are numerous examples of this in Buddhism, in Daoism, and in Hinduism.

Even the Samkhya Karika, that I am discussing in this book, can be said to be one such example of a text revealed to mankind from a spiritual source of high rank. In Colebrooke (1837)'s translation of the Samkhya Karika, there is included a commentary by Gaudapada, an eminent sage who was one of the founders of Advaita Vedanta, a spiritual philosophy also discussed in this book. Of Kapila, a being of high rank to which the Samkhya Karika is attributed, Gaudapada had this to say:

"The divine Kapila, the son of Brahma indeed : as it is said, "Sanaka, Sanandana, and Sanâtana the third; Asuri, Kapila, Borhu, and Panchasikha : these seven sons of Brahma were termed great sages", Together with Kapila were born Virtue, Knowledge, Dispassion, and Power : for he being born, and observing the world plunged in profound darkness by the succeeding series of worldly revolutions, was filled with compassion; and to his kinsman, the Brahman Asuri, he communicated a knowledge of the twenty-five principles; from which knowledge the destruction of pain proceeds." (p.1)

To put the quote above into context, we can think of Kapila as an incarnation of the Creator or Supreme Being, Brahma, within creation. Who is this Brahma? Well, Brahma can be thought of as a Hindu aspect of "God". When I traveled across India for months a few decades ago, I continually came across Hindu holy men and philosophers describing the Vedic trinity as "Generate, Operate, Destroy". Notice that the first letter of each of those three words, when put together, makes the word "God". It was repeatedly explained that Brahma generated the world, Vishnu, another heavenly being of this trinity, operates the world, while Shiva, yet another being of this trinity, is the world destroyer. It should come then as no surprise, that Gaudapada, himself an adherent of Advaita Vedanta, would be interested in the Samkhya Karika enough to write an influential commentary about it. Since the Supreme Being in Advaita Vedanta is Brahma, it is logical that a source of spiritual and worldly teaching from Brahma in incarnation, as Kapila, would be of great interest to a sage propounding a spiritual philosophy whose Supreme Being is Brahma. Anyone who takes the time to read the Samkhya Karika would realize that it is not a text about some "airy fairy" spiritual teachings. Rather, it is a text that propounds a supremely logical framework that is largely grounded in understanding experience in reality.

At any rate, let us not lose sight of the main point about the third means that the Samkhya Karika suggests for gaining knowledge, which Colebrooke (1837) translates as "right affirmation", a process that can lead to revelation. The point is that it is not only through processes of body and mind that we can gain knowledge. We can also gain knowledge through processes of spirit. This is a key difference in what constitutes knowledge, among those cultures that integrate spirit in a foundational way into their ontologies and epistemologies, and those that do not.

I however prefer a translation of the notions of perception, inference and right affirmation instead as perception, deduction, and correct witness. I came across this alternative translation of these three notions from the Samkhya Karika as I studied yet another text known as the Yoga Sutras of Patanjali. Specifically, the translation of the Yoga Sutras of Patanjali I read is the version made available in the Alice Bailey materials and that is titled *The Light of the Soul – The Yoga Sutras of Patanjali*. These Yoga Sutras are an ancient yoga training manual of sorts, that are said to have been composed or at the very least compiled by Patanjali, a scribe of Ancient India. A fascinating aspect of this yoga training manual is that it appears to be based on the Samkhya spiritual philosophy. This manual was suggested to me for reading by one of my spiritual teachers from the early 2000's. In it, I resonate more with the statement of these three modes in the following stanza, which is the seventh in part one of the Yoga Sutras of Patanjali from Bailey (2012):

"The basis of correct knowledge is correct perception, correct deduction and correct witness" (n.p.)

In place of "right affirmation" given in Colebrooke (1837), Bailey (2012) gives "correct witness". I resonate more with "witness" than with "affirmation" because the term gives me more information about this process for gaining knowledge. Here, the witness, is the being, the observer. It is the awareness, the consciousness, the spirit. It is that part of ourselves that can witness or observe its own thoughts, because it is *not* its thoughts. It is the ever-present presence that has awareness even before we as humans develop capacity for language, speech and logical thought. It has been called the "observer", because even though it is ever-present and it occasionally or frequently (depending on the individual) offers insights, it does not impose its input nor does it overrule the machinations, ruminations and thoughts of the conscious mind that most of us grow, develop, and learn to identify with during incarnation.

So, the witness, witnesses. However, to bear correct witness, is to manage to correctly convey the witnessing of the "witnesser", to the conscious mind. This is why I prefer the term "correct witness", over "right affirmation". For the sections that follow, I shall defer to these terms, "perception", "inference", and "witness", as I discuss the ways other cultures obtain knowledge as seen through the lens of this three-term framework given by the Samkhya Karika for the modes through which knowledge can be gained.

Perception, inference and witness in Indigenous thought

After I became aware of the three ways of gaining knowledge through my study of the Samkhya Karika, I realized that I had gained a means to understand other knowledge systems as well. This is because it occurred to me that this three-term Samkhya framework applied not only to ways of gaining knowledge within the Hindu-Vedic epistemology but to other knowledge systems as well. Being of Akan background, my own culture is steeped in indigenous knowledge. Being generally curious to learn about peoples and cultures beyond my own, I have also devoted much time studying cultures and traditions of other indigenous people in Africa, the Americas, Asia, Europe and the Pacific as examples. What I have come to learn is that the disparate groups of indigenous peoples within these regions have knowledge systems that draw on perception, deduction, and witness.

As has already been discussed at the beginning of this chapter on ontologies and epistemologies of indigenous people, spirit has played a foundational role their knowledge systems. The knowledge traditions within these "spiritual" cultures also drew on deduction as a way of understanding the world. Logic and rationality involve analyzing, categorizing, evaluating, and synthesizing data. The data can be from facts pertaining to physical or to non-physical sources. In regard to the use of logic universally across most if not all cultures on Earth, we find the practice of aphorisms or idioms. These pithy sayings often require thinking to deduce their meaning. Indigenous people also made use of their knowledge of the environment, such as knowledge of the seasons to determine when to plant crops, what to hunt at which time, and how to best use of resources found in their physical environment. This can be seen in how for example Native American "plains Indians" used as many parts of the bison they hunted. Meat was used for food, fat for dyes (among other uses), bone sinews for bows and as binding cords for tents, bones for arrows, and fur for clothing and for tents.

An example from Africa (and elsewhere in the world) are the many uses of the moringa tree. Different parts of the tree, such as the flowers, the fruits, the leaves and the seeds are eaten as food. The leaves can be used by themselves as a tea, while the seeds can be processed further in order to extract oil from them. The plant itself is highly nutritious while also containing substances that are high in antibacterial, antifungal and antiviral components. The roots, when properly prepared, can be used in a number of therapeutic capacities. Moringa has antidiabetic, anti-inflammatory and anti-aging properties. Although modern research has contributed to further unveiling the many properties of moringa, this is one example of a plant that has been studied and used by indigenous people for centuries because of its many benefits.

The point in this section is that in order for indigenous knowledge to unveil the many uses of the bison, or of the moringa tree, and to use these qualities, there would have been processes involving perception, deduction and possibly even witness, that aided them in generating and demonstrating their knowledge.

Perception, inference and witness in Western thought

Where Eastern and Indigenous knowledge systems have drawn on perception, deduction and witness, the same cannot be said of modern systems of knowledge that have developed in the West. Western scholarship from medieval times till the present time has struggled with the question of spirit and its existence. The root of this struggle in my view can be seen in what I call the "starting points" or "premises" of Western spirituality. What do I mean by that?

Well, in the West, the predominant form of spirituality over the past two thousand years has been Christianity. This refers to both the Orthodox and non-Orthodox varieties. Certainly, there were forms of spirituality among the peoples in the countries now known as the West. Some of what I have referred to as indigenous knowledge was practiced in Europe among various groups of people. These indigenous practices incorporated knowledge of spirits. The early Christians collectively called such practices paganism, wicca, or witchcraft, although there were also certain organized and larger groups such as the druids, who had a name for themselves, even where their practices were similar to others who practiced indigenous knowledge.

The "starting point" for Christianity, however, is the notion that Jesus Christ came to the world as a saviour of mankind. This is why he died on the cross. Even though he died, the Christian faith also believes that Jesus resurrected from the dead, and subsequently ascended into heaven. Because Jesus was said to have been able to do this, he is thought of as one who conquered death. For Christians to reach heaven the way Jesus did, a great majority of them believe that they have to accept Jesus as their personal saviour. What this means, is that it is through him that they would be able to also reach the non-spiritual realm. Where before, in Europe and elsewhere (and still in Africa), indigenous people work through ancestors and the spirits of nature to intercede on their behalf, they now had Jesus Christ.

To become a Christian, one has to believe in Jesus Christ as their personal saviour. This belief effectively takes away your own power and agency as a being, and gives it to Jesus, to be the saviour. And many people really and truly believe in this. They believe in this so strongly, that once Europe was turned, after centuries, when the Christian faith became the faith of the Roman empire, which proceeded to convert its citizens, and make war on those nations with large populations of pagan citizens, Europeans then became the instrument of Christianity, traveling to other regions of the world as missionaries to convert to convert those 'pagan' people into Christianity, just as it was done to Europeans by the Roman empire, and by the Holy Roman Empire that followed.

If believing in Jesus Christ as one's personal saviour is all that is needed to achieve liberation, then the stronger one's belief, the greater the likelihood of being saved, in order to be with Jesus and God in heaven. So, that became the methodology of Christianity. *The emphasis on belief in a savior who intercedes on behalf of the believer in order to bring about the goal of liberation has led Christianity away from an esoteric path and more toward a mystical path.* This, in my view, is the root of the difficulty later European scholars have had in their attempts to integrate spirit into Western epistemology, and I aim to explain why.

Before explaining that, permit me to expand a bit on the terms esoteric, exoteric, and mystical. First, let us discuss the word "esoteric", and its opposite, "exoteric". The word esoteric connotes "inner". That is, "inner knowledge", "inner circle", "inner reality", and so on. Conversely, the word exoteric connotes "outer". For this latter term, we can think of outer practices and observances. Esoteric knowledge refers to "inner" or secret knowledge. Here, inner means the inner workings of things. The mechanism. The methodology underlying the apparent. In other words, how is it that Jesus was able to turn water into wine? How did he walk on the sea? How did he ascend to heaven? How is it that Jesus fed five thousand people with five loaves of bread and two fish?

The exoteric teachings of Christianity state that these actions by Jesus were miracles. That is the explanation you get, when you inquire into the mechanism of these manifestations. From the exoteric point of view, it can be seen as not the place of the Christian believer to ask questions about how Jesus performed miracles, for Jesus is God. The Christian believer must only believe, trust in and obey what the Bible says, in order to get to heaven. Now, this in my view, is both fantastic and insidious, because as aspects of the one infinite creator, we can create whatever we wish for. This includes wishing for a being to save us. It does not mean that the being will indeed save us, however it does mean that we may manifest our reality in a manner that reflects this belief.

The esoteric teachings of Christianity would offer something else. Rather than merely stating that some of Jesus' actions, such as turning water into wine, or feeding five thousand people with five loads of bread and two fish, are miracles, the esoteric approach, even where it acknowledges a miracle having taken place, would also offer an explanation of the mechanism underlying the miracle. Not only that. An esoteric approach may also offer a means to reproduce the miracle by oneself, so that the miracle transcends the realm of the magical into a phenomenon that can be studied as a science.

A mystical approach, on the other hand, may seek not to understand and reproduce the phenomenon in the esoteric way. Rather, it is given to devotion to the figurehead, in this case Jesus the saviour. The mystic follows the exoteric teachings of Christ the teacher, thereby emulating him so as to be as close to Christlike behaviour as possible.

Unfortunately for Christianity, those early Christians who sought to follow an esoteric path, those such as the Hermetic Gnostics and others, were persecuted by more powerful Christian groups that saw the esoteric Christians as heretics. A heretic is an individual or a group that does not follow established dogma. In this case, the dogma is that Jesus is God, one born without sin. However, we are not God, but are sinners, since Adam, our ancestor, and his wife Eve, disobeyed God, and were both thrown out of the Garden of Eden. This is known in Christianity as the original sin. The Christian faith sees ordinary people as sinners, born of original sin, who need to accept Jesus Christ as their personal saviour in order to have a chance to enter into heaven. The persecution of heretics was very strong, especially during Roman times. This oppression resulted in the esoteric Christian path becoming a minority path. Those Christians who wanted to follow a more esoteric approach to their spirituality had to join secret Gnostic orders or other secret orders such as the Rosicrucian order which shares the same Hermetic (that is, Ancient Egyptian) basis as the Hermetic Gnostic orders. This occurrence was unfortunate because the esoteric has a scientific quality to it. Phenomena are studied to be understood, not only with the mind but also with the spirit.

The esoteric approach to gaining knowledge is similar to the scientific one in the sense that it focuses on discovering principles and laws that govern repeatable behaviour. In fact, the esoteric approach can be termed a science, only that it is not merely limited to studying material physical existence. The esoteric approach integrates the outer scientific study of material reality with the inner scientific study of spiritual reality. It integrates physics and metaphysics and to do that, it draws on perception, deduction and witness. Perception involves data that may be registered quantitatively, witness involves data that may be registered qualitatively, and deduction involves making sense of data from both approaches. The methodology that enables correct witnessing to occur can be made available within an esoteric approach, but not within an exoteric approach. The methodology, that would allow a Christian adherent to become like Jesus, in the sense of being able to perform miracles, and even to ascend into heaven, would then not be seen as 'magic' but instead understood as esoteric spiritual science, governed by principles and laws which, if followed carefully, could lead to repeatable behaviour just as is the case with the principles and the laws that govern natural phenomena.

The result of these two approaches to engaging in Christianity is that the history of Christianity is replete with saints, whose approach to Christianity and whose orientation is that of the mystical, rather than of the esoteric. Through the mystic path, it is in fact possible to achieve transcendence. Modern day examples of individuals who have followed this path of devotion, such as the late Mother Theresa, can also achieve a lot through their compassion and through their service to humanity. It is only to say that even where the mystic achieves breakthrough, reaching transcendence, the methodology to reach there is not necessarily repeatable.

It should therefore not come as a surprise that European scholars who spearheaded the development of Western thought from medieval times, through the European enlightenment and to the modern time struggled to integrate spirit into Western epistemology. There was already no room for esoteric knowledge to be developed in an open way within the Christian paradigm. Remember that esoteric knowledge was frowned upon in the Christian Bible, since it was seen as the reason for Adam and Eve becoming outcasts from the Garden of Eden and achieving the status of original sinners, a status that was to pass onto their progeny for posterity. Because esoteric knowledge was frowned upon, and even openly oppressed, as in the case of those early Christians whose views clashed with established dogma because they hoped to pursue an esoteric approach to Christianity, there was very much lacking those methods and means that would lead aspirants to enlightenment, spiritual and material.

So, European scholars, caught in the intellectually and spiritually disempowering dogma of Christian Europe rejected the view that Jesus Christ was their only personal saviour. Perhaps a personal saviour for their souls, but not for their material existence. They did what some current conscious blacks in Africa and within the African diaspora are doing. They did what is called in the Akan language 'san ko fa'! This phrase means 'go back and retrieve'. Those intellectuals of medieval Europe went back into history to retrieve the intellectual traditions that flourished in Greek culture, which was itself influenced by Ancient Egyptian and Mesopotamian scholarship established long before Greek culture came into its own. In so doing, the medieval Europeans and those that followed them in later centuries resolved their intellectual challenge. They became their own intellectual saviours, thereby taking up the role of God in this matter, as Christianity had thrust upon Europe. Europe to this day is very much the product of a Christian culture, however mankind in Europe took up the role once entrusted to God by becoming their own intellectual saviours at least as far as matters relating to the physical world is concerned.

Where a reversion to Ancient Greek culture can be said to have provided intellectual deliverance for European culture, the same cannot be said for the case of spiritual deliverance. For the Greeks, being the great thinkers and philosophers that they were, did not appear to have an openly spiritual culture where individuals had achieved spiritual enlightenment and had left a record of how others could also achieve the goal. In other words, there appeared to be no openly established spiritual traditions in Ancient Greece that championed approaches to spiritual practices that could lead to enlightenment and that were openly discussed and developed just as other philosophical schools in Ancient Greece did. There were of course the Pythagoreans, a secret society modeled after the secret priesthoods of Ancient Egypt, and who also taught practices common to the Ancient Egyptian priesthood. In Ancient Greece, mind, and not spirit, was supreme.

Therefore, in the knowledge traditions that Europe has developed since medieval times, mind, and not spirit, has become supreme. Successive Europeans practiced philosophy in the manner of the Ancient Greeks. Their philosophy influenced every area of knowledge, from medicine, to law, to politics, to biology, physics, and the other sciences, and the many other areas of knowledge that we have today. As we shall discuss later in this chapter, some European philosopher made genuine efforts to include metaphysics and spiritual considerations in the development of European philosophy however materialism ultimately won the day.

Considering the Samkhya knowledge triad of perception-inference-witness, European knowledge systems that have had such a powerful influence in modern times promote gaining knowledge through perception and inference, and not so much through witness. The two reasons for the latter have been given above, which are that (1) the Christian spiritual tradition offered no open methodologies for gaining knowledge through spiritual means, and (2) when European thinkers rejected Christianity in favour of the intellectual tradition of Ancient Greece, they started over with traditions strong in gaining knowledge through processes of perception and inference, and not so much through correct witness. With the exception of secret government bodies in powerful Western nations (e.g., in the US, UK, and France) that have succeeded in operationalizing methodologies such as remote viewing, that effectively integrate both science and spirituality, it is only fairly recently that Western culture, by embracing spiritual philosophies such as Buddhism and Yoga, is opening up in a mainstream way to methodologies that can empower individuals to operationalize this third aspect of the triad for means of gaining knowledge. The next section discusses some of these aspects within the spiritual tradition of Buddhism.

Perception, inference and witness in early Buddhism

In reading about the early teachings associated with Gautama Buddha concerning the nature of impermanence and the need for each individual to arrive at personal understanding as part of their path for awakening, I cannot help but notice some similarities with Samkhya teachings concerning understanding the impermanence of discrete events and also the need to become a thinking soul (sutras 2, and 10, for example, of the Samkhya Karika). In the early teachings of the Buddha, there is also the notion of humanity being afflicted by pain, or suffering (duhkha), and the need to remove this pain. This is a similar or perhaps the same idea found in sutra 12 of the Samkhya Karika which also highlights the concept of apriti, a term synonymous with duhkha (Wilson, 1835).

So, both the ancient Raja Yoga adepts who formulated the Yoga Sutras of Patanjali (the latter sometimes thought of as a compiler), and the early teachings of the Buddha seem to parallel some of the ideas from the Samkhya philosophy. This should not surprise us, since the Buddha is said to have first learned from Raja Yoga masters, before subsequently turning to teachers of asceticism (Winters, 1994). It is therefore possible that as part of the Buddha's earlier training, he came across the ideas set forth in the Yoga Sutras, itself having a conceptual foundation based on the Samkhya philosophy, and that he integrated these ideas into his own understandings that subsequently led to his awakening.
I find the Samkhya philosophy to be an intriguing middle ground between the primarily quantitative approach adopted by Western materialist science and the primarily qualitative approach

adopted by spiritual science. In the West, at least in mainstream endeavours, energy and spirit are less emphasized or ignored altogether in the scientific quest for generating knowledge and understanding reality. The Buddha taught the middle way, which is the way that avoids extremes. According to Winters (1994), "the middle way is the principle that infuses the entire corpus of moral teachings of Buddhism" (p. 10).

I believe there is a gap in the use of Samkhya as a theoretical basis in the Yoga Sutras of Patanjali. As a system, Samkhya to me appears to be complete (i.e., no contradictions) when applied to the physical world. When speaking beyond the physical world, however, I believe that Samkhya as detailed in the Samkhya Karika does not speak directly to this condition. Patanjali, or whomever the original compilers of the Yoga Sutras were, it would appear that they managed to find a way of adapting Samkhya, a philosophy that applies primarily to physical conditions, to the Raja Yoga, a philosophy that extends beyond physical reality. Eliade (1958) opines that the Yoga Sutras of Patanjali are informed by Samkhya philosophy. What makes the situation even more interesting, is that I am convinced that the manner of thinking outlined in Samkhya Karika can be successfully applied to other non-physical realms. This is what the Yoga Sutras of Patanjali succeeded in doing.

Nagarjuna's Mulamadhyamaka Karika

My thesis that the Samkhya philosophy or way of thinking as found in the Yoga Sutras of Patanjali was tacitly adopted by early Buddhist spiritual philosophy but not fully integrated in a manner that accounted for the extent of spiritual realization that Gautama Buddha achieved can be underscored in the struggles that Buddhist thought appeared to go through, a few centuries after the Buddha died. While the Buddha was alive, he had hundreds of arhats as companions and fellow teachers and showers of the way. These individuals had already realized the level they were helping others achieve, and so in the true spirit of correct witnessing, they could directly show those people the way, without having first worked out all the details of the logic that would lead them there. Those who got to the goal were effectively leaping there, and not thinking their way there.

And so, after the Buddha died, over time, over the centuries, Buddhism grew to become a larger and larger spiritual paradigm and practice, with more and more practitioners, more and more thinkers of its philosophy and proportionally less of those arhats or "stream enterers", those that were already en route to the goal, or had achieved the goal, and could show others the way to get there, without having to explain all the steps. With the growth of Buddhism came a struggle, which was that in the absence of these enlightened or realized ones, Buddhist practitioners more and more began to fall to deduction, logic or inference, to map out a way to reach the goal. The problem they encountered was that this logic had never been fully worked out during the time the Buddha was alive, so it was left to different Buddhist scholars to do it. There were a number of approaches, and one which succeeded in putting forth an awesome framework of logic, based on what he saw to be the very core of the Buddha's teaching, which has since allowed Buddhists to work recursively backward from their awareness of ordinary conditions to awareness of the subtle and the sublime, the realm of enlightenment and realization.

Enter Nagarjuna, a personality in Buddhism who is arguably the most important to have emerged after Gautama Buddha himself. What Nagarjuna achieved was nothing short of extraordinary, perhaps even sublime. Nagarjuna resolved a crisis in Buddhism, a spiritual philosophy tacitly based on a version of the Samkhya philosophy adapted to the non-physical, but one that had not been fully worked out to account for the extents of the Buddha's realization. Through the logical framework Nagarjuna presented in his Mulamadhyamaka, it was now possible to lead Buddhist practitioners to the ultimate goal of realization, through logic. Knowing the goal, as was presented by the Buddha, Nagarjuna was able to work out and present a logical path to reach it. It was a path that not only he could follow, but others could as well. That is the story of this part the discussion. But first, let us build the story up to where Nagarjuna comes into the picture, by first providing some historical context.

Confusion came about as a result of the lower mind attempting to realize Buddhist teachings not as a result of making the leap after being introduced to the doctrine but by studying the body of Buddhist materials left behind. This happened centuries after the Buddha died and left, with attempts to codify and to canonize his works. An interesting aside here is that those arhats who were by the Buddha during his time and who were succeeding in getting so many people on the path of enlightenment were not simply speaking words in their teachings. These were realized beings, who were also transmitting meaning behind the words they spoke. This is similar to receiving an empowerment in today's Buddhist practice. The power of realization of the being transmitting the message can impact the consciousness of the recipient and lead them also to achieve a certain degree of realization. With the Buddha leaving and advising that each monk was an island onto their own, it was now left for individuals or groups to figure out how to arrive at the goal, with teachers who would be at different levels of realization or perhaps in some cases having to figure it out all by themselves. In such a scenario, different philosophical and scholarly positions arose.

Knowledge of a fundamental layer is not a necessary condition for consciousness to make the leap. Samkhya taught dependent origination (or dependent arising) thinking, but limited the process to that which occurs in physical reality. The Yoga Sutras of Patanjali, which drew postulates from Samkhya included the notion of dependent origination in a spiritual system (Raja Yoga). Although Samkhya provided the notion of a fundamental layer for physical events, prakiti, it does not appear to provide an analogous notion for non-physical events. Therefore, the Yoga Sutras of Patanjali, although it had managed to extend the Samkhya philosophy to Raja Yoga, appeared not to have an analogue of prakriti for non-physical events. The Buddha however did something that very few had done, which was to arrive at realization and enlightenment through his own experiences. Now, Buddhism, arguably, has operationalized two of the key tenets of Samkhya, dependent origination, and impermanence, however because the practice of Buddhism deals not only with physical events but also with non-physical ones, there has been a problem of that gap, which is what to do about the lack of a fundamental layer for non-physical events. Buddhists have been able to sidestep this gap, without the need to understand the mechanism.

The beauty of Nagarjuna's achievement is that his approach allows consciousness to logically arrive at the level of the formless. In this regard, Nagarjuna did a great service to Buddhism and to Buddhist thought. The underpinnings of earlier Buddhist teachings, showing influence from the kind of thinking found in the Samkhya Karika, was only understood tacitly. What kept Buddhism going in the earliest days was that there were individuals, along with the Buddha who had reached enlightenment and who could transmit the truth of their realization through their words and teachings in ways that got other individuals to the goal without necessarily having to logically work out how to get there. Centuries after the Buddha passed away, this "empowerment type" energy had dissipated, because Buddhism had spread to many other places, and there were fewer of these enlightened individuals gathered in any one place to transmit the reality of the teachings. This led Buddhist adherents more and more to rely on their own logical understandings and insights to get to the goal of enlightenment.

The method that Nagarjuna used is based on an awesome logic that is true to the spirit of the middle way. In my reading of the Mulamadhyamakakarika, after examining many of his verses, I noticed that Nagarjuna frequently proves his stated postulates through modus tollens, a form of propositional logic that involves denying the consequent, and that takes the form: if p, then q. Not q, therefore not p. In this structure of formal logic, p is the antecedent, and q is the consequent. One example of his verses, from Kalupahana (1986), is "If that effect, being non-existent [in the conditions] were to proceed from the conditions, why does it not proceed from non-conditions?" (p. 115). To be clear, however, Nagarjuna uses many other constructs linguistics and from formal logic, such as declaratives, interrogatives and postulates to successively set up and prove his essential thesis, stated in the very first verse of the first chapter of his Mulamadhyamakakarika, which is that there is nothing which exists, which arises from something else that exists. In essence, that all is empty of inherent existence.

What amazed me the most, however, is how frequently his arguments, accounting for aspects and their polar opposites, assumes a form that demonstrate his adherence to the middle way. For instance, the example given above from page 115 first addresses conditions, and then it address, its polar opposite, non-conditions. The middle way is about eschewing either extreme. One way to argue from the standpoint of the middle way, is to simultaneously consider both extremes. This effectively "cancels out" the individual positions of either one. I noticed that Nagarjuna also uses this literary approach a number of times in his verses.

To conclude this part, I am essentially making the argument that Buddhism advanced some key elements of Samkhya philosophy beyond physical events, however beyond the notion of "emptiness", Buddhism lacked the notion of a fundamental layer of reality. Nagarjuna was able to come up with a coherent logical framework that sidestepped the need for acknowledging a fundamental layer while simultaneously providing a path that can lead Buddhist adherents and practitioners to the goal of enlightenment.

Perception, inference and witness in Daoism

Daoism is a fascinating and wonderful body of knowledge with a unified spiritual philosophy but with approaches that encompass different methods and schools. The underlying spiritual philosophy of Daoism, is based on the idea that energy pervades all things, and that this energy, in its primordial form, is undifferentiated. As it differentiates, it configures into two qualities, one being yin, and the other being yang. From the interactions of yin and yang, the "ten thousand things" come into existence. Ten thousand is merely a number to denote the many, many things that come into existence that result from the interactions of yin and yang. From this basis of yin and yang, and the things created in existence, it is possible to study them, by understanding how yin changes to yang and how yang changes to yin. And therefore, the permutations of these fundamental qualities then provides the conceptual basis of the entire spiritual philosophy of Daoism.

Within Daoism, there is what can be called a shamanic origin or connection, where I would say that of the three modes of gaining knowledge, perception plays a role. This is in the discovery of the Hetu and Lusho representations of the I Ching. Explained briefly, the Hetu is a diagram that was perceived on the back of a turtle, that provides a magic square, from which can also be derived the permutations of yang and yin in the I Ching. The story is that the Hetu was perceived by people after a "great flood" that affected the entire globe. I also find that Daoism incorporates gaining knowledge through correct witness, in this case through revealed texts. One of those texts, attributed to the Quanzhen or "Complete Reality" school of Daoism, is the text known as the Ling Bao Bi Fa, which is an incredible treatise on the manner in which changes in yin and yang and in their flow within the body of the Earth the solar seasons and the lunar cycle.

Perception, inference and witness in Advaita Vedanta

In my view, in regard to the three modes of gaining knowledge, Advaita Vedanta draws the most on correct witness. This view stems from the idea that within Advaita Vedanta, there is a study of major texts, such as those of the Upanishads, that can be termed as revealed texts.

Comparing Eastern, Indigenous, and Western positions

When the standard for acquiring and developing knowledge consists of people arguing amongst themselves, then there is rarely agreement. It comes down to the most convincing argument winning. The most convincing argument, however, is not necessarily the truth. It is simply, the most convincing argument. When others concede to the most convincing argument, it becomes the consensus reality, until a better argument comes up. This has come to be seen as a means for ascertaining knowledge, in a system of epistemology where rationality and empiricism are held up high, but where revelation has no place. In systems with revelation, those with the deepest spiritual insights can bring forth material inspired by spiritual processes and sources that are taken as direct knowledge (by the authority of the spiritual source) and not material to be debated. This process of receiving instruction by revelation is common among Asian and indigenous cultures. In Asian cultures, the material could be texts or visions. In indigenous cultures, it has mostly been visions and other forms of spiritual direction. These are not up for doubt. They are discussed primarily for understanding and use.

What about analogous approaches among indigenous peoples the world over? From my studies of different indigenous knowledge systems, I find that their approach is closer in orientation to Asian paradigms already discussed than it is to the Western influenced science. In indigenous knowledge systems, there remains the notions energy and of spirit, and an understanding of how to use them. Rather than having a philosophy or a way that leads to enlightenment, I have observed that indigenous knowledge systems rather have paradigms for understanding manifest reality, and their role in it. There is often not the drive to dominate reality (Western mainstream science) or to transcend or escape it (Eastern spiritual enlightenment approaches) but rather to understand and to participate in the role of the individual and the community in the schemes of manifest reality.

So, for example, indigenous systems often have a reverence for ancestors and also for tutelary deities or spirits of nature, including ultimately the Earth and other celestial deities that serve as intermediaries between divine first cause the world of humanity. This position has also led some indigenous people to build knowledge systems that operationalize knowledge of ancestors and spirits of nature to see and to learn about events. Similar to the discussed paradigms, indigenous knowledge systems also gain knowledge through the use of perception, inference and seeing, unlike Western epistemology that is mostly centered around processes involving perception and inference. Having just written that, I also must add that there are some exceptions to this apparent trend. One of those exceptions is Don Juan's Yaqui way of knowledge, that Carlos Castaneda introduced to the world. I am a huge fan of this spiritual system, and have practiced tenets of it for many years now. I find Don Juan's spiritual paradigm to be similar to the enlightenment path approaches of Buddhism and Daoism. Don Juan claims that his lineage is very old and from my previous writings, I have proposed that Don Juan's Nagual path is perhaps influenced by, or even the same as that of the Nahuatl path or that of the Nagas/Naacals, who originated in Lemuria, who to many parts of Asia and who also travelled to different parts of the world. That calls to question whether Don Juan's spiritual paradigm is indigenous or not, where I define indigenous as characteristic of peoples or cultures who were the first known inhabitants of a region or country.

Perception, inference and witness in Keylontic Science

Keylontic science is one of those paradigms that incorporates all three modes for gaining knowledge. This is because it has within its paradigm a philosophy, a science, and spiritual practices. The philosophy draws on revealed texts, the science draws on deduction and inference, and the spiritual practice incorporates practices that pertain to both correct witness and perception.

There are entire sections on Keylontic Science coming up in this chapter.

Merging of science and spirituality

The predominant currents of knowledge in modern society are lost, and yet there is the perception that they are not lost. Since modern science has not integrated spirit into its epistemology, modern science as it currently stands has not integrated "spiritual sight" or guidance into its method. As such, processes of perception and inference are given almost free reign, where just about anything goes, as long as it sounds logical and has an interesting hypothesis. In the absence of spiritual input, the mind that infers also became its own moral compass. As such, the concrete mind unrestrained is given full recourse to explore scientific extents without acknowledged spiritual guidance, rather guided when so by moral restraints which are another process of mind.

This brings up once again the notion of a human who can see and yet walks around blindfolded and with a stick, like a blind man. Because modern scientific theories do not have a spiritual vision of where they are ultimately going, these scientific theories come and go. In fact, within the very nature of modern scientific thinking, theories are meant to fall, over a period of time. This is the idea shared in Thomas Kuhn's book The Structure of Scientific Revolutions. The main thesis of this book is the idea that, rather than progressing slowly and cumulatively, science progresses in leaps and bounds, that occur as complete paradigm shifts. Hence the term 'scientific revolution'. After the revolution, a newer paradigm becomes mainstream, taking the place of an older one. That modern scientific advancement is said to evolve this way is due to the fact that the current "scientific method" paradigm that underlies the work of most scientists attempts to build an understanding of reality from the bottom up. This is done by collecting and measuring data (i.e., via processes of perception), and then analyzing and making sense of the data in order to synthesize understandings into theories and laws (i.e., via processes of deduction or inference). Any important new data that does not fit established models necessitates a new model.

One very interesting book on this topic of the need for scientific revolutions is *The Case Against the Nuclear Atom*, by Dewey Larson. I discovered Larson's work while reading the RA Material. The main point Larson tries to make in this book is that the nature of scientific endeavour requires ideas and models to go through revolutions, in order to improve the accuracy of the models in the face of available data, especially new data that was not present at the time older scientific models were conceptualized. In the case of quantum mechanics, this scientific paradigm, according to Larson, has become more like a religion for the scientific community. Even where new data contracts the theory, extensive attempts are then made to salvage the theory, with exclusions, exceptions or patches, even where the theory as it originally stands does not fit with currently available data. In Larson's view, this attitude of science being defended religiously goes against the very nature of scientific enquiry, with theories standing only as long as they align with experimental findings, and with new paradigms replacing older ones when the older ones become untenable.

In order to instantiate his thesis, Larson explains that scientists during Erwin Rutherford's time came up with theories to help explain the nature of the atom based on limited data available to them at the time. These theories that developed into the fields of nuclear physics and quantum mechanics were incomplete at best, and have as such led to challenges among physicists. One such challenge is determining what the nature of the electron is, given that experimental evidence was showing atoms as discovered by Rutherford were not stable. Rather, they were susceptible to external pressures such as thermal collisions. In view of this instability, Larson argues that physicists decided that phenomena within atoms followed laws of their own instead of previously established laws of physics. In other words, the model of the atom given by physicist Neils Bohr that has electrons in fixed orbits was an attempt to explain the behaviour within atoms based on data available at the time. As more experimental data became available, other physicists postulated further theories that veered further away from established physics laws in attempts to explain away the behaviour of the atom. This led to the idea of the development of elementary particles and of quantum mechanics spearheaded by Neils Bohr, Werner Heisenberg, Erwin Schrödinger and others. In Larson's view, attempts by these physicists, and successive attempts by others since then are all aimed at patching a scientific paradigm that needed to be changed, rather than propped up.

Larson states that "Perhaps the most surprising discovery that awaits anyone who turns the light of critical inquiry on the current theory of the atom is the extent to which the scientific profession has been willing to sacrifice logic and consistency in order to keep this cherished theory from being destroyed by the advance of knowledge" (Larson, 1963, n.p.) In other words, the data need not be forced to conform with an explanatory hypothesis. If the data conforms, fine. If not, then change the hypothesis. The notion that science needs to go through periodic revolutions is because scientific theories are plausible models with which to try to explain observable data. The scientific method works to build understandings of reality from the bottom up. In other words, collected data is modelled into theories and further tested through experiment, which, if they hold, graduate theories into laws. Over time, new data that does not fit existing models, especially if the data is critical, necessitates the emergence of new scientific models and theories. In essence, science is continuously "guessing" about the nature of reality, based on collecting data (i.e., perception), and the subsequent analysis, synthesis and explanatory modeling in the form of theories and further experiments working up toward becoming established physical laws (i.e., deduction, or inference). The processes available to material science as it functions in these modern times cannot delve into intention and cause, behind that which is measured and analyzed. In order to access the level of intention it will have to be revealed, through processes of spirit, because it is through spirit that we humans can access the subtlest levels of existence, including becoming one with Creator-Source to know of its intentions. For this, correct witness is needed in addition to perception and deduction.

So, how does material science deal with the fact that it struggles to access spirit using processes that involve physical perception, and deduction? Material science says, "if it cannot be measured, it does not exist". Speak nothing of the 'mind of god' or of a purpose in creation. These questions continue to remain outside the realm of material science, because the tools available to material science are inadequate. As long as material science precludes consciousness and spirit, its methods will forever remain guesswork, with continual iterations of theories and laws based on new data collected in bottom-up processes. Material science will forever progress from one revolution to the next, because there is little to no idea of possible top-down intentions and conditions that brought about manifest reality.

As with many things, there is more to it than meets the eye. For those who are wondering how consciousness and spirit can or has made it into science, there are actually at least one well-known and well-established example which, in my view, provide exactly the kind of methodology that can revolutionize the practice of doing science. This approach has however, to my knowledge, remained all but completely ignored by mainstream scientific endeavour, even though the one who modelled the methodology was incredibly successful as a scientist, having successfully filed, it is said, 112 scientific patents with the US patent office, and at least 278 scientific patents in 26 countries attributed to him? This individual has been a popular subject of discussion in non-academic circles for decades, and his work, it appears, was thoroughly researched and reproduced in secret by the USA and by the USSR (i.e., the Soviet Union) during the Cold War.

Who is this person? I am speaking of Nikola Tesla, a personality who has now become a household name in contemporary times. What is so remarkable about Tesla was that he conducted scientific work in a reverse manner to the way scientific work is done conventionally in a mainstream way. According to the book Secrets of Cold War Technology by Gerry Vassilatos, Tesla relied almost exclusively on visions he received, that then inspired the quality and the direction of his work. Once Tesla received a vision, he knew that the answer was correct and exact. He then worked backward, from the vision, to the physical manifestation of the vision which was then the work he produced. This is the methodology Tesla adopted, over and over again, to come up with hundreds of amazing scientific inventions that revolutionized science from the 20th century until the present moment. While mainstream academia largely rejected Tesla and his work as a matter of habit, according to Vassilatos (2000), military researchers on both sides of the "Iron Curtain" (i.e., the Cold War divide) worked feverishly to reproduce his work and to incorporate the resultant new technologies into military hardware. Because of this, Vassilatos (2000) claims that military hardware articles of the 20th Century that he was able to access are replete with designs and ideas attributed to Tesla.

I was amused however, when I read that the military folk, try hard as they might, have only been able to approximate Tesla's designs. They have been unable to duplicate them exactly, even as they continue in their efforts to integrate Tesla's ideas. My amusement stems from the realization that it would seem the military people are "doing science" just as science is conducted in a mainstream way, and not in the way Tesla did. As I have mentioned earlier in this chapter, and in this section, mainstream science conducts scientific enquiry in a "bottom-up" fashion. That is, collect some data, and then apply methods of deduction or inference to it, in order to come up with explanations and answers. This approach is adopted not only among scientists such as biologists, physicists and so on. It is pervasive! To my knowledge, it is the same approach applied in medicine and in law enforcement, including in the judiciary. The attentive reader will realize draws on the first two (perception and deduction) of the three-triad modes of gaining knowledge that are a central theme of discussion in this chapter are what we are all taught to use, as the "scientific method". One salient drawback with this approach to acquiring knowledge, is that it can lead to approximations and to probable solutions, rather than to exact ones. Most of us may have been educated in a manner to believe that exact solutions are not even possible. But that is the best that the scientific method as it currently stands can give: a solution that is highly probable. This is also the reason why medical practitioners occasionally make mistakes, and also why law enforcement officials and legal practitioners occasionally incorrectly administer justice, where an innocent person is occasionally jailed, or where a guilty person occasionally walks away. When this happens, it means that the most probable outcome that was judged by the medical practitioner or by the Judge came up with a solution that was deemed of highest probability to be true, when in fact it was not.

If what I am suggesting here is disturbing to you, or feels uncomfortable, then it should be. It has been for me as well, however to me, it underscores the extent to which modern education can indoctrinate a mind to think in a particular manner. We are taught to think in terms of probabilities and to accept margins of error as best-case scenarios. This is origin of the notion of making a decision with the best available information or data at the time. We are taught to think that this is reasonable, or even the most reasonable manner. And in fact, it is my opinion that it is reasonable to think in think in terms of probabilities, from the standpoint of what our minds can achieve, given available data. But what if there is another way? What if, it is possible to arrive at exact solutions? I offer to you, the reader, that this is a possible, if we draw on other resources we have as conscious human beings, to arrive at exact solutions.

Nikola Tesla used visions, a spiritual process, to arrive at exact solutions for his inventions. In pre-modern cultures, indigenous peoples in many parts of the world, including Africa and the Americas, treated visions as exact solutions. By this, I mean a vision obtained by a member of a tribe among Native Americans for instance was treated as importantly as a scientific discovery would be, even to the extent of the entire tribe making changes to its orientation to account for the discovery that was the vision. This is because understood by the tribal members that the vision was an exact solution. It was inherently true, and therefore would come to pass. It was in their best interest, then, to align with the information in the vision, in order to make best use of the truth of it. One example of this scenario among the Native Americans of yesteryear, was a powerful vision revealed to a member of the Crow Tribe, wherein it was made apparent that white European settlers would eventually overcome the resistance they were facing from Plains Indians to prevail across the land. With this vision/discovery, the entire Crow tribe decided to orient itself in a manner that aligned with the vision. The tribe, knowing that the approaching white settlers would eventually prevail, made a strategic decision to aid them in ways that would avoid conflict with the settlers and that would preserve their lives, their land their way of life as much as possible. This decision brought them into conflict with some of their traditional Plains Indians adversaries, such as the Lakota Sioux, who instead chose to oppose white settler occupation. True to the vision, the white settlers eventually prevailed, and the Crow also managed to hold onto much of their traditional lands and hunting grounds unlike several other Plains Indians, a feat that would not have been likely had the Crow chosen to be adversaries rather than strategic collaborators.

The point of the Crow example is that through visions, it is possible to arrive at an exact solution, or an exact truth. It is a different way or being, to arriving at conclusions through deduction. Visions make use the means of gaining knowledge termed correct witness, a term which is also being discussed in several places in this chapter. On the topic of the three modes of gaining knowledge, a favourite example of mine that illustrates each approach in the arena of trials are three types of trials each of which arguably relates to one of the three modes of gaining knowledge. The three trial types are trial by combat or duel, trial by a jury, and trial by ordeal. Many of us would recognize trial by combat or duel from 'Western' movies. One version of this kind of trial is when two individuals face one another. Whomever gets to his pistol first and pulls the trigger quickly enough and accurately enough may win this type of trial, at the expense of the opponent. Another version uses knives, swords or some other type of weapon. Or it could be a raw fight between two people, sometimes to the death, with or without weapons. This is an ancient form of settling disputes which is now more or less outlawed in most if not all countries around the world. It relies on knowledge from the senses, so it is a form of knowledge gained primarily through perception. The second kind, trial by a jury, is a common form of trial in the modern world, especially in Western nations. In this form of trial, the means of gaining knowledge is primarily through both perception and deduction. In the modern law courts of the world that admit a jury, the two opposing sides in the conflict, one represented by a prosecution team, and the other represented by a defense team, both strive to convince the judge and the jury of the guilt (in the case of the prosecutor) or innocence (in the case of the defense). In order to support their respective positions, each team presents physical evidence and fields arguments. The physical evidence draws on knowledge through perception, and the arguments draw on knowledge through deduction. It is then the duty of judge and jury to work at reaching a verdict, taking into account the physical evidence and the arguments as the best information available at the time. This approach, or a version of it, is held as a 'gold standard' and is a norm in many parts of the world.

The third form of trial is arguably the least known in the modern world, and at the same time arguably the one that receives the most derision or is frowned upon the most amongst people educated in the modern way. This is the trial by ordeal. It is also an ancient form of trial, perhaps the most ancient. In this form of trial, the accused faces an ordeal. The ordeals, at a surface level, sound unbelievably cruel, because they bring the accused close to real and certain danger, which can cause great harm or even end the life of the accused. For instance, the accused may be required to have their tongue touch a glowing red-hot piece of iron, or even hold the iron in their hands, while taking an oath of innocence. Or the accused may be put in an enclosure with wild animals. These are just two examples. The idea is that if the accused is innocent, they will pass the trial unharmed. If on the other hand, the accused is misrepresenting the truth then there would be a form of natural justice meted wherein the danger the accused is exposed to would subsequently cause harm, or even death.

Understandably, this form of trial has been seen as a most barbaric and primitive application of justice by early Europeans interacting with indigenous people. The trial was seen as a superstitious act that randomly caused harm to people rather than mete justice that was required in the situation. But, as with many things, there is perhaps more to the situation that meets the eye. The general idea behind various forms of trial by ordeal is that the accused stands trial not in a human court of law but rather in a divine court of law. Unlike Christians who might have to wait to be judged by God after death, various indigenous peoples found ways to collaborate with spirits of nature. It is a spirit of nature, in the capacity of a judge, that runs a court in a trial by ordeal. The humans there are observers, just as they do in a regular modern court of law. The point of confusion that has baffled many a mind educated in modern scientific ways is how this can be a form of justice. Well, let us take the example of the red-hot iron rod. The idea is that there is a spirit of nature, a spirit that governs the fire element having control over this element to the extent that the spirit can protect the accused from great injury, if the accused is innocent. In the trial by ordeal court of law, there is no need for arguments. All that tends to be needed is for the accused to declare their innocence, plead guilty, or lie. The spirit judges the situation and is thought to be powerful enough to protect or to allow harm to happen.

So, that is the idea underlying the trial by ordeal. This form of trial is seen to produce exact solutions. There is of course the inherent trust in the capacities of the assumed spirit administering the situation. One might object that the spirit could be untrustworthy or make mistakes. Again, such a view would reflect a lack of knowledge about nature spirits. In my own dealings and experiences with nature spirits of the elements, some of which I shared in my book titled *Out of Body into Life*, I came to experience the truth of the notion that nature spirits are not necessarily like humans. There are some spirits that have a way. What they respect and follow is their way. If you want to work with them, what you respect, is their way. You cannot simply argue or negotiate with a nature spirit in a manner contrary to their way. It does not work like that. I tried it, so I know. Our ways as humans do not necessarily translate to the ways of other beings. The point here is that there are certain nature spirits whose purpose and role is to administer justice, if you will. Such spirits have traditionally entered into collaboration with humans for the purpose of administering justice. One modern example of such a spirit, that is found in Ghana, elsewhere in Africa and now in the African diaspora, is a spirit known as Tigaare (Bannerman-Richter, 1982). As a spirit that administers justice, one of Tigaare's functions is to "arrest" negative polarity spiritually powerful humans", if you will. Some of these have been called witches and witchdoctors. Here is how it works. This still happens in Africa, to this day. When Tigaare "arrests" a "negative polarity spiritually powerful person", the spirit gives the individual an ultimatum. That individual can either confess their sins in front of the community, or the spirit may cause the person to lose their life. If the accused chooses option one, which is to confess, they also typically lose their spiritual power. Obviously, we can imagine what option two entails. As a result of Tigaare, there have been individuals who have made strong confessions of their misdeeds, often under the duress of losing their power or even their lives if they do not fully and honestly confess. To the community people who witness such an event, they fully take to be true what is said under confession, because it is part of their ontology and epistemology to admit data obtained as a result of spiritual means.

I give this last example to show that although the Christian and Muslim cultural norms and traditions have deeply penetrated the indigenous world in a place like West Africa, in certain areas, often rural areas, there are still episodes of events such as an "arrested" individual confessing under duress of Tigaare, and possible consequences. Add colonization to foreign religions, and we can say that many indigenous peoples have internalized non-indigenous norms and traditions. One of these norms is to frown upon an event like a trial by ordeal, because it is backward, primitive, and superstitious. And yet the historical account seems to show that many of the diverse people across Africa practiced forms of trial by ordeal, and that the people of those times responded very favourably to such a trial. People did the 'right thing' because they knew if they were caught, they would not be able to escape the consequences. These trials kept law and order, possibly because the people realized that if guilty, the justice was an exact solution fitting the crime of an accused. If not, an innocent person walked free. This is an application of spiritual knowledge in human life, and one that is in the set of outlawed and despised practices. Meanwhile, we still read accounts of individuals falsely accused who spent decades in jail, only to be released once some new information prove their innocence. We have become accustomed to accepting this latter situation, because of the way we have been educated to think.

Let us however return to Nikola Tesla, and other scientific issues. I was glad when I read Vassilatos (2000) describe Tesla as a 'qualitative scientist'. I thought that was exactly correct, because it underscores the nature of the instrument used to perform the scientific operation. In qualitative science, the scientist is the instrument. It is the quality of the scientist to receive visions, through revelation, and to correctly register those visions in the awareness of the concrete mind that then facilitates the work to be done. To be a recipient of visions does not mean that you cannot think, or think well, or use your logical and deductive faculties. Rather, the scientist who receives visions is akin in the story we talked about earlier about the blindfolded individual to an individual who has been able to see all along and who one day removes the blindfold. Now, with the individual's eyes, they know where they're going. They still use logic and rationality, as well as their senses, to get there. They no longer need the blindman's stick (i.e., scientific hypotheses) to feel their way around. Their goal is determined once they can see, therefore logic leads the way, or, in some cases builds a bridge between where they are, and where they need to get to.

There you have it. Tesla's model for doing science has been around for almost a century, and yet it is still marginalized. In a world where many things seem to be upside down, or where that which is in front should in fact be behind, it does not surprise me that Tesla's top-down approach to doing science is in the opposite orientation to the bottom-up approach that mainstream science uses. In esoteric science, manifestations occur from the subtle realms into the gross physical. Tesla's top-down approach advances from the subtle realm of the vision to the gross physical invention, which then generates data. With the bottom-up approach, the starting point is the hypothesis, which is then tested to generate data, which is then analyzed and synthesized into theories and laws, which are of a subtler nature. So, this is how the orientations are opposite. Even with someone as famous as himself, I doubt that this way of thinking and doing has penetrated the consensus mindset deeply enough to take root in a way that is actively practiced and developed by a community of scholars. Otherwise, those secret military programs would not be scratching their heads trying to duplicate Tesla's models. They would instead invest in finding and training individuals gifted in the capacity to receive visions useful for scientific work and who also have the mind to do scientific work. This is what we need.

Just as academia invests a great deal in finding and promoting amazing minds, the Einsteins of the world, it would be great if there was a culture to also find and nurture amazing spirits, or those who can access their spirits in a way that allows their minds to do great work. Tesla's ability was not simply a natural phenomenon. In his own written works about his life, he talks about how he trained his ability to hold images in his mind. He trained his visual capacity to such a degree, that once he received his visions, he was able to design and test the model of his invention, in his mind, and to know that it worked before he proceeded to build it. This kind of ability, to hold and to manipulate images in our minds, appears to be more natural and easier for some than for others, however the ability can be developed via Hermetic and Raja Yoga spiritual sciences (as examples) that teach an individual to progressively hold and manipulate images in their minds. In my view, it is fine that not everyone will have the same ability with visions, just as not everyone has the same ability for languages, for mathematics, for art, for engineering or for the social sciences. The point I hope to make is that there may be individuals out there similar to Nikola Tesla who have a rare and unique ability to tap into knowledge beyond what just the concrete mind by itself can give, and that Tesla, a Westerner educated within the Western tradition left behind to the world a methodology for aiding such individuals as himself to share their gifts with the world. This methodology would likely also be a valuable addition to the education of individuals who may not be extraordinarily gifted in this means of gaining knowledge but who can nonetheless enrich their lives and the lives of others with their gifts.

Apart from Tesla, another example of a program that has had a shroud of secrecy around its development, again in connection with powerful militaries of the world, is the psychic spying program known as remote viewing. It is now no longer a secret that during the Cold War, both the West (US and NATO) and the Soviet Union explored whether they could garner advantages spying on one another by operationalizing psychic and spiritual abilities. Out of this research emerged the practice of remote viewing. Remote viewing is another example of a qualitative science, where the researcher-as-instrument, following specific scientific protocols, is guided to conduct a viewing when given a target. While being guided, the viewer captures and reports data pertaining to the target. In the US, the government, in collaboration with the Stanford Research Institute (SRI) worked with particularly gifted individuals to come up with protocols for remote viewing. It is now known that not only the US, but several European nations as well as other nations around the world have teams of remote viewers that work in or alongside "lettered agencies" conducting official government espionage and research. As such, remote viewing is another successful practice of integrating spirituality and science. The field of remote viewing is however yet to advance into academia and the secular world in a mainstream way, at this time of writing. For a reader interested in accessing scientific studies done on remote viewing that are also accessible in the public domain, one book to possibly check out is *Mind at Large*, first published in 1979, and edited by Charles Tart, Harold Puthoff, and Russell Targ.

To bring this part of the discussion to a close I would like to return to Dewey Larson, his drive to point out the deficiencies of the nuclear atom, and his call for scientific revolution in the manner of Thomas Kuhn's scientific paradigm shifts. It happens that first of all, although some scientists have shown interest in Larson's work and indeed in his arguments, the scientific establishment as a whole has largely ignored him and his work. So, I decided to examine his work, and his ideas a little bit more closely. On one hand, he forwarded arguments for the inadequacy of the nuclear atom. On the other hand, he advocated for an alternative model of the physics of the nuclear atom. In Larson's view, the notion of sub-atomic particles is incorrect. To account for what Larson viewed as an incorrect conceptualization of the atom, he conceptualizes what has been called sub-atomic particles, as incomplete atoms, and of their energies as various forms of vibratory motion. In Larson's view, motion is the only constant in the universe, whether it is at the celestial level where that motion can be described by extant laws of physics (i.e., Newton's laws of motion) or at the atomic level, where it can be described by different kinds of vibratory motion. With this viewpoint, there is no need for quantum mechanics, sub-atomic particles or even of particle physics. However, there is a need to understand what complete and incomplete atoms are.

Naturally, this viewpoint has been almost completely ignored by established academia, although there are small groups of researchers that have tried to advance Larson's work. What struck me as amazing as I read Larson's viewpoint was that it had an uncanny similarity with the scientific ideas promoted by the Inner Circle, spoken of earlier in this chapter. Specifically, the Inner Circle teach that at the beginning of Creation, atoms smashed into one another, resulting in two possible scenarios. The first scenario was that at the time of collision, the larger atom would exert a more powerful force on the smaller one, smashing it and leading to a fusing of the two atoms to create a new atom. The second scenario was that the collision would result in the larger atom smashing the smaller one, but rather than fusing, the two atoms would separate, with the smaller one becoming an incomplete atom while the larger one took on parts of the smaller atom. It occurred to me that both accounts by the Inner Circle and by Dewey Larson likely refer to scenarios that are studied today under a field known as plasma physics, which deals with both fusion of atoms and the creation of ions, which both the incomplete atoms and the larger atom that collected parts of the smaller atoms would be. To make matters more interesting, I also made a link with Tesla's work, where it is clearly in Vassilatos (2000) that Tesla worked with high voltage electricity and with gas plasmas, and through his experiments, he was able to the energy of the ether. This single discovery got him into trouble with "the establishment" of his time.

The dots were connecting. I was beginning to think and possibly even realize that if quantum mechanics was not necessarily the answer to understanding what happened at the level of the atom, then there had to be a field of physics which involved the study of forces of electricity and magnetism, but went further than that to describe the forces within the atom. This is what quantum mechanics had sought to do. Bringing together the ideas of the Inner Circle, of Larson, and of Tesla, my interest in the field of plasma physics has grown. Plasma physics involves the study of plasmas which exist throughout the universe, at the macro level of stars, solar and celestial winds and at the micro level of atoms. It is also through working with plasmas that Tesla chanced upon a discovery of the ether. Unfortunately, neither Larson nor Tesla left behind detailed mathematical equations and formulations of their ideas. I have found the lack of detailed formalism to be one of the weakest aspects of Larson's work. Fortunately for us, another scientist, the British physicist and mathematician James Clerk Maxwell, came up with mathematical formalisms for the study of electromagnetism. Similar to Larson, Maxwell thought of electromagnetic fields as being created by matter in motion. This would be the case, if such matter are ions, for example gaseous plasmas that are in motion. Unfortunately, the versions of Maxwell's equations that were taken up by scientists and developed into the theory of electricity and magnetism were severely watered down by some scientists, a story which would be told in later in this chapter.

The reason for my enthusiasm concerning plasma physics is that it may serve as scientific basis for where science meets spirituality. Plasma physics, especially some of the work Tesla did, enables material science to break out of the confines of the five physical senses into the realm of energy/ether and beyond. The mathematical formalism and framework that can go with studying and developing this branch of science is not limited to only that which can be experienced in physical reality. Maxwell's equations, in their original unified form, gives us a way to discuss how to link the physical world and its phenomena, which the non-physical and subtle worlds. It begins to take us to the realms where mind, matter, spirit and energy meet. And bringing it all together are the ideas from Keylontic Science which has been mentioned numerous times earlier in this chapter. Keylontic

Science is the "unified field theory" we were waiting for, that brings together science and spirituality in a multidimensional and a multi-density way. In the sections that follow, I shall explain the concepts behind Keylontic Science in greater detail. I shall then show how Keylontic Science relates to indigenous knowledge, to esoteric traditions of various cultures, such as Buddhism, Daoism, Kabbalah, and Sufism, and to science, specifically to plasma physics and to other branches of science I have found interesting. The aim of this endeavour is to suggest a framework that may be capable of healing the rift between science and spirituality that are represented by the two sides of the Magic Bag.

Keylontic Science ties it all together

In the CDT-plate teachings, the concept of partiki is the fundamental unit or layer of manifest reality. They emanate from a central source known in these teachings as the Yunasai. The partiki is an energy that has certain qualities. The energy is its own identity. It is electro-tonal in nature. This means that the energy is electrical and it also has sound vibration, which is frequency. It has a quality that generates light and sound. Both of these imply vibration. It embodies the energy of consciousness. It is in a state that precedes matter. It is self-regenerating, through a fission-fusion process. Partiki, being a pre-matter substance, fissions into two parts: particum, which is matter, and partika, which is anti-matter.

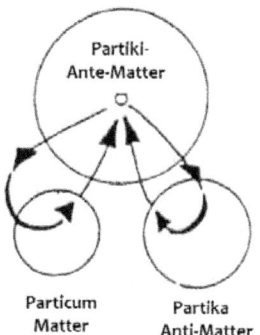

Source: Deane (2001)

The fusion process entails the merging of partiki and partika back into particum. This fission-fusion process, known in the CDT-plate teachings as 'partiki phasing' and which mimics the process of breathing, continues unceasingly, the expansion phase or fission bringing about manifestation (particum and partika) and the contracting phase or fusion bringing about de-manifestation (the union of the two, back in to partiki).

In its basic form, the partiki units form the 'mind' of manifest existence. They are everywhere, and in everything, as a most subtle basis of all that exists, including our multidimensional selves and the various the dimensions and densities. From Deane (2011), we learn that:

"The "mind" is an attribute of consciousness. The mind does not produce consciousness, consciousness is not a product of mind, but rather the mind is a structure of energy that consciousness creates and uses in order to participate within realities that have their basis in differentiated perception...The mind is the portion of your identity that allows you to experience individuality. The mind exists as a large conglomerate of electromagnetic energy units called Partiki, which span multiple dimensional fields. Consciousness itself does not possess form other than the units of electrotonal energy of which it is composed (Partiki), but consciousness uses form constructions such as mind to create the experience of differentiated perception. The form construction of the mind is created through organized groupings of Partiki units or "electrotonal units of consciousness"" (n.p.)

What this quote above tells us is that partiki units come together to create structures which result in what we know of as the "mind", but the partiki units themselves embody consciousness. The mind we speak of here is a first differentiation of pure consciousness into mind, which is a part of ourselves that exists in a higher density. Our first layer of identity, out of the pure consciousness that is common to all that exists in manifest reality. Not only do partiki constitute what we know of as primordial consciousness, this fundamental unit also then goes to constitute what the CDT-plate teachings view as the "divine substance" (Deane, 2002). Partiki are the starting point for building any kind of form that exists in manifest reality. Together with the fission pair partika and particum, whatever form that exists in the antiparticle or the particle realities comes into existence as a result of the rhythm and pulsation interactions between partiki, partika, and particum:

"*Partiki are the smallest units of energy in the cosmos* (one could find 800 billion billion Partiki units in an average 3-dimensional photon). They exist within and beyond all particle and matter substance and represent the "divine substance" out of which the cosmos is composed...Partiki manufacture two intrinsic sub-units of crystalline morphogenetic substance that serve as blueprints for rhythms of pulsation through which particles and antiparticles manifest. The Partiki sub-units that pulsate the fastest are called Partika and they set the pulsation rhythm through which Partiki units will group to form anti-particles. Partiki sub-units that pulsate more slowly and appear in conjunction with the Partika are called Particum. The Particum set the pulsation rhythm through which Partiki units will group to form particles that are a slower pulsating reflection of the Partika anti-particles." (Deane, 2002, p. 453)

There are a number of points I would like to comment on here. The first is the idea of anti-particle structures that are reflected in particle structures. This brings to mind theories in physics pertaining to antimatter and to antiparticles, and the search for examples of these, that has been a research interest in physics for at least the last hundred years. The second is mention of morphogenetic substance. The term 'morphogenetic' is the idea that physical structures can be built on the basis of non-physical or energetic "blueprints". The term was arguably made popular by Rupert Sheldrake, in his book *The Presence of the Past: Morphic Resonance and the Habits of Nature*. For example, in biology, cells that respond to influences in the field around them, in order to build structures that they are programmed to build. The third is mention of 3D photons and the number of partiki in them. What I find interesting about this is the manner in which partiki units are described in the CDT-plate teachings as forming strands that then further organize into grids which constitutes structures of different kinds. This brings to mind ideas from superstring theory, which Professor Silvester James Gates who teaches that in reality, the most fundamental objects, instead of being thought of as being particles, should instead be thought of as being like spaghetti. It would seem to me that the 'spaghetti' of superstring theory could in fact be likened to strands of partiki, as the units self-organize. How then do the partiki self-organize, in order to create all that exists? Let us return to the CDT-plate teachings to learn more about partiki self-organizing:

"Each Partiki perpetually breaks down into Particum and Partika, particle and anti-particle, while simultaneously replicating the original Partiki, through the act of internal fission. The replication serves to retain the pattern of the original, while the Particum and Partika serve to draw other Partiki units from the Unified Field. The Particum and Partika are then magnetically drawn back together in an act of fusion, through which they merge with the replica of the original Partiki out of which they were created. During fusion the Particum and Partika draw new energy patterns in the form of Partiki units back into the morphogenetic structure of the original Partiki, which expands the original pattern while retaining its organic integrity. Through this process crystalline composite forms are created, which serve as the morphogenetic blueprints through which individuated forms and identity will manifest" (Deane, 2002, p. 454)

In order to unpack the content of the quote above, let us refer to the diagram introduced earlier. First, let us imagine that there is a single partiki unit, before any fission. Then, fission occurs. At the point that fission occurs, instead of one particle vanishing, leaving two behind, there are three particles. These three particles comprise the partika and particum of the partiki that just underwent fission, along with a partiki drawn from the unified field to replace the one that just underwent fission. Now comes fusion of the partika and the particum that resulted from fission. At the end of the fusion, there are now one partiki unit that was drawn from the unified field, along with one partiki that just resulted from the fusion of partika and particum. Therefore, after fission and fusion, where there was one partiki, there are now two. The process can be illustrated thus:

1 partiki: [a] fission --> 1 replica partiki from unified field, 1 partika, 1 particum; [b] fusion --> 1 partiki: the replica from unified field, fused with 1 partika and 1 particum

Now, imagine that each partiki that exists is undergoing this mechanism. This is the manner in which more and more partiki are drawn into manifest existence from the unified field. It is this expanding and contracting motion of the partika and particum, from partiki and back to it, that maintains the structure of manifest reality. We are told in Deane (2002) that "Through this dynamic a perpetual motion, expanding and contracting universe and parallel universe are perpetually re-created and eternally sustained...*Partiki can be viewed in spiritual terms as units of identity of God, the central creative source*" (p. 454).

The last two points offer a segue into a discussion of the next level of abstraction beyond partiki as a fundamental unit, with its fission-fusion processes that correspond to partika and particum, and their related antiparticle and particle realities. Now, according to the CDT-plate teachings, the units of partiki can bundle together or 'congregate' to form more complex structures.

The next complex structure beyond the fundamental partiki unit, is the partiki strand. These partiki strands further organize into structures known as partiki grids. It is these partiki grids that create morphogenetic substance:

"Partiki units group by like polarization, electrical partika to partika, magnetic particum to particum, forming strings of energy units called partiki strands. Partiki strands group with other such strands to form geometrical "fabrics" or grids of electro-tonal, electromagnetic energy that serve as a template of light spectra and sound tones upon which particle and anti-structure forms. These templates of Partiki units are called Partiki Grids and they form a unified field of living energy substance through which all things in the cosmos are energetically united" (Deane, 2002, p. 454).

So here, we find that the first law of the universe, like attracts like, being applied. That is, instead of imagining just one partiki undergoing fission-fusion, we could imagine countless numbers of them doing so. During this process, the law of attraction begins to aggregate partiki strands based on electric and magnetic polarity. The first aggregate is in strand form. The strands then weave together into grids, also through the process of like attracts like. Once these grids are formed, they constitute different qualities of energy substance. We can for example think of a pot of soup that, in addition to the liquid "soupy" parts, also contains different vegetables floating in the soup. These vegetables could be carrots, peas, tomatoes, and peppers. Also in the soup would be small bits of each of these vegetables floating in the liquid. We could then liken the water to partiki units (plants take up water to make their food). The really small bits of each vegetable that make up the "solid" of the liquid but are not large enough to for instance make an entire pea, these could be likened to partiki strands, and a small piece of pepper or tomato could be likened to a partiki grid. As this is an analogy, it is not exact. Rather, it is only to give an idea of scale. And now, let us further abstract in terms of complexity, some levels of congregation in the formation of structures in manifest reality. Just as units of partiki bundle together to form partiki strands, which bundle together to form partiki grids, these grids also bundle together to form what are known as Keylons. So, the next level of abstraction beyond a partiki grid is the Keylon:

"Partiki Grids represent the morphogenetic fabrics into which tapestries of crystalline matter blueprints are laid and are the third state of being between pure consciousness and manifestation of form...Keylons are dimensionalized, geometrically formed Partiki composites, composed of more complex arrangements of Partiki Strands that form around the base structure of the Partiki Grids. Keylons are minute crystalline structures composed of Partiki that form the dimensionality of consciousness and matter." (Deane, 2002, p. 455)

The quote above indicates that if partiki grids are the fabrics, then keylons are those fabrics woven together to create a structure that has an identity such as a mitten, a hat, or a jacket. In the example of the vegetables, if those vegetables can be thought of as partiki fabrics, then an example of a keylon, extending this analogy further, would for instance be a veggie pizza of a certain kind. Relating these ideas of levels of abstraction to material reality, keylons would for example constitute different, what we know of as sub-atomic particles. One kind of keylon could be an electron, another could be a neutron, and so on. There is a level of abstraction beyond the keylon, and those are known as keylontic codes. So, where a keylon may be an electron or a proton, a keylontic code would be an atom of one kind or another. This would imply then that all of material reality is made up of combinations of keylontic codes. Keylontic science then, is the study of keylontic codes, and the science around them. So, to summarize, the progression of levels of abstraction and complexity of organization of units of partiki can be termed in the following way, where complexity of organization increases, progressing from left to right:

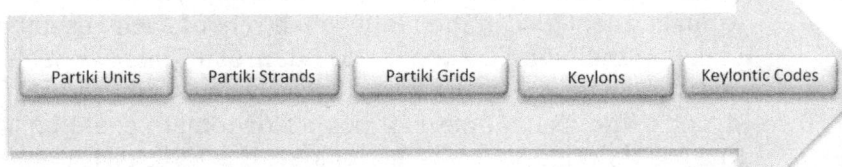

I have often wondered about the quest by particle physicists to discover the particles (and antiparticles) that make up the nucleus by smashing nuclei in particle accelerators to study what comes of the result. From the perspective of Keylontic Science, the processes and outcomes that emerge in their particle accelerators occur are at the keylon and keylontic code levels.

Keylontic Science and Akan spirituality

When it comes to Akan spirituality, we find that the "fundamental level" is that of the creator, known by the epithets Borebore (meaning: creator, architect, originator, inventor), Oboadeè (also meaning creator), Odomankoma (meaning: infinite, boundless, absolute, eternal), Obiannyèw (meaning: uncreated). Linking these epithets to Keylontic Science, the equivalent notion is that of the Yunasai, which is the notion of creator or source.

Keylontic Science and Ancient Greek metaphysics

So, what is metaphysics? Let us give it a definition now, since the term has been introduced and since we will be discussing it some more in this section. Metaphysics is the branch of philosophy that studies the first principles of being, identity and change, space and time, causality, necessity and possibility. Basically, metaphysics is a branch of philosophy that can help address questions like the big ones I posed at the beginning of this book, such as who we are, what we are doing here, what is the nature of change, life and death, do we have a purpose, does God exist, can every human being ascend, and so on.

In Ancient Greece, there were different schools of thought, and a number of philosophers are well-known for their thoughts, including thoughts on metaphysics. The diversity of thought in Ancient Greece was due to their culture of encouraging thinking. As there were different personalities, different thoughts arose as a result of the thinking activity of those personalities. Of the many metaphysicians that came out of Ancient Greece, one of my favourite is Heraclitus, whose ideas sounded like a Daoist and at the same time like a Buddhist. Heraclitus is said to have forwarded the idea that the central tenet of reality was the idea of change and flow. That sounds to me like the Dao and its ideas from the I Ching. It also sounds to me as akin to the idea of the partiki from Keylontic Science that is ever moving, ever flowing, ever changing. His sayings are as those of a Zen master or of a mystic. Heraclitus is also said to have been forwarded ideas of harmony, balance and from this quote, his words remind me of Nagarjuna, who espoused the middle way in Buddhism, "Thou shouldst unite things whole and things not whole, that which tends to unite and that which tends to seperate, the harmonious and the discordant; from all things arises the one, and from the one all things." (Burnett et. al., n.d.). This quote also brings to mind the Law of One teachings.

When discussing Ancient Greek philosophers, we cannot overlook Plato, who also wrote about metaphysics. Plato is well-known for his theory of forms. In this theory, there are forms or molds, if you will, that exist in non-physical worlds and that are unchanging. The forms that we perceive are but physical representations of the abstract forms existing in non-physical worlds. This is an interesting theory to me, because I have in the esoteric works I have studied, this idea of form or blueprint surfaces. The idea is not exactly as Plato expressed it. In Plato's version, the forms seem to be unchanging. In the versions from my esoteric studies, forms may change. What both have in common is that the forms that can exist in non-physical existences can influence objects in physical reality.

And yet what makes Plato's theory of forms also quite interesting, is that if we take Plato at his word, that the forms in the abstract world do not change, and also think of those solids attributed to Plato (that is, the tetrahedron, the cube, the octahedron, the icosahedron, and the dodecahedron), then we can make some fascinating links with Keylontic Science. First of all, in esoteric studies, the Platonic solids tend to be associated with the classical "elements". These are fire, air, water, earth, and the ether. So, fire is often associated with the tetrahedron, air with the octahedron, water with the dodecahedron, earth with the hexahedron (i.e., a cube), and the ether with the icosahedron. In my rendition, I assign dodecahedron to water, and icosahedron to ether, because of the number and geometric correspondences of these solids. The fascinating thing is that if we think of these Platonic solids as shapes ultimately taken up by keylontic codes (see section above on Keylontic Science), then we could say that Plato may have been correct in saying that their forms do not inherently change. In that case, the Platonic solids would serve as the fundamental level of reality. These Platonic solids could merely be seen as less abstract grades of partiki that are eventually taken up as keylontic codes.

Among other thoughts, Plato also forwarded the notion of the existence of the soul and the possibility of life after death. Now, the empiricism and rationalism both developed out of Western schools of philosophy which were themselves strongly influenced by Ancient Greek philosophers. The Ancient Greeks, having learned from others of the ancient world such as the Chaldeans and the Egyptians had a broad range of ideas and philosophies that certainly included their own ideas. As a result, among the mix ideas of Ancient Greek philosophy are those that today can be termed scientific, as well as those that can be termed metaphysical. Some of these ideas would be dropped by later European philosophers, and other ideas would be taken up and developed into modern philosophy and science. As an example, some of the ideas of Plato's famous student, Aristotle, the arguably most well-known natural philosopher among the Ancient Greeks, have been dropped, while others have been taken up seriously and developed as part of today's modern logic, mathematics, philosophy, and science. Aristotle's ideas around the five elements (i.e., earth, water, air, fire, and ether) have not really been taken seriously and developed by Western philosophers and scientists. These are ideas from metaphysics. On the other hand, other ideas attributed to Aristotle, such as syllogistic logic, ideas on proportionality and motion, and his ideas on observation of living things have influenced modern logic, physics and biology respectively.

Taking some of the ideas of philosophers of Ancient Greece such as Aristotle as a point of departure, the thinkers of the European Enlightenment appeared to veer more away from metaphysics and further into empiricism and rationalism. In particular, it would appear that in their attempt to advance the philosophical and the scientific work of their ancient European predecessors, European Enlightenment era philosophers struggled to find a place for metaphysics in their intellectual theories, unlike the Ancient Greeks. Increasingly, metaphysics became the opponent of philosophy and science, in the thinking of European Enlightenment era philosophers. Hagenbruber (2012) tells us that "The differentiation between "science" and "natural philosophy" and the understanding of philosophy as its own discipline alongside physics has been accepted since the 18th century. The meaning of these concepts however, has continually undergone changes since then. In the middle of the 18th century, philosophers grappled with the meaning of philosophy, then opposing the metaphysical approach against the scientific one." (p.viii)

In reference to two of the three modes of gaining knowledge suggested by the Samkhya Karika, we can see here that the European philosophers during the medieval and enlightenment periods appeared to be alternating between having perception as basis for knowledge (i.e., the empiricists) or deduction as the basis for knowledge. European enlightenment philosophers and scientists were often either of the empiricist camp, with the likes of Francis Bacon, John Locke and David Hume, or of the rationalist camp, with the likes of Immanuel Kant and Gottfried Leibniz. Some, like Kant, although of the rationalist camp, also fell into the empiricist camp. Briefly, the empiricists hold that knowledge is gained primarily through what can be perceived with the five physical senses. So, according to the French philosopher Voltaire, who was supportive of British empiricist John Locke's views, "If something is available to our senses and thus to reason, it can be known. If not, it cannot be known, says Voltaire." (Hagengruber, 2012, p.7). The rationalists on the other hand, hold that knowledge is gained primarily through acts of reason, such as deduction and inference. For the rationalist, the ability to reason is held supreme, as we find with Rene Descartes's famous quote "cogito ergo sum", translated as "I think, therefore I am." Descartes is himself counted as one of the rationalists.

There was little to no room, among European philosophers at the time, for the third mode, correct witness, or revelation. Metaphysical enquiry, for the most part, can be said to have 'died' in Europe, with the British philosopher David Hume, and his empiricist predecessors. Empiricism later developed into materialism. The rationalists did not help much either. There were however at least two prominent philosophers at the time, who kept the possibility of integrating metaphysics into European epistemology alive. These were Christopher Wolff, who lived in Germany, and Emilie du Châtelet, who was a philosopher and mathematician that translated Newton's Principia Mathematica into French. Wolff's metaphysics were termed as rational cosmology, rational psychology and rational theology. He addressed metaphysical questions from the standpoint of the first two modes of gaining knowledge, perception and deduction, and not the third, correct witness.

Du Châtelet was different. This fiercely independent thinker who was for a time Voltaire's partner and confidant (before her early and untimely death) was neither convinced by the positions of the empiricists nor was she convinced that the rationalist position was the way to arrive at the most fundamental knowledge. She also appeared not to be convinced that being both of empiricist and of rational orientation would get to the goal. It appeared that she understood the need for a causal level. To me, this borders on the notion of dependent origination that was discussed in the sections of the Buddha, Buddhism and Nagarjuna. Working backward from causes, there has to be an initiating first cause, must have thought. Hagengruber (2012) has this to say about Du Châtelet:

"Du Châtelet claims the necessity of a universal presupposition, because if there is no such beginning, all our knowledge is relative: The foundations of knowledge would then have to be proven again and again and would never be secure in any respect...the possibility that something can be known must be based on a metaphysical principle which is beyond experience and the natural development of reasoning. Otherwise there can be no conclusion, no order and no continuity, no before and no after." (p. 9)

I imagine Du Châtelet would have enjoyed reading the Samkhya Karika, and the Yoga Sutras of Patanjali, had she had the opportunity to do so. The comment above about her is I believe what is fully addressed in the theory of Keylontic Science.

Keylontic Science and Buddhism

I should point out that one can achieve emptiness and nirvana without the need for understanding that there is a fundamental layer undergirding all of physical and non-physical reality, as I argue is the case of the 'partiki' idea from Keylonta. In other words, it was not necessary for the Buddha and other arhats and realized ones to have an understanding of 'partiki' to reach transcendence. The doctrine of impermanence is however a necessary requirement to be able to reach emptiness and to transcend. In the absence of an understanding of 'partiki', the higher mind naturally makes the leap, as a stream-enterer (Thera, Bhikkhu, and Hecker, 2003) once the personality wills it and moves consciousness in that direction. Becoming a stream-enterer is an early step to gaining full enlightenment. This is when there occurs a deep realization of the nature of reality.

Of course, introducing this notion of 'partiki' from kelontic science will make Buddhism no longer 'Buddhism', so it will therefore only be an intellectual exercise. The intellectual exercise could for instance take the following form: what if we were to assume that, similar to 'prakriti' in Samkhya, there could be 'partiki' in Buddhism? How would that change Buddhist thought? Such deliberation could determine how close Buddhism is to a show how close Buddhism had come to being a generalization of Samkhya, which I assert that Keylontic Science could possibly be seen as. Such a comparison is relevant because in the past years, I have come across attempts to unify science and spirituality, or the approaches of East and West. Two of the Eastern systems I have come across that have been juxtaposed with science, either by material scientists, or by spiritual scientists, are Buddhism and Samkhya. Buddhism more so by people who have an interest in both science and spirituality. I think the reason why the union with science has been attempted with both systems is because the key idea of dependent origination appears in both Buddhism and Samkhya, and this idea can allow for the discussion of just about anything and everything in reality, including things at the quantum level.

Keylontic Science and Daoism

In Daoism, it is understood that all things follow the way, and that the way itself follows a notion called 'ziran' which can be understood as "self-becoming", or "what is so of itself" (Roberts, 2001, p. 12). This, existence, that is self-becoming, is like the primordial first cause. It continues to evolve, and to change, and to self-become. Within the macrocosm of this "what is so of itself" we have constant change, that manifests as seasons, nature on Earth, the celestial mechanism in the skies, and beyond that, to the source.

Daoist philosophy beautifully puts it this way: humanity follows the changes in the seasons, the seasons follow nature on Earth, Earth follows Heaven, Heaven follows the Way (the Dao), and the way is modelled after Ziran, which means that the way follows change, and an ever evolving, self-becoming "what is so of itself".

This, to me, is one of the most beautiful spiritual philosophies, that is easy to grasp, and perhaps not so easy to realize. In relation to Keylontic Science, the spiritual philosophy of Daoism makes total sense if we are to imagine that the notion of ziran, or "what is so of itself", can be likened to the idea of the Yunasai, that ever-infinite source from which all springs.

When it comes to partiki, this fundamental particle that is everything, the closest concept I can relate it to, in Daoism, is the concept of 'ling guang'. This is a very subtle level of light, that pervades all of reality.

Keylontic Science and Kabbalah

Similar to the notion of the primordial first beginning, of source, that infinity from which all that exists emanates, this is the Ain Soph. In the Kabbalistic tree of life, the highest sphere is the Kether. It is the highest heaven, if you will. But the Ain Soph is even higher than that. The Ain Soph is the source from which all manifest reality emanated. The closest comparisons I can make of the Ain Soph based on what has already been written in this chapter are the accounts given by the Inner Circle and by the late Zulu high Sanusi Credo Mutwa under the section *Concepts of source* at the beginning of section 9.3. In the Sefer Yetzirah (Kaplan, 1997), we get some insight into the concept of the creator in the esoteric Kabbalistic tradition:

"In general, none of the names of God refer to the Creator Himself. The Creator is only referred to as Ain Sof, which means Infinite Being, or simply, the Infinite. The names used in scripture and elsewhere merely refer to the various ways through which God manifests Himself in creation" (p. 7)

In comparison with Keylontic Science, the Ain Soph would be the source from which all the partiki emerged, as they became the manifest reality, which is the Yunasai.

Keylontic Science and Material Science

As pointed out in its dedicated section above, Keylontic Science begins at the very fundamental level of consciousness, embodied in the self-becoming evolution and changes of partiki. A single partiki is a unit of electro-tonal energy, that is, electricity and sound or vibration energy. As such, in Keylontic Science, the entire existence is composed at the most fundamental level of electric and vibrational energy. These partiki units self-organize into all that exists in manifest reality, including the physical and non-physical realms of existence, and the multidimensional aspects of ourselves that can exist in these realms.

Much as the theory and philosophy of Keylontic Science all-encompassing, and one might even say, beautiful, as it is stated by Ashayana Deane in her materials, it does not include a logico-mathematical framework that can assist the concrete mind to understand and apply the principles of Keylontic Science at a level that is relatable given the disciplines and the tools available in conventional academic work. I think there is a need to bridge the spiritual principles of Keylontic Science (which do not need a logico-mathematical framework to function) with the scientific disciplines of academia. It is important to do this, because it will help heal the divide between science and spirituality.

In the section above titled *Keylontic Science ties it all together*, I hinted that of all the spiritual paradigms I have surveyed to date, Keylontic Science is the only one that provides a framework that in my view satisfies both scientific and spiritual work. I have shown in various parts of this chapter how Keylontic Science relates to a variety of spiritual disciples. In this section, I aim to also show how Keylontic Science also relates to the natural sciences, and specifically to physics. Obviously, there are other natural sciences. I choose physics because it is a branch of natural science that attempts to explain all natural phenomena.

As I think in a top-down fashion, I reasoned that if partiki embody electric and vibrational energies, then this quality in varying aspects and degrees must pervade all of manifest existence. As manifest existence includes physical reality, I gathered that a study of the science of and its relatives, magnetism, electromagnetism and such, should be my starting point in physics. Therefore, I began my revisit of physics (which I took at college, but not since) with investigating electricity, magnetism and related topics. I should also mention that my decision was strongly influenced by the teachings of the Inner Circle given in the Magic Bag. The fascinating account of creation given by Yada Di Shi'ite of the Inner Circle at the beginning of section includes strongly electrical phenomena in the creation of manifest reality. So it was, that I decided to delve more deeply into a study of electricity.

In my readings, it was not long before I realized that physics does indeed theorize that electric and magnetic phenomena explain much of the behaviour that holds all of matter together. Strong electrical forces keep the integrity of the atom intact and in fact keep atoms together to form molecules and ultimately, solid matter according to Kip (1962) who wrote an excellent text that introduces electricity and magnetism titled *Fundamentals of Electricity and Magnetism*. It is a great book to read and study the subject, especially if you have a background in college level calculus, or can quickly and easily work up to it.

Kip (1962) teaches that "Familiarity with the electrical rules of behavior is thus essential for understanding much of nature" (p. 26). Within this statement is the claim that much of nature is governed by electric behaviour, hence understanding electric behaviour helps understand nature. This is good to know, because it means that if all of manifest reality is electric and vibrational in nature, then physical reality must also display electric and vibrational qualities since physical reality is part of all of manifest reality.

It gets more interesting when we also learn that the part of reality that is not adequately explained by classical theories of electricity is when we begin to discuss phenomena at the quantum or sub-atomic level. Kip (1962) teaches that "the behavior of all matter is understood through the laws of quantum mechanics and of electricity" (p. 38). This was an eye-opener for me, because by this point, I had already read Larson (1963) whose misgivings with the quantum theory of the nucleus and of sub-atomic behaviour was discussed earlier in this chapter. For that reason, it came as a real eye-opener when Kip (1962) admitted in what I deemed to be an ever so subtle manner that quantum mechanics had thus far not completely succeeded in explaining the phenomena for which the theory was designed. Arthur Kip was a mainstream scientist, a well-known professor of physics at the University of California, Berkeley. He was unlike Dewey Larson who did not have these academic credentials and was actually not but rather a commercial engineer whose deep insights into physics stemmed from his practical application of physics theories to his work and to data generated by others that led him to doubt quantum mechanical theories.

Kip (1962) noted that "the ultimate problem of the existence of electric charge and of protons, neutrons, electrons, and all the other particles of physics is still with us" (p. 38). Unless I am misinterpreting this statement, it sounds to me as if he meant that most phenomena in nature can be explained by studying electrical behaviour, however when it comes to particle physics, although electrical behaviour is apparent, there is more going on than simply that. The field of quantum mechanics has attempted to explain this "more", that is going on, however quantum mechanics had not completely succeeded in explaining phenomena related to electrons, neutrons, protons and other the other particles studied in relation to the atom.

This got me thinking, because I have been fascinated with quantum mechanics since I was in high school, even though I never fully understood it. My mind also went back once again to the teachings from the Inner Circle pertaining to creation. In Yada di Shi'ite's account earlier, of creation, there were particles, there was electricity, there was magnetism, but then there was also heat, incredible heat, and cold, and collision of particles creating what amounted to ions moving at incredible speeds and creating vibrational energies. As I thought about these things, I thought, well, perhaps quantum mechanics may be looking at the sub-atomic scenario from one perspective. What if there are other perspectives that attempt to explain the same phenomena of the happenings in within and around atoms, but from another angle. In these musings, I had an epiphany. I realized that the extreme heat and cold conditions that were described as existing at the time of creation, coupled with the highly electrical nature of the endeavour all seemed to point to the field of physics known as plasma physics. So, I thought, here is a possible alternative to focusing mainly on electricity and quantum mechanics. Plasmas exist throughout much of nature, from within atoms, to planets, stars, and whole galaxies. Apart from the electric quality, plasma is another feature that seems to pervade much of manifest physical reality. In this section, I will argue that plasmas exist not only in physical objects, but also that humans have the capacity to work with and to generate plasmas of a high degree or intensity, through the manipulation of bioenergy known as chi in China, prana in India and nyama in Africa. In my research and studies, I have not yet come across a work that links plasma physics with bioenergy so in this section, I intend to explain what I mean by this association. Let us first discuss plasma physics from a scientific perspective, however. After that, I will elaborate on how plasma physics and spirituality are associated.

According to Chen (2016), "A plasma is a quasineutral gas of charged and neutral particles which exhibits collective behavior" (p. 2). By "quasineutral", he means that taken together, the overall charge of a plasma is zero, since all the positive and negative charges cancel out. However, within the collective that is the plasma, there are particles that are charged as either negative or positive, and other particles that are neutral. By "collective behavior", he means charged and neutral particles act as a unit, whether the unit is a cloud of particles, or a beam of particles. Peratt (1992) gives a much more straightforward definition which bring together the concepts explained in Chen (2016), "Plasmas consist of electrically charged particles that respond collectively to electromagnetic forces. The charged particles are usually clouds or beams of electrons, ions and neutrals but also can be charged grains or dust particles" (p. 1). As such, plasmas can exist in diverse formats, from charged and neutral particles at the atomic level, to charged and neutral particles in a stellar cloud, as examples.

One of the most astounding aspects of the account given by the Inner Circle in connection with their version of creation and with plasma physics is the degree to which it matches with the spiritual practice of one approach to Daoism. In the book *The Magus of Java*, Kostas Danaos shares with the world, the spiritual practice of a Daoist practitioner who has mastered the principles of yang and yin to an extreme degree. This practice involves bringing yin and yang together in a region of the etheric body around the abdomen area known as the 'dan tian'. When the yin and yang come together, they create electricity. This sounds exactly like what happens at the cosmic level in the account at the creation of existence. The creation of existence is the creation of life. In the account of the Inner Circle, the two forces that came together to form light and electricity were heat and cold. Heat can be thought of as yang energy, and cold can be thought of as yin energy. Similarly, in plasma physics, we have heat and cold energies, that are both involved in the creation of plasmas. Therefore, I see this connection between plasma physics, or a version of it that includes the ether, or chi/qi (as energy is called in Daoism), which involves the same principles at the macro level of the cosmos as well as in the micro level of the inner spiritual universe.

Keylontic Science and Samkhya

Earlier in this chapter, I expressed a view that there was a gap in the use of Samkhya as a theoretical basis in the Yoga Sutras of Patanjali. The gap, I hold, lies in what the higher density analog is, for prakiti. Prakiti, the idea from Samkhya, appears to me to be tied to matter, and to the physical world, where it can be sensed with the five senses. The Yoga Sutras of Patanjali appear not to generalize the notion of prakiti beyond what the Samkhya philosophy provides, or at least, not explicitly. Yet, this yoga philosophy draws on the same ways of thinking that is applied to events in the physical world that according to Samkhya are ultimately based on prakiti. This to me implies then, that there must be yet another fundamental basis, similar to the idea of prakriti, that pertains to higher densities beyond third density physical. Otherwise, when reasoning backward, as Samkhya teaches us to do, effects would eventually end in causes that are not fundamental, or do not exist. It leads to an "empty place", which defeats the idea that effects must have causes, an idea fundamental to Samkhya.

This is where Keylontic Science comes in. Where the Yoga Sutras of Patanjali provides a workable system based on an adapted version of Samkhya that is incomplete for the higher densities, Keylontic Science fills in that gap. This is because the principles outlined in Samkhya apply beyond third density, although Samkhya, as given originally, was meant to help people dispel confusion and ignorance in dealing with aspects pertaining to third density. The reason why I am convinced of this is that the Yoga Sutras of Patanjali have been able to successfully adapt the Samkhya philosophy to the practice of Raja Yoga, which deals with phenomena that goes beyond third density existence. This, notwithstanding the inability of the Yoga Sutras of Patanjali to reconcile the incongruity of the notion of prakriti, when speaking of phenomena beyond physical existence.

There must therefore be an even more fundamental root or layer, similar to the idea of prakriti, but one which pertains to and can be applied to phenomena beyond third density existence. This idea, as given in Keylontic Science, is the notion of "partiki". Now, in Keylontic Science, partiki is the most fundamental layer of existence within manifest reality, which pervades all of manifest reality, from the subtlest of levels deriving from the Creator or Source, to the level of gross physical reality. The equivalent notion, in Keylontic Science, to that of the pratiki notion in Samkhya, is the keylontic code. With the name partiki being quite similar or perhaps even arguably the same as pratiki, a question that in earlier days arose in my mind, was whether these two ideas originate from the same source. That is, whether Keylontic Science is derived from Samkhya, or Samkhya from Keylontic Science, or both from a third source.

Now, I shall actually speculate. From my studies of both Keylontic Science and Samkhya, I have come to conclude two hypotheses. The first is that Samkhya and Keylontic Science have the same source and if that this source is directly from the Creator Source and the Guardians who work under them. Why do I hold this view? This is because Keylontic Science, if we are to take as true what is said about it, is a system that was revealed to humanity on Earth by the Creators and the Guardians over 200,000 years ago in a specially given compilation of texts that could be accessed holographically using some special technology based on plates. Over this period, these texts have been guarded by factions of these guardians who have remained on Earth.

This information has only been released during periods of the ends of cycles, when humanity may gain advanced knowledge in order to work toward ascension. So, that is for Keylontic Science. Since Earth humanity is said to be currently going through the end of a cycle, a large cycle in fact, it would appear that the Creators and the guardians sent a group of emissaries in the person of Ashayana Deane and her team to expound on this information for Earth humans. Ashayana Deane and her group have in fact claimed to be associated with the guardians and the creators they represent, so if that is true, then it would appear that Keylontic Science comes from the creator source and the guardians. For Samkhya, we are told that the philosophy was originally revealed by Kapila, an ancient sage who is thought to be an incarnation of Brahma. When you hear Brahma, think Creator. Therefore, Kapila was either the creator source in incarnation, or an aspect of the creator source. Samkhya is actually a very old philosophy. If we are to take what is written about it as true, then it is old indeed. That is, if we are to assume to be true, that which has been written about the Yoga Sutras of Patanjali. According to Bailey (2012), citing Hindu sources, the Yoga Sutras of Patanjali are at least 12,000 years old, dating back to at least 10,000BC. If indeed the Yoga Sutras of Patanjali adapted Samkhya philosophy as revealed by Kapila and not some other, older or other philosophy from which Samkhya may also derive, then this would mean that Samkhya is at least 12,000 years old. Otherwise, it would mean that these ideas are at least that old. In any case, this first hypothesis or point I hope to make is that both Keylontic Science and Samkhya originate from the creator or source level.

The second hypothesis is that Kapila's Samkhya philosophy can be thought of as being a subset of Keylontic Science. It can be seen as a subset of the same ideas, but one that pertains to physical reality. In other words, Keylontic Science and Samkhya are the same insofar as the principles and ways of thinking apply to both. However, the main difference is in what the fundamental or root layer is. In Keylontic Science, it is the idea of 'partiki', that fundamental layer that pervades all of manifest reality, including physical matter. In Samkhya, it is the idea of 'prakriti', that fundamental layer that pervades all of nature, which is physical matter. Furthermore, I hold that with Keylontic Science as a generalization of Samkhya, we can find a resolution of one of the difficult points in Samkhya, which is that while prakriti, the root or fundamental layer produces (i.e., it is not produced by something else), soul, is neither produced nor does it produce (Wilson, 1835). Within Keylontic Science, both prakriti and soul would have the same basis, which is partiki.

Keylontic Science and Sufism

Sufism has teachings which give us a view of some of the esoteric philosophy of Islam. One of these teachings comes from Sufi mystic Ibn Arabi, in whose metaphysical teaching we learn about the names of God. It is from a discussion of God's 'most beautiful names' that we can learn something about the creator, from the Sufi perspective:

"Al-Haqq, praise be to Him, wanted, through His most beautiful names which are innumerable, to see the essences (a 'yān') of the names – of the names – or, if you will, to see Himself [or his own 'ayn, essence]. He wished to do this through an all-encompassing being (*kawn jāmi`*) who embraces the whole matter: a being which embodies the attributes of existence. Through this being, God's secret would then be revealed to Himself" (Nettler, 2003, p. 19).

I cannot help noticing a similarity between the Kabbalistic notion of Ain Soph, and the Sufi notion of 'ayn, both of which refer to a sublime concept of the creator, or God. It could be that the two concepts are related.

Within Keylontic Science, we may associate the notion of 'ayn with the Yunasai, or the source of all creation. Similarly, the idea of an all-encompassing being, that which in Sufi metaphysics is called the kawn jāmi`, can be associated with the concept of partiki.

Keylontic Science and Ra's Law of One teachings

The Law of One teachings give one fascinating concept that I think directly relate to Keylontic Science. This is the concept of infinite energy. Infinite energy pervades the entire existence. In Keylontic Science, the equivalent idea to infinite energy of the Law of One teachings is the idea of partiki. Partiki, similar to infinite energy in that it is infinite. It keeps producing more of itself, because it has a self-regenerating quality, therefore it is infinite. What is also important and related to the concept of infinite energy is the concept of infinite intelligence. In the Law of One, infinite energy emanates from infinite intelligence. The equivalent concept to infinite intelligence in Keylontic Science is the Yunasai.

Keylontic Science and Vedanta

Vedanta is a fascinating spiritual philosophy in which manifest reality can be thought of as a cosmic illusion (Comans, 2000) brought forth by Brahma, that, according to the Hindu sage Gaudapada, can be likened to a dream. Here, we have a connection with dreams, which has been a recurring theme in this book. In connection with Keylonta, the dream of Brahma would be the equivalent of the entry of partiki into the void, from the level of the Yunasai.

Keylontic Science and the metaphysical science of the Inner Circle

In the Inner Circle teachings, the Overlords and the High Archangels are the Yunasai.

Keylontic Science and Zulu spirituality

In the cosmogonic scheme shared by Credo Mutwa in his book *Indaba, my Children*, we learn that the name of being he refers to as the Great Spirit, is uNkulunkulu. uNkulunkulu is what we may refer to as the "first cause". This being manifested reality, and through this manifestation was born Ma, the Goddess of creation, as she is referred to by Credo Mutwa, who, according to the account, is self-created. She then proceeds to execute the plan of creation on hewing out the sun, the moon, the stars and all that physically exists. Of uNkulunkulu and Ma, we are told:

"The eternal Iron Mountain
She stood erect, a pillar of incredible beauty
Such as no mortal has ever, or will ever see.
Her golden glittering eyes pierced the dark of the starry sky
And peered into the remotest reaches of Infinity
Where, far, oh so far away

She could vaguely discern the blaze of Light
The formless, ageless, immortal *uNkulunkulu,*
The Highest of the High" (Mutwa, 1999, p. 10)

In relation to Keylontic Science, uNkulunkulu would be the equivalent of the Yunasai, who are the creator level, the Goddess Ma would be the equivalent of the notion of partiki, which is the fundamental layer within Keylontic Science, that which is self-generating and which creates all else.

9.4 Becoming God

In this book, we have covered a lot of structure, of ideas and of paradigms. We can think of these ideas, paradigms and structures as helping aids, as scaffolds, as ways of putting into finite moulds some of the expressions we experience within the infinite. It is well to do this. In fact, there is a part of us that may enjoy the process of thinking, conceptualizing, categorizing. Apart from the enjoyment, it also serves a purpose. It is a skill that, having been developed, can lead us to gain merit in our interactions with ourselves in reality, and it plays a role in helping us reach a state where we no longer need any structure. Or rather, where the structure become subordinate to the no-structure. And yet, it is also well to know, that there is a part of us that is infinite. There is a part of us that transcends structure, thinking, concepts, categories, and that can know anything and everything instantly, without going through the thinking process. This infinite part is eternal. It is always present, always simply in a state of being. This part is one with All.

While incarnated, we can access this part, by being this part. Simply by placing our attention on this part, keeping it there, and becoming this part, we become this part. We become this part because we have always been this part, and will always be this part. The way to know about this part, is to be this part. Talking about this part in terms of concepts or descriptions or structures does incomplete justice to this part. At best, it just points the way. To progressively stay being this part, simply by intending to. And the more you place conscious attention on this part, the more this part can become a conscious part of being. This part does not have an ego, in the sense of separated consciousness that needs to be defended. This is because it is one with All. This was the start, and this is the end, and this is the in-between. Even in separated consciousness, this part still remains. It shall never die, so it is not afraid of death. It simply is. It simply was, and it simply will be.

AFTERWORD

As the final section of this book, I would like to remark that it can be a choice, to experience the world in an engaged manner. In our mundane life, in our spiritual life, in our thinking life, and in our professional life. In being engaged, it means we gain experiences through our multidimensional selves. Especially for our non-physical selves, since many of us do not get formally trained in practical ways to apply these parts of ourselves. If we want to have ways to personally ascertain the truth of spiritual phenomena, then we would have to consider empowering ourselves through spiritual education. It may mean going out of your way to pursue learning what you would otherwise not get through formal or mainstream education. It may also mean finding ways to remain motivated during your studies, and persevering through them since, unlike the case of the mundane school system, there may not be a mundane consequence resulting from a lack of motivation and inadequate performance, such as not getting into a college or not getting a job, or being reprimanded by a superior at work.

The spiritual path that can lead to empowerment involves developing clear understandings and applicable skills based on correct practice. *It is important to consider developing spiritual practices and ways that can empower you to personally witness spiritually some of what you may read about and understand intellectually.* On your spiritual path, it would be good to seek out competent teachers who can assist you reach competency in an aspect of spiritual endeavour you wish to be empowered in. I would like to encourage you to persevere, and to try to learn the specific content and skills as well and as correctly as you are able. As you develop your skills, there may be some learning pains involved, however the benefits of perseverance would be well worth the effort.

It is possible to live consciously while also being fully engaged. It is possible to hold the consciousness of having awakened to your nature as an infinite being, hold on to the awareness that what you perceive as physical reality when considered from the standpoint of a sea of energy may be seen as an illusion generated by your minds to give structure to sense data registered from energy and vibrations. You can be aware of all of this and still be fully engaged and present in your life and your experiences.

SOURCES

Bailey, A. (2012). *The light of the soul: its science and effect: a paraphrase of the 'Yoga sutras' of Patanjali with commentary by Alice A. Bailey*. New York, NY: Lucis Pub Co; London: Lucis Press

Bannerman-Richter, G. (1982). *The practice of witchcraft in Ghana*. California: Elk Grove

Baum F. L., & Sabuda, R. (2001). *The wonderful wizard of oz*, London: Simon & Schuster

Blavatsky, H. P. (1888). *The Secret Doctrine, A Synthesis of Science, Religion, and Philosophy - Volume I: Cosmogenesis*. London: The Theosophical Publishing Company

Bloom (1968). *The Republic of Plato: Translated with notes and an interpretive essay*. New York: Basic Books

Browne, H. (1973). *How I found freedom in an unfree world*. New York: Macmillan

Burnet, J., Fairbanks, A., & Freeman, K. (n.d.). *Fragments By Heraclitus*. Retrieved December 20, 2021, from https://antilogicalism.files.wordpress.com/2016/12/heraclitus_fragments_final.pdf

Campbell, J. (2008). *The hero of a thousand faces*. Novato, California: New World Library

Chen, F. F. (2016). *Introduction to Plasma Physics and Controlled Fusion*. Cham, Switzerland: Springer

Churchward, J. (1931). *The Children of Mu*. New York: Ives Washburn

Cleary, T. (1987). *Understanding Reality: A Taoist Alchemical Classic*. Honolulu: University of Hawaii Press

Comans, M. (2000). *The Method of Early Advaita Vedanta: A Study of Gaudapada, Sankara, Suresvara, and Padmapada*. Delhi: Motilal Banarsidass Publishers

Danaos, K. (2000). *The Magus of Java: Teachings of an Authentic Taoist Immortal*. Rochester, Vermont: Inner Traditions

Deane, A. (2001). *Angelic Realities*. NC: Wildflower Press

Deane, A. (2002). *Voyagers 2, 2nd Edition*, NC: Wildflower Press

Deane, A. (2011). *Voyagers 1, 2nd Edition*, NC: Wildflower Press

Eliade, M. (1958). *Yoga: Immortality and Freedom (Vol. 56)*. New York: Pantheon Books

Greer, S. M. (2017). *Unacknowledged: An Exposé of the World's Greatest Secret*. West Palm Beach, Florida: A&M Publishing, LLC

Grindal, B. T. (1983). Into the Heart of Sisala Experience: Witnessing Death Divination. *Journal of Anthropological Research*, 39(1), 60–80.

Gyekye, K. (1987). *An essay on African philosophical thought: The Akan conceptual scheme*. Cambridge, UK: Cambridge University Press

Jamison, S. W., & Brereton, J. P. (2014). *The Rigveda: The earliest religious poetry of India, vols. I–III*. Oxford, UK: Oxford University Press

Hagengruber, R. (2012). *Emilie du Châtelet between Leibniz and Newton*. New York: Springer

Kalupahana, D. J. (1986). *Mulamadhyamakakarika of Nagarjuna: The Philosophy of the Middle Way*. Albany, NY: State University of New York Press

Kaplan, A. (1997). *Sefer Yetzirah: The Book of Creation*. Boston, MA: Weiser, LLC

Kip, A. (1962). *Fundamentals of electricity and magnetism*. New York: McGraw Hill Book Company

Kuhn, T. (1962). *The Structure of Scientific Revolutions*. Chicago: The University of Chicago Press

Larson, D. (1963). *The Case against the Nuclear Atom*. Portland, OR: North Pacific Publishers

Linderman, F. B. (1962). *Plenty-Coups, chief of the Crows*. Lincoln: University of Nebraska Press

Lobaczewski, A. (1998). *Political Ponerology: A science on the nature of evil adjusted for political purposes*. Grande Prairie: Red Pill Press

Long, M. F. (1948). *The Secret Science Behind Miracles*. New York: Robert Collier Publications

Miller, R. L. (2017). *Psychedelic Medicine: The Healing Powers of LSD, MDMA, Psilocybin, and Ayahuasca*. Toronto, Canada: Park Street Press

Monroe (1985). *Far Journeys*. New York: Harmony Books

Mutwa, C. V. (1999). *Indaba, my Children*. New York: Grove Press

Nabokov, P. (1967). *Two-Leggings: the making of a Crow warrior.* New York: Thomas Y. Crowell

Neal, J. H. (1969). *Jungle magic: my life among the witchdoctors of West Africa.* New York: Paperback Library

Nettler, R. L. (2003). *Sufi Metaphysics and Quranic Prophets Ibn Arabi's Thought and Method in the Fusus Al-Hikam.* Cambridge, UK: The Islamic Texts Society

Obenga, T. (1990). *La Philosophie Africaine de la Période Pharaonique: 2780 – 330 avant notre ère.* Paris: L'Harmattan

Peniel, J. (1997). *The last days of Atlantis.* Alamosa, CO: Network

Peratt, A. (1992). *Physics of the Plasma Universe.* New York, NY: Springer

Probert, M. (1963). *The Magic Bag: A Manuscript Dictated Clairaudiently to Mark Probert by Members of the Inner Circle.* San Diego: The Inner Circle Kethra E'Da Foundation, Inc

Puharich, A. (1975). *Uri: A journal of the mystery of Uri Geller.* New York: Bantam Books

Schlemmer, P. (1994). *The Only Planet of Choice: Essential Briefings from Deep Space.* Bath: Gateway Books

Shafton, A. (1995). *Dream reader: contemporary approaches to the understanding of dreams.* Albany: State University of New York Press

Somé, M. P. (1995). *Of water and the spirit: ritual, magic, and initiation in the life of an African shaman,* New York, NY: Penguin

Steigler, B. & Steigler, H., S. (2014). *Real Encounters, Different Dimensions, and Otherworldly Beings.* Detroit: Visible Ink Press

Tart, C. (1969). *Altered states of consciousness.* New York: Doubleday & Company, Inc

Tart, C. E., Puthoff, H. E., & Targ, R. (2002). *Mind at Large: Institute of Electrical and Electronic Engineers Symposia on the Nature of Extrasensory Perception.* Charlottesville, VA: Hampton Roads Pub

The Stanzas of Dzyan. (n.d.). Retrieved, January 13, 2022, from http://prajnaquest.fr/downloads/BookofDzyan/StancesOfDzyan/StanzasofDzyan.pdf

Thera, N., Bhikkhu, B., & Hecker, H. (2003). *Great disciples of the Buddha: their lives, their works, their legacy.* Sri Lanka: Buddhist Publication Society

Vassilatos, G. (2000). *Secrets of Cold War Technology: Project HAARP and Beyond.* Kempton, IL: Adventures Unlimited Press

Wambach, H. (1978). *Reliving Past Lives: The evidence under hypnosis.* New York: Bantam

Wambach, H. (1979). *Life before life: is there life before birth? 750 cases of hypnosis.* New York: Bantam

Werner, E. T. C. (1922). *Myths and Legends of China.* London: George G. Harrap & Co. Ltd

Colebrooke, H. T. (1837). *The Sánkhya Káriká, Or Memorial Verses on the Sánkhya Philosophy.* London: A.J. Valpy

Winters, J. (1994). *Thinking in Buddhism: Nagarjuna's Middle Way.* Reed College

ABOUT THE AUTHOR

Kwame Adapa is an intellectual and a spiritual being with diverse interests, currently incarnated in an early middle-aged male Akan physical body. He strives to achieve mastery of self, on the physical, emotional, intellectual and spiritual levels of experience while incarnated. Kwame has been writing about and sharing his thoughts and experiences for a decade and a half. Recently, he has been guided to reach a wider audience by sharing his experiences and thoughts with the world. Kwame continues to expand the limits of his knowledge and experience and he continues to develop himself spiritually. To this day, Kwame still practices the out of body projection skills he first learned in 2005, as well as other methods from internal alchemy. Get linked with Kwame:
Email – akwadapa@hotmail.com
Homepage – https://www.theakan.com
Facebook – https://fb.me/KwameAdapa
Instagram – https://www.instagram.com/Kwameadapa
Twitter – https://www.twitter.com/Akwadapa

OTHER BOOKS BY KWAME ADAPA

The Akan, Other Africans & the Sirius Star System: Egyptian and Sumerian gods in African culture – The traditions and the culture of the Akan people of West Africa are a treasure trove of clues to an ancient past, linking to extraterrestrials associated with the Sirius star system who influenced the ancestors of the Akan and other Africans.

Out of Body into Life: Journeys into spirit worlds and how to get there on your own – through out of body journeys, also known as astral projection, Kwame explores the regions that human souls go to after passing through death. He also found answers to who he is as a soul, what ancient civilizations lie within the Earth's caverns, about nature spirit entities that cohabit our planet and about the inhabitants of other star systems.

The Guardians, Earth Humans and Ascension: Spiritually hacking your awareness and DNA – as a sequel to The Akan book, this book discusses the guardians and the Earth human experiment in significant detail, including but going beyond the Akan and other Africans, to human groups from across the globe. There is also a discussion of techniques to bring about spiritual ascension. These techniques ultimately come from the guardians.

DID YOU FIND ANY TYPOS?

Although I went to great lengths to find and remove any typos, there is a chance that you might have chanced upon some. In the event that you did, I would very much appreciate a heads-up from you, if you could kindly drop me a message at the following address: https://www.theakan.com/contact/

Thank you for reading my book!

Please allow me to thank you for choosing my book. I sincerely hope you found some of what I shared useful to you on your path and I know that you could have picked up another book on dreams but chose to read mine so I thank you again.

If you enjoyed reading this book, and found some value in it, I would be most grateful to receive a five-star rating from you. It would only take less than a minute. Your feedback would also help me continue to write more books such as this one, to promote learning and knowledge. Thank you again!

Regards,
Kwame Adapa

Printed in Dunstable, United Kingdom